Mechatronic Milestones

Englisch für Mechatronikberufe

von
Dr. Wolfgang Schäfer (Hrsg.)
Irene Hildenbrand
Annely Humphreys
Jason Humphreys
Andreas Morbitzer
Mary Schäfer

Ernst Klett Verlag
Stuttgart · Leipzig

Mechatronic Milestones

Englisch für Mechatronikberufe

Autoren: Dr. Wolfgang Schäfer (Hrsg.), Irene Hildenbrand, Annely Humphreys, Jason Humphreys, Andreas Morbitzer, Mary Schäfer

Werkübersicht:

Schülerbuch, 978-3-12-808279-0

Milestones Workbook für alle technischen Fachbände mit Prüfungsvorbereitung KMK-Fremdsprachenzertifikat und CD-ROM, Übungsbegleitheft für alle technischen Berufe, 978-3-12-808285-1

Milestones Lehrerhandbuch für technische Berufe inkl. Digitalem Lehrer-Service mit Medien-DVD-ROM + Lehrer-Audio-CDs (6), 978-3-12-808287-5

1. Auflage

1 7 6 5 4 3 | 22 21 20 19 18

Alle Drucke dieser Auflage sind unverändert und können im Unterricht nebeneinander verwendet werden. Die letzte Zahl bezeichnet das Jahr des Druckes.

Im Lehrwerk befinden sich ausschließlich fiktive Internet-Adressen, die deshalb auch mit ww#. beginnen anstatt wie üblich mit www.

Die im Buch abgedruckten Mediencodes führen zu interaktiven Zusatzübungen und Hörverständnistexten auf www.klett.de. Die Mediencodes leiten ausschließlich zu optionalen Unterrichtsmaterialien, sie unterliegen nicht dem staatlichen Zulassungsverfahren.

Projektleitung: Matthias Rupp
Redaktion: Helen Smyth, Volker Wendland
Herstellung: Angelika Lindner

Satz und Gestaltung: Satzkiste, Stuttgart
Umschlaggestaltung: Projektteam des Verlages
Reproduktion: Meyle + Müller Medien-Management, Pforzheim
Druck: PASSAVIA Druckservice GmbH & Co. KG, Passau

Printed in Germany
ISBN 978-3-12-808279-0

Mechatronic Milestones bietet Ihnen praxisorientiertes Fachenglisch für Mechatronikberufe an Berufsschulen, Berufsfachschulen, Fachschulen sowie für technisch ausgerichtete Englischkurse in der Erwachsenenbildung.

Mechatronic Milestones im Überblick:

- Konsequente Berücksichtigung neuester Lehrpläne (Lernfelder) sowie durchgängiges Sprachkompetenztraining nach dem Gemeinsamen Europäischen Referenzrahmen (Sprachstufen A2 – B2).
- 19 kompakte 4-seitige Module: Fachmodule mit Schwerpunkt auf Fachenglisch wechseln sich mit Modulen (A – H) ab, in denen der Schwerpunkt auf der beruflichen Kommunikation liegt.
- Schnelle Orientierung im Buch durch Übersicht der Lernziele jeweils am Modulanfang.
- Die Kompetenzen auf einen Blick: Viele Aufgaben bereiten bereits gezielt auf die Anforderungen des KMK-Zertifikats hin. Diese Aufgaben sind mit den Kürzeln R (Rezeption), P (Produktion), I (Interaktion) und M (Mediation) gekennzeichnet.
- Typische Sprachhandlungssituationen im Berufsalltag werden multimedial mit Audio- und Videounterstützung (u.a. Originalvideos der BBC) trainiert.
- Zahlreiche Partner-, Gruppen- und Internetaufgaben werden durch Texte und Aufgaben zur Arbeitssicherheit *(Safety first)* abgerundet.
- In den Modulen befinden sich hilfreiche Verweise auf die nach beruflichen Situationen geordneten Redewendungen *(Phrases)*.
- Unter der Überschrift *Understanding technical English* befinden sich Hinweise und Aufgaben zum richtigen Umgang mit englischem Fachvokabular.
- Möglichkeit zur Binnendifferenzierung durch anspruchsvollere Aufgaben sowie Aufgaben zur Vorbereitung auf das KMK-Fremdsprachenzertifikat in verschiedenen Stufen.
- Auf den Fachwortschatz in den jeweiligen Modulen kann über die *Word Bank* (auf jeder Doppelseite) direkt zugegriffen werden.
- Online-Grammatiktraining über die Milestones-Codes ⊕ 3u5mw9 in den Modulen A – H.
- Vertieftes Grammatik- und Hörverstehenstraining im Workbook mit Prüfungsvorbereitung auf das KMK-Fremdsprachenzertifikat inklusive CD-ROM mit allen technischen Milestones-Fachbänden- und Workbook-Audios (MP3).

Weiterführendes Material

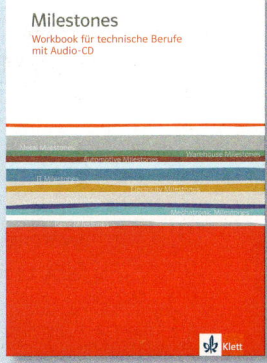

Milestones Workbook für alle technischen Fachbände mit Prüfungsvorbereitung KMK-Fremdsprachenzertifikat und CD-ROM

Lehrerhandbuch für alle technischen Milestones-Fachbände mit 6 Audio-CDs + Digitaler Lehrer-Service (Lehrer-Software mit multimedialen Schülerbüchern, Audios, Videos, Lösungen, Übungsmaterial, Übungsgenerator, Dokumentenpool mit veränderbaren Materialien)

Appendix

Umschlagseiten

Moduleelemente	
Nach diesem Modul	Lernziele
WORD BANK	Fachvokabular
UNDERSTANDING TECHNICAL ENGLISH	Hinweise und Aufgaben zu englischem Fachvokabular
SAFETY FIRST ⚠	Aufgaben zur Arbeitssicherheit
→ Phrases: Telephoning	Verweis auf Phrases (Telephoning) im Anhang

Symbole	
⊙ A 1.27	Audioverweis mit Tracknummer (CD1 – Track 27)
P, M, I, R	Produktion, Mediation, Interaktion, Rezeption
⊕	Aufgabe mit Internetrecherche
▲	Anspruchsvollere Aufgabe (advanced)
👥 👤	Partner- und Gruppenaufgaben
⊕ 3u5mw9	Grammatiktraining online über www.klett.de
KMK II	Aufgabe zur Vorbereitung auf die Prüfung des KMK-Fremdsprachenzertifikats (Niveaustufe II)

01

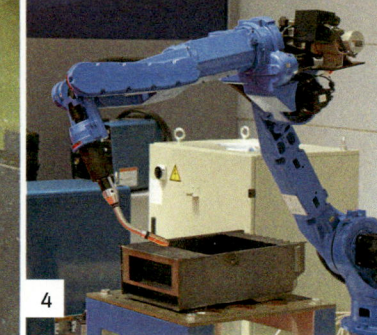

1
2
3
4

Tooling devices and robots

Mechatronics is applied to the design of products and production processes.
For example, much of manufacturing is automated using mechatronics and robot
systems. Mechatronics describes a branch of engineering that includes electronics,
IT and control theory. Therefore you will find tools and other equipment from each
of these branches in a mechatronics workshop: wire strippers, multimeters, long
nose pliers, spanners and different types of screwdrivers.

1 Make a word web like the one below with the tools and equipment in the photos.

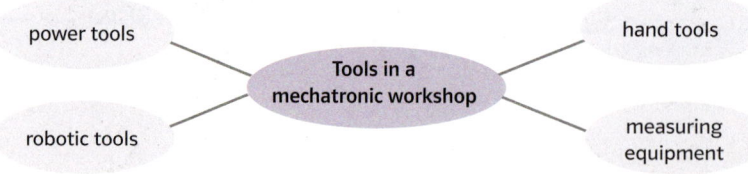

power tools

hand tools

**Tools in a
mechatronic workshop**

robotic tools

measuring
equipment

2 Describe what you can do with the tools and equipment using the verbs.

measure · cut · drill · mill · place · strip · grip · drive in · bend · screw

A | General tools

I/M **1** Alan comes from Brighton in England and he is doing an internship in your firm. Work in groups of three. Your trainer speaks very little English so you help him to explain the tools in the pictures on page 8. Use the verbs in exercise 2 on page 8 and follow the example below.

Example:

Trainer: Wir lernen heute verschiedene Werkzeuge kennen. Dies ist eine Messlehre. Wir benutzen sie zum Messen von Werkstücken.

You: We use this tool to measure workpieces.

Alan: It's called a vernier calliper in English.

You: …

P **2** Write definitions for three of the tools in the pictures on page 8.

Example:

A mains tester is a tool you use to check whether a wire is live or not. A lamp lights up when the wire is live. Only then can you decide what to do with the wire.

B | Working with tooling devices

Apart from general tools, you will also find power tools and robot systems like power drills, feeders, welding equipment and CNC machines in the mechatronic workshop. These tools make it possible to automate manufacturing processes.

I **1** Match the tooling devices in the box with the photos below.

> robotic gripper · crimping device · PC panel · column drill ·
> grinding machine · soldering iron

1

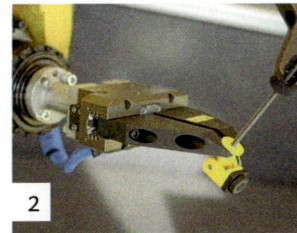

2

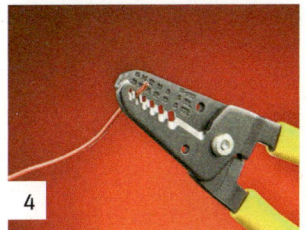

4

3

5

6

WORD BANK

automate (v) – automatisieren
feeder – Beschickungsapparat, Füllvorrichtung
test leads – Prüfspitzen
welding equipment – Schweiß-ausrüstung

2 Explain what you can do with the tooling devices in exercise 1. Use the words below and make complete sentences.

1. solder	a hole	on a conveyor belt
2. drill	wires	in a sheet of metal
3. start	a fuse	of a workpiece
4. lift and place	an object	on a CNC machine
5. cut and strip	the surface	in one step
6. smooth	a working process	to a circuit board

R **3**

⊙ A 2.1

Alan Gates, an exchange student from London, comes across a new lathe in the workshop. He asks Detlev, one of the German apprentices, a lot of questions. Listen to the dialogue and look at the photo. Say which machine parts they talk about.

a. digital measuring system

b. guard

c. headstock

d. clamping device / chuck (spindle inside)

e. toolholder

f. tail stock

g. spindle sleeve

h. top slide

i. cross-slide

j. handwheel

R **4**

⊙ A 2.1

Listen to the dialogue again and decide whether the statements are true or false. Correct the false statements.

1. Alan and Detlev are interested in how much the lathe costs.
2. The lathe was only installed the week before.
3. The lathe moves the cutting tool towards a rotating workpiece.
4. A lathe and a milling machine work in the same way.
5. The workpiece or tool can be fastened to the chuck.
6. The lathe is operated by a PC-control.
7. The lathe is widely used to machine precision parts.

5 Ask your partner what one of the following parts is for. He / she gives its function. Then swap roles.

handwheel · toolholder · guard · chuck

C | Robots

M 1
KMK II

Alan hat ein paar englische Fachzeitschriften als Geschenk für die Lehrwerkstatt mitgebracht. Die Auszubildenden interessieren sich für einen Artikel über Roboter, können aber nicht alle genug Englisch, um ihn zu lesen. Stellen Sie die wichtigsten Argumente auf Deutsch in einer Liste zusammen. Schreiben Sie ganze Sätze.

Robots and robotic systems

Robots and robotic systems are commonly used in manufacturing industry. But what are they exactly? Some robots look like arms with flexible joints while others look more like humans. Controlled by a PC and equipped
5 with tools such as grippers and spray painters, industrial robots perform various movements both quickly and precisely. Robots are widely used in the automotive and packaging industries, for example. Researchers and technicians are continually searching for new ways of using robots and robotic systems. Japanese experts are developing a robot care assistant for the
10 elderly in hospitals and old people's homes. Experts predict that robots will help out in normal households in the future and they are even experimenting with teaching robots to replace traditional school teachers. Robots are often used in situations like big fires or nuclear accidents, which are too hazardous for humans. They are versatile, flexible, precise, and able to work 24 hours
15 a day. This makes them popular but at the same time highly competitive workmates in manufacturing processes.

R/P 2
KMK II

List the advantages and disadvantages of robots in a table. Add your own ideas.

D | Safety at work

R/P 1
KMK II

SAFETY FIRST ⚠

1. Complete the statements about safety in the workshop. Then compare your answers with a partner and tell him / her why you think your choices are correct.

1. When working at a milling machine you should …
   a. wear your new baggy trousers.
   b. wear an overall.
   c. tie back long hair.
2. While you are using the column drill to drill holes, you …
   a. wear your goggles.
   b. talk to your workmate at the drill across from you.
3. Your workpiece isn't finished. When somebody calls you over, you …
   a. walk away while the machine is running.
   b. finish the job, switch off the machine and go over to them.
   c. tell them that you are busy and ask them to wait five minutes.

2. Make a list of some important safety regulations in the workshop.

WORD BANK

goggles – Sicherheitsbrille
install (v) – installieren
lathe – Drehbank, Drehmaschine
machine (v) – mit einer Maschine bearbeiten
operate (v) – betreiben
precision – Präzision
spray painter – Farbsprühdüse
workpiece – Werkstück

WORD BANK ⊙

catcher – Auffangschale
clamp (v) – befestigen
cutting tool – Schneidwerkzeug
milling machine – Fräsmaschine

A

NACH DIESEM MODUL:

✓ weiß ich, wie man sich auf Englisch begrüßt,

✓ weiß ich, wie ich mich selbst und andere einander auf Englisch vorstelle.

Meeting people

In the world of work you will often meet new people and it will be necessary to introduce yourself. In all industries developing relationships with colleagues and customers is the key to success. Not only is it important that you are polite, confident and friendly, but also that you know what to say, what information to include, and what the differences between formal and informal situations are.

1 Match the parts of the dialogues to form short conversations. Start with Speaker A.

Speaker A	Speaker B
1. Morning, Tom. That was a great game last night, wasn't it?	a. Nice to meet you, too, Hannah.
2. Hi guys, my name's Natalie.	b. Goodbye, Mr Horvath. It was nice meeting you.
3. Goodbye, Mr Bauer. See you next week.	c. Morning Chris. Yeah, it was amazing!
4. It's nice to meet you, Simon.	d. Hi Natalie, I'm Mark. Welcome to the team.

2 Now match the conversations above with the appropriate picture (1–4) and decide which are formal and which are informal.

P **3** Which other phrases do you know for greeting somebody and saying goodbye? Make a list.

A | Saying "hello" and "goodbye" and giving your name

A trainee from Denmark has just arrived at Neureuther und Söhne in Kiel for a three-month internship.

R **1** Listen to the two dialogues and write down the names of the people and their
⊙ A 1.1 positions in the company.

R **2** Listen again and write down the phrases the people use for greeting and introducing
⊙ A 1.1 one another.

R **3** Match the replies to the greetings and goodbyes in the two boxes.

Formal greetings/goodbyes	Formal replies
1. Good morning. How are you today?	a. Good morning. I'm fine, thanks. And you?
2. Good night. Have a nice evening, Mr Dachs.	b. Goodbye, Mr Schäfer, and thanks for everything.
3. Goodbye, Mr Horvath. Have a nice journey home.	c. Good night, Ms Kistner, you too.
4. Good night, Silke.	d. Good night, Ms Hornbach.

Informal greetings/goodbyes	Informal replies
1. Hello, Mike. Haven't seen you for a long time.	a. Bye, Thomas. Give me a call, will you?
2. Lena, how are you this morning?	b. You, too, Florian. Thank you.
3. Morning. How was your weekend?	c. Fine, thanks. How about yours?
4. Bye-bye, Sevda.	d. I'm good, thanks. Yourself?
5. Have a nice weekend, Joe.	e. Yes, I was away on a trip last week.

P **4** Make dialogues from the following prompts and present them to the class.
Look at your lists of phrases from exercise 2 and check the info box on the next page.

Example:
A: Hello, my name is Marina Kohler. I represent Toolcell in Leipzig.
B: Hello, Ms Kohler. I'm Amy Strong from Easytools in Bern. Nice to meet you.
A: Nice to meet you, too, Ms Strong.

Names: Denise Hofmann · Marina Kohler · Alice Campbell · Abel Kazich ·
Tanja Neuhäuser · Rudolfo Orvieto · Ursula Braun · Stefan Helm ·
Gerard Mathieu · your name

Job descriptions: I'm a trainee/intern · I work for … · I come from … ·
I represent … · I'm training to be a … · your job

Companies: Toolcell GmbH in Leipzig, Germany · Easytools in Bern,
Switzerland · Tools Expert Pontypridd, Wales · DWT Electronics,
Stuttgart · Smart EDV, Kiel · Xiang Piong Ltd, Hong Kong ·
Naturholz GmbH · your company

Situations: a first meeting with a new customer · a meeting with an existing
customer/a colleague · a party · a company open day · a trade
fair · a job fair for trainees · the first day in a new company

5 Introduce the people to each other according to the following structure. Use the prompts on the previous page.

→ PHRASES: Meeting people

A: Fragen Sie **B** und **C**, ob sie sich schon kennen. **B** und **C** antworten mit Nein.
A: Stellen Sie **B** und **C** einander vor.

B: Begrüßen Sie **C** freundlich.

C: Sie grüßen **B** zurück und stellen eine Frage zu **B**s Firma

B: Sie geben eine Auskunft über Ihre Firma. Sie fragen **C** nach seiner Tätigkeit.

C: Sie beantworten **B**s Frage.

INFO BOX: Meeting people

First meeting / Formal introduction
A: Hello, my name is Ines Sacher.
B: Nice to meet you, Ms Sacher. My name is Joshua Hamsung.
A: Nice to meet you, too, Mr Hamsung.
Women – married or not – are addressed as Ms, not Miss.

A: Mr Jacobs, this is Mr Sykes.
B: How do you do?
C: How do you do?
"How do you do?" is rarely used for first introductions.

A: I'm Frank Warren of Wood Tools in Manchester.
 Please call me Frank.
B: Pleased to meet you, Frank. My name is Joanne McNeill.
 Do call me Joanne.
In English-speaking countries first names are often used from the start of a
business realtionship. In South America or Asia, however, you don't usually use
first names right away.

I hope you had a good trip. /
I hope you had no trouble finding us. /
Welcome to our stand.
Phrases like these are used to break the ice after an introduction.

Second meeting
A: Good morning, Ms Sacher. Do you remember me?
 I'm Joshua Hamsung from Bell & Co in Chicago.
B: Good morning, Mr Hamsung. Nice to see you again.

Informal meetings
A: Hello Ines. Great to see you again. How are you?
B: Hi Joshua. Lovely to see you, too. I'm fine. And you?

B | Intercultural awareness

M **1**
KMK II

Ihr Betrieb wird in Zukunft für einen amerikanischen Auftraggeber arbeiten. Ihre Vorgesetzte interessiert sich daher für folgenden Artikel aus einer englischen Fachzeitschrift. Sie bittet Sie, die wesentlichen Aussagen des Artikels stichpunktartig in übersichtlicher Form für sie auf Deutsch herauszuarbeiten.

Intercultural awareness

Politeness, pleasantries and profitability

Americans are known to be direct, but they do like to take a few minutes to chat before getting down to work. They may ask after
5 your health, or if your trip was pleasant, or about where you are from. This gives both parties a chance to form an impression of the other and establishes a basis
10 on which to do business.

Americans, including the president, like to be called by their given name. This is not an invitation to be personal, as
15 you would expect in Germany if someone suggested using the familiar "Du". It is a way to set a framework for working together. While it is usual in business, it
20 would not be expected in dealing with a doctor, a teacher or a professor, and in any case, you should wait until it is offered: "Hello, I'm James Smith, vice-
25 president in charge of sales. Call me Jim." "Pleased to meet you! I'm Walter König; please call me Walter." (Note that in the United States you state your *given*
30 name and then your *family* name, and not the other way around, except perhaps on a form that you have to fill out.)

Americans don't like to waste time. They get to the point, 35 in conversations as well as in conferences. Although Milton Berle, a comedian from the 1950s and 1960s, is quoted as saying: "A committee is a group of people 40 that keeps minutes and wastes hours."

Americans are generally very polite, and they tend to smile much more than we are used to. 45 An American tourist was quite upset that perfect strangers didn't smile back at her when she walked through the streets of a small town in Germany. On the other 50 hand, a German woman in New York became quite tired of being asked, again by perfect strangers, the person at the cash register, the bus driver: "How are you 55 doing?" and commanded to "Have a nice day!" These pleasantries are intended to show that you are noticed and respected. More than "Thanks!" is not expected. 60

P **2**

Check the Internet to see what advice people from other countries get to prepare for meetings in Germany. Make a list of ten useful tips.

02

NACH DIESEM MODUL:

√ kenne ich die englischen Fachbegriffe für elektrische Einheiten,

√ kann ich einen elektrischen Stromkreis auf Englisch beschreiben,

√ kann ich die Stromarten auf
Englisch unterscheiden.

Electricity and electronics

Two important areas of mechatronics are electrical engineering and electronics.
Electronics is seen as a sub-field of electrical engineering and it deals more with low
voltages. Electrical engineering deals with high voltages. However, both fields of
engineering work with the basic principles of electricity and the different types of
electricity.

1 Use some of the words in the box to name the devices in the photos.

> substation · TV · sliding · GPS navigator · flat-screen · computer ·
> portable · TV · closed circuit · doors · on-board · with switches · cameras

2 Decide whether the applications in the photos are based more on electrical
engineering or electronics. Use a table like the one below.

Electrical applications	Electronic applications

3 Add more applications of electricity and electronics to your table in exercise 2.
Use a dictionary.

A | A complete circuit

Both electrical and electronic applications are based on circuits. A circuit is a closed
path along which the electrons can flow. Its basic components are a power source,
a path and a load. In the case of electrical circuits, the load can be anything from a
light-bulb in the home to a milling machine in a workshop. Examples of the loads
placed on electronic circuits are transistors and resistors. Electrical circuits normally
use alternating current (AC) whereas electronic circuits are more likely to use direct
current (DC).

1   Give the English terms for the words.

1. Bauteil
2. Stromkreis
3. Gleichstrom
4. Ladung
5. Wechselstrom
6. Stromquelle

2   Complete the text using the English terms from exercise 1. You will need the plural
forms of some of the terms.

An electrical circuit is a combination of one or
more electrical **1** such as batteries. **2** such as
lamps, resistors and switches are examples of
different **3** on the circuit. The parts are linked in
5 a circuit so that the **4** , or the **5** as is the case in
an electronic circuit, can be transported.
If the current cannot flow, electricians call it an
interrupted **6** . This interruption can be caused

unintentionally by a faulty lead, for example.
The circuit can also be interrupted when
components are missing. The user can switch the   10
current on or off as needed, which also interrupts
the circuit. An unwanted connection between
components in the circuit may lead to a short-
circuit. When there is too much current in the   15
circuit, we talk about over-current.

M   **3**   Summarize the main points of the text in exercise 2 in German.

P   **4**   Identify the parts of the circuit diagram, a – d. Two components are not in the diagram.

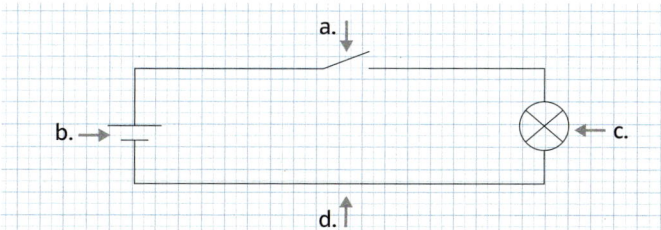

battery
resistor
lamp
fuse
switch
wire

WORD BANK

circuit diagram – Schaltplan,
Schaltbild
current – Strom
device – Gerät, Vorrichtung
lead – Zuleitung, Zuführung
milling machine – Fräsmaschine
over-current – Überstrom
resistor – Widerstand
short-circuit – Kurzschluss
transistor – Transistor
voltage – Spannung
workshop – Werkstatt

R   **5**   Listen to the two mechatronics students Daniel Weber from Hamburg and Joanna
◉ A 2.2   Holmes, an exchange student from Liverpool. They are talking about some home-
work they did for an electronics class.
1. Make a list of the mistakes Joanna made.
2. What mistake do they both make?

R   **6**   Listen to the dialogue again and correct the mistakes in Joanna's diagram. Then use
◉ A 2.2   your notes to draw the circuit correctly.

WORD BANK ◉

blow (v) – durchbrennen

B | Working with electronic components

Electronic components may be quite basic elements or more sophisticated ones with two or more electrical connectors. The components are usually connected to an electronic circuit using a soldering iron. A circuit diagram shows where electronic components, such as resistors, switches, capacitors, power sources, sensors, diodes and other conductors or semiconductors, have to be connected.

1 Identify the components in the photos.

2 Match the symbols and abbreviations with the components you found in exercise 1. Two of the abbreviations do not match.

Abbreviations
Z/ZD · C · Tr · SCR · R · S

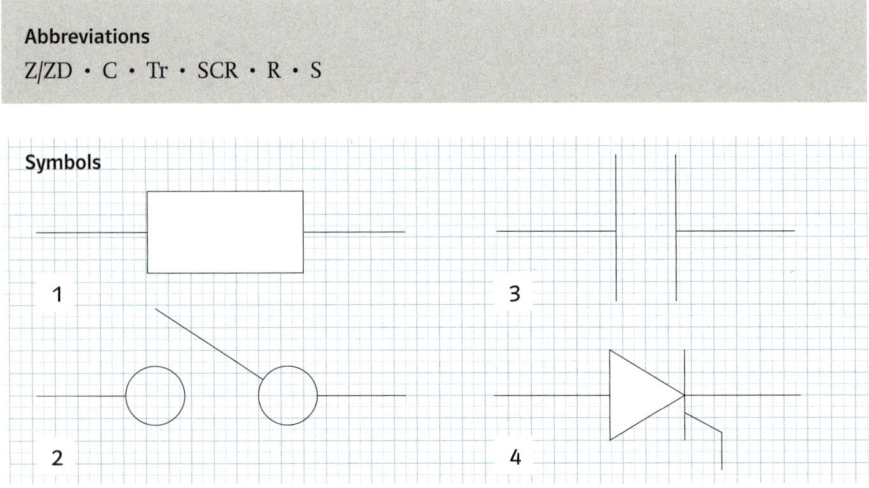

P **3** Check the Internet for an example of a circuit and describe it.

Example:
I recognise a symbol for resistors. It is connected with two other resistors.

C | Electric current

M **1**
KMK II

In einem englischen Fachbuch haben Sie eine Erklärung beider Stromarten gefunden.
Tragen Sie die wichtigsten Informationen auf Deutsch in eine Liste ein.

> **Types of electric current**
> Electric current is divided into two types: direct current (DC) and alternating
> current (AC). There is a DIN classification and a special symbol for appliances so
> that users know which current a particular device needs.
> 5 If you have an electrical current which flows only in one direction, it is called
> direct current. Almost all electronic devices, such as computers, work with DC.
> If electronic devices do not use batteries or accumulators but receive their power
> supply through a mains supply circuit, then a rectifier is needed. As solar cells can
> produce DC too, a lot of devices that use solar energy are supported by DC.
> 10 Alternating current (AC) periodically changes direction. The movements of the
> electrical charges can be monitored and look like sinusoidal waves. Electricity
> supplies worldwide are provided by alternating current. Its popularity is based
> on its easy production and ease of transformation. Photovoltaic systems need
> inverted rectifiers to feed AC into the national grid.

P **2** Compare the notes below with the text in exercise 1 and correct any mistakes.

> 1. Both DC and AC flow in two directions.
> 2. There is a special symbol on appliances to show users
>   which type of electrical current is needed.
> 3. Computers work with AC because it is the cheaper type
>   of current.
> 4. Solar cells and photovoltaic systems have no problems
>   supporting the grid.
> 5. AC is used for the long distance transfer of electricity.

3 UNDERSTANDING TECHNICAL ENGLISH

1. Find the general and technical meanings of the words in an English-German
   dictionary or in an online dictionary.

   a. conductor   b. circuit   c. charge

2. Translate the sentences into German.

   a. Two good examples of poor conductors of electricity are glass and
      plastic.
   b. There is a charge of 20 euros if you want to drive your car on the motor
      racing circuit.
   c. The conductor interrupted the rehearsal because there was a problem
      with the lighting in the hall.
   d. An electric charge can be a flow of current through a circuit.

WORD BANK

conductor – elektrischer Leiter,
Draht
electrical connector – elektrischer
Anschluss
semiconductor – Halbleiter
sensor – Sensor
soldering iron – Lötkolben

B

NACH DIESEM MODUL:

√ kann ich verschiedene Firmenab-
teilungen auf Englisch erklären,

√ kann ich Arbeitsplätze und Tätig-
keiten auf Englisch beschreiben,

√ kann ich eine Firmenstruktur auf
Englisch beschreiben.

Your company

Regardless of whether your company builds houses, repairs cars, or makes furniture, there is likely to come a time where you will be required to talk about yourself, your job and your company in English. Whether you are greeting an English-speaking visitor, giving a tour of the factory, or talking to suppliers from another country, it is important you have the skills and vocabulary to express yourself clearly.

1   **Work on your own. Look at the photos and brainstorm words that describe what is shown in each of them.**

I/P **2**   **Compare your list of words with your partner and work together to describe the pictures. Use these words to help you:**

> building site • cable • construction worker • grease • hard hat •
> car mechanic • overalls • ratchet • server • timber • tools • wires •
> work gloves

WATCH OUT!

She ~~wears~~ a hard hat.   She <u>is wearing</u> a hard hat.

P **3**   **With your partner, think of three questions you would like to ask each of the four young workers shown in the photos.**

A | The company and its departments

P **1** **Use the words and phrases in the table to explain what the departments of Krone Elektronik GmbH do.**

Example: Sales and Marketing advertises and sells the products.

Department		
Sales and Marketing	distribute	the products are not damaged.
Production Planning	*advertise and sell*	new employees.
Accounts	check	raw materials.
HR (Human Resources)	buy	*the products.*
Production	deal with	the computer network.
Logistics	recruit and train	the finished products.
Purchasing	maintain	customer problems.
Customer Service	handle	the company's finances.
R&D (Research and Development)	make	new products.
IT (Information Technology)	organize	production schedules.
Quality Control	develop	the products to the customers.

P **2** **Use the information in the table to form sentences using *responsible for / in charge of*.**

Example:
The Production department is responsible for making the products.
The Production Planning department is in charge of …

P **3** **Look at the departments again and write down three questions. Then close your book and ask your partner.**

Example:
A: What is the Quality Control department responsible for?
B: It is responsible for …
A: Which department is in charge of …?
B: The … department is in charge of …

R **4**
KMK I
⊙ A 1.2 **Der Ausbildungsleiter von Krone Elektronik, Herr Kirchner, zeigt Sean, einem Elektrotechnikstudenten aus Belfast, das Firmengelände und die einzelnen Abteilungen. Hören Sie sich das Gespräch an und beantworten Sie die folgenden Fragen auf Deutsch.**

1. Wann wurde Krone Elektronik GmbH gegründet, und von wem?
2. Wo hat die Firma ihren Hauptsitz?
3. Wie viele Produktionsanlagen hat Krone Elektronik insgesamt?
4. Wo wird nächstes Jahr eine neue Produktionsanlage eröffnet?
5. Wie viele Leute beschäftigt die Firma?
6. Woran arbeitet die Forschungs- und Entwicklungsabteilung gerade?
7. Welche drei Abteilungen befinden sich in dem Hauptgebäude?
8. Wo wird Sean zuerst arbeiten?
9. Wie viele Zylinderköpfe werden jährlich bei Krone Elektronik hergestellt?
10. Was passiert momentan in der IT-Abteilung?

WORD BANK

grease – Fett, Schmierfett
ratchet – Knarre
raw materials – Rohmaterialien
recruit (v) – anwerben
tool – Werkzeug

B | Tasks and responsibilities

Industrial companies are made up of many different people, who all have a variety of tasks and responsibilities. DWG Tech GmbH in Stuttgart manufactures machine parts for the automotive and aviation industry. Below, Tim Schieber, a DWG Tech GmbH employee, talks about his job and daily activities on DWG Tech GmbH's English website.

R **1** **Read the text and answer the following questions in your own words.**

1. What do CNC machines do?
2. What problems can occur with CNC machines?

Hi, my name is Tim Schieber and I work as a CNC machine operator here at the DWG Tech headquarters in Stuttgart. I've been with the company since completing my apprenticeship three years ago and next summer I am going to work at the DWG Tech branch in Detroit.

5 In my opinion, what we do here is very important. CNC is all about precision, and it is therefore essential that I concentrate at all times. These machines drill, shape, cut and polish the parts for automobiles and aeroplanes. As a CNC machine operator I am responsible for one machine. As I said, this job is all about precision, and the machines are programmed specifically for each job. I do not do the programming
10 myself, but I learnt programming during my apprenticeship and I sometimes have to intervene when something goes wrong – such as a vibrating workpiece or broken cutting tools.

The CNC process is almost entirely automatic. It is my job to set up the machine for the production process, which means loading the machine with the correct tools and
15 workpieces. Once the programming for an operation is done, I enter the commands into the machine. To do this we use a computer network. The next step is to let the machine work its magic.

The main part of my job is to monitor the machine and spot problems. This means checking that the machine is running smoothly, measuring finished workpieces to
20 check that the dimensions are correct, and sometimes replacing tools. It is also important that the machine is kept cool and lubricated with a special lubricating oil – but this is also done automatically. Of course, another of my tasks is to make sure the machine is kept clean, and that the working area is safe.

My working day depends on what shift I am on. We generally work either early shift
25 or late shift. Early shift is from 6am until 2pm, and the guys on late shift begin at 2pm and clock out at 10pm. Sometimes, if we have a lot of work to do, there is also a night shift – but that doesn't happen too often. I actually prefer early shift. Even though I don't enjoy waking up at 4:45am, it is great to have the afternoon to do whatever I like – especially in the summer.

30 I really enjoy my job and I am proud to be working for an international company like DWG. My colleagues and I are always very busy and it can be fairly stressful. But I love working with the machines and it is interesting to see the many technological developments in the industry.

2 **Find the synonyms in the text for the following words:**

1. to finish
2. very important
3. cars
4. accuracy
5. to observe
6. usually
7. to like
8. workmates
9. quite

R   **3** **Decide whether the statements are true or false. Give reasons for your decisions in German.**

1. Tim is currently doing an apprenticeship as a CNC machine operator.
2. Once the machine starts running, Tim's work is over.
3. One of Tim's tasks is making sure that the cutting tools are not broken.
4. Tim rarely works in shifts.
5. Accuracy is very important for CNC work.
6. The technology used in CNC machining has hardly changed over the years.

P   **4** **Your boss has asked you to write a short text for your company's English website. Make sure you include some basic facts about your company and details about your daily tasks and responsibilities. Use some of the phrases in Tim's text, e.g.** *I work as, I've been with the company since,* **etc.**

→ **PHRASES:** Your company

P/I   **5** **Check the Internet for a job in your industry that interests you. Make notes on the daily tasks and responsibilities.**

I   **6** **Explain the job you researched to your partner, but don't mention the job title. Your partner must guess what the job is from the description you give. Then swap roles.**

C | Organisational structure

P/M   KMK II **Sie sind Auszubildende(r) in der DWG Tech GmbH. Ihr Vorgesetzter benötigt eine Übersicht über die Ingenieursabteilung der DWG Tech GmbH Niederlassung in Detroit. Auf deren Firmen-Homepage finden Sie die folgenden Informationen zu den Mitarbeitern. Zeichnen Sie ein Organigramm nach der vorliegenden Beschreibung.**

Who's who in DWG Tech GmbH Detroit's engineering department?

DWG Tech GmbH Inc. employs around 60 people in its engineering department. The department is led by Chief Engineer Dr. Adam Foster, who is supported by his Personal Assistant Helen Green and DWG Tech's Assistant Chief Engineer Dr. Tim Bayliss. The engineering department is split into two core areas: automotive and aviation. Shift leaders Chris Falsone and Sandra Borowski report to Michael Kellermann, the foreman. They all belong to automotive which is run by experienced Chief Automotive Engineer, Dr. Torben Brinkema. DWG Tech's aviation department is in the capable hands of Dr. Judith Sommer, Chief Aviation Engineer, who has

been with the company for over 15 years. Dr. Sommer is supported by foreman Frank Kapowski. Barry Richardson and Jens Schmelzer are the two shift leaders and work closely with Mr Kapowski.

WORD BANK

aviation – Luftfahrt
CNC (computerized numerical control) – CNC (computerisierte numerische Steuerung)
dimensions – Maße
drill (v) – bohren
lubricated – geölt
lubricating oil – Schmieröl
measure (v) – messen
polish (v) – schleifen, polieren
precision – Genauigkeit
shape (v) – fräsen, formen
vibrate (v) – vibrieren
workpiece – Werkstück

WORD BANK ◉

braking system – Bremsanlage
cylinder head – Zylinderkopf
interface – Schnittstelle
manufacturing plant – Produktionsbetrieb
operating system – Betriebssystem

03

Electronic devices

Complex electronic devices such as transistors, rectifiers, varistors, zener diodes, capacitors and op-amps all work with electricity in some way. Some devices amplify the current, for example, and other devices can switch or break the current. Other electronic devices control voltage or store electric charge. The devices are usually connected together on a circuit board. They are represented on circuit diagrams by various symbols.

1 Identify the electronic devices in the photo. Then give the German words for the devices that you have identified.

P **2** Match the definitions with six of the devices in the photo.

1. It amplifies and switches electronic signals.
2. It converts AC to DC.
3. It conducts increased current and protects circuits.
4. It allows current to flow forwards and also in the opposite direction.
5. It stores energy.
6. It produces an output voltage that is much higher than the voltage difference between its input terminals.

3 Think of other electronic devices that you know. Find the English term and a definition for each device.

A | A frequency converter

Frequency converters or frequency changers are electronic components, which are used in applications such as motors, pumps and fans. They do exactly what their name suggests: they convert or change the frequency of alternating current (AC) from the national grid, for example. The current can then be used to drive devices that require direct current (DC).

P **1** **Read the text and answer the questions.**

1. Why are frequency converters necessary?
2. For which applications does the automobile industry need frequency converters?
3. Which other industries use frequency converters, and why?

Frequency converters

The national grid transmits electricity at a frequency of 50 Hz. This frequency is not suitable for some devices and this is where a frequency converter comes in. Frequency converters are often applied in the automobile industry
5 to control the speed of pumps and fans as well as the torque of AC motors, for example. Frequency converters are also used in the aircraft industry. As aeroplanes are often powered with much higher frequencies, 50Hz converters are needed to power aeroplanes while they are still on ground or later to provide power in the planes when they are in the air. The nuclear power
10 industry uses frequency converters to regulate operations in power stations. Production lines in industry include frequency converters to guarantee the accuracy of products.

P **2** **Check the Internet for other applications of frequency converters and present your results in class.**

3 **SAFETY FIRST** ⚠

⊙ A 2.3 1. **Markus Schröder is in the second year of his mechatronics course at a college in Dortmund. He meets Peter, an exchange student from London, after a class about safety regulations when working with electricity. Peter wants to make sure that he has understood everything correctly so he asks Markus for help. Listen to the dialogue and make a list of the German safety regulations they talk about.**

⊙ A 2.3 2. **Listen to the dialogue again and make a list of the English safety regulations that correspond to the German ones in exercise 3.1.**

👥 3. **Think of accidents that can happen when working with electricity in the workshop if you don't follow the safety rules. Use if-clauses as shown in the example below.**

Example:
If you don't disconnect the machine from the electric circuit, you will get an electric shock.

WORD BANK

amplify (v) – verstärken
circuit board – Leiterplatte
conduct (v) – leiten
convert (v) – umwandeln
electric charge – elektrische Ladung
frequency converter, frequency changer – Frequenzumrichter
input terminal – Netzeingang
torque – Drehmoment

WORD BANK ⊙

circuit – Schaltkreis
circuit breaker – Sicherung, Leitungsschutzschalter
disconnect (v) – abschalten, abklemmen
earth (v) – erden
guard – Schutzschild, Schutzgitter
live wire – stromführender Draht
multimeter – Mehrfachmessgerät
short-circuit (v) – kurzschließen
tag – Zettel, Anhänger
tag (v) – beschildern, mit einem Zettelanhänger versehen

B | Semiconductors

Semiconductors are materials which conduct electricity. Although semiconductors
are less conductive than conductors, their conductivity can be adjusted easily.
For this reason, they are often used in the manufacture of electronic components.
The conductivity of semiconductors is highly dependent on temperature.
The resistance of semiconductors decreases as the temperature increases.
Semiconductors are important materials in the electronics industry where they
are used in the manufacture of transistors, diodes, rectifiers and sensors.

P **1** Find and correct the mistakes in the definition of a semiconductor.

> **Semiconductor** [ˌsemikən'dʌktə] *(noun)* The word 'semiconductor' describes a
> material with a much higher conductivity than conductors. When the
> conductivity of a semiconductor is changed, it can no longer be used in
> electronic devices. By raising the temperature of a semiconductor, you
> automatically raise its resistance, too.

2 Complete the text about semiconductors using the words in the box.

> adding · charged · computers · conductivity · electronic · holes ·
> insulators · jump · materials · metallic · properties · resistors ·
> semiconductive · temperature

Semiconductors

Semiconductors are widely used in the production
of **1** devices where they can function both as
conductors and insulators. The chemical structure
5 of semiconductors gives them an electrical **2**
between these two ranges. Semiconductors are
used as basic elements in transistors, light-emitting
diodes, rectifiers and other **3** components.
These components are found in appliances such
10 as radios, telephones and **4** where they control,
convert and carry out other processes.
Current flows in **5** conductors when the electrons
move. In semiconductors, however, the flow of
current is usually described either as the flow of
15 electrons or as **6** in the flow of electrons. These
gaps can be filled by other electrons which **7** into
the spaces. Thus the current is considered to be
moving and it is positively **8** .
Semiconductors are extremely dependent on **9** .
Therefore they are used as thermistors or NTC 20
(negative temperature coefficient) **10** . Depending
on the chemicals used in their manufacture,
semiconductors can also function as **11** . Silicon is
commonly used for semiconductors, but lots of
other **12** are also in use. By **13** different chemicals 25
called dopants, you can influence the conductivity
of a semiconductor as well as its electronic **14** .
These 'doped' semiconductors are called extrinsic
semiconductors whereas pure semiconductors are
called intrinsic semiconductors. 30

3 Define the following words in the text in your own words.

1. thermistors
2. dopants
3. extrinsic semiconductors
4. intrinsic semiconductors

4 Find examples of applications of semiconductors and present your results in class.   → **PHRASES:** Presentations

C | Ohm's Law

M 1
KMK II
Als Vorbereitung für ein Referat über das Ohmsche Gesetz bittet Ihr Lehrer Sie, folgenden Artikel aus einer englischen Fachzeitschrift auf Deutsch zusammenzufassen. Fassen Sie die wichtigsten Informationen in dem Artikel zusammen.

Georg Simon Ohm, a German physicist, discovered a basic law according to which direct current (DC) reacts.
5 He experimented with three components: current for which he used the letter I, voltage named in English V and the resistance of the conductor
10 which he labelled R. The letters I, V and R are commonly used when we talk about Ohm's Law (in German U is used instead of V). Through his experiments
15 Ohm found out that the current (I) flowing through a resistor is proportional to the electric voltage (V). He also discovered that the resistance (R) is
20 dependent on the material, the length and the cross-section of the resistor as well as its temperature. Resistance increases with length and
25 decreases with an increasing cross-section.
Ohm presented his findings with this equation which later became known as Ohm's Law:
30 **R = V / I**
There are three conventional representations of the law. The three equations are interchangeable and they all
35 lead to the same result: current = voltage/resistance; voltage = current·resistance; resistance = voltage/current. Scientists later agreed to
40 measure voltage in volts, current in amperes (or amps) and resistance in ohms, using Ω, the Greek letter omega (Ω).

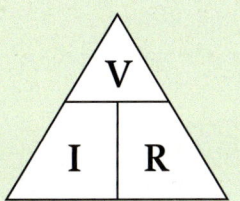

Ohm's Law

P 2
KMK II
Entscheiden Sie, ob die Aussagen richtig oder falsch sind und begründen Sie Ihre Meinung auf Deutsch.

1. Georg Ohm hat herausgefunden, nach welchen Grundsätzen Wechselstrom sich verhält.
2. Ohms Experimente waren auf Strom, Spannung und Leitungswiderstand abgestellt.
3. Um seine Ergebnisse darzustellen, zeichnete Ohm einen Kreis und teilte ihn in drei Abschnitte mit den Buchstaben I, V und R ein.
4. Das Material, die Länge, der Durchmesser und die Temperatur des Leiters sind unabhängig voneinander und können jederzeit frei gewählt werden.
5. Der Widerstand verkleinert sich mit einem anwachsenden Durchmesser des Leiters.

3
UNDERSTANDING TECHNICAL ENGLISH

1. **Find the general and technical meanings of the German words in a dictionary.**
   a. Spannung   b. Strom

2. **Translate the German version of Ohm's Law into English.**

Das Ohmsche Gesetz besagt, dass die Stromstärke I in einem Leiter und die Spannung U zwischen den Enden des Leiters direkt proportional zueinander sind. Als einfache mathematische Merkformel dient URI.

WORD BANK

4
⚠ **Use the Internet to find out why current is measured in amperes and voltage is measured in volts. Then report your findings to the class.**

cross-section – Querschnitt
equation – Gleichung

NACH DIESEM MODUL:

✓ kenne ich die wichtigsten Redewendungen um ein Telefongespräch zu führen,

✓ kann ich Maße, Namen und
Adressen am Telefon auf Englisch
weitergeben.

Telephoning

When you are on the job, chances are you will have your mobile phone with you –
it does not matter what line of work you are in. Whether you are repairing a server,
fixing a leak, or installing a telephone line, your phone can ring at any time. It could
be a customer with a complaint, you may have to ring a supplier or check the status
of an order. And if you have to talk in English, you need to have the necessary skills
to understand and be understood, no matter what the situation.

P **1** **Look at the photos. What might the people be talking about on the telephone?
Compare your answers with a partner. Use these words to help you:**

materials · problem · delay · support · help · breakdown · repair ·
solution · angry · confused · crash · computer network room

2 **Match the German words below with the English equivalents.**

1. Handy	a. message
2. Anrufbeantworter	b. hands-free device
3. Festnetz	c. extension number
4. Nachricht	d. mobile/cell phone
5. Durchwahl	e. answering machine
6. Freisprechanlage	f. area code
7. Vorwahl	g. country code
8. Ländervorwahl	h. landline

A | Making and receiving a phone call

R **1** Which of the following phrases are used for making calls and which ones for receiving calls? Make a list.

1. Could you put me through to Mr Warren, please?
2. I'm sorry, but Mr/Ms … is in a meeting at the moment.
3. How can I help you?
4. Thank you. I'll ring back later.
5. Can I ask what your call is about?
6. Would you like to leave a message?
7. Thank you very much for your help.
8. My name is Barry Potter and I'm calling from …
9. May I take your name, please?
10. I'd like to speak to somebody in the production department, please.
11. Hold the line, please. I'll put you through.
12. Could you tell him/her that …?

M **2** Read the telephone conversation below and find the English equivalents for the following German expressions.

→ **PHRASES:** Telephoning

> 1. Haben Sie etwas zum Schreiben?

> 2. Soll ich Ihnen seine Handynummer geben?

> 3. Er ist leider zurzeit nicht im Büro.

> 4. Ich hätte gerne mit … gesprochen.

> 5. Einen Moment, bitte.

> 6. Wie kann ich Ihnen helfen?

Christoph: Smart EDV, Christoph Fink.
Caller: Er, yes, hello. Do you speak English?
Christoph: Certainly. How can I help you?
Caller: This is the Smart IT company in Kiel, isn't it?
Christoph: Yes, that's correct.
Caller: Great. My name is Erik Pedersen and I'm calling from Danske Onlinebank Copenhagen. I'd like to speak to Mr Gebhardt, please.
Christoph: Sorry, but Mr Gebhardt is not in the office at the moment. Can I take a message, or would you like his mobile number?
Caller: Can you give me his mobile number, please?
Christoph: Ok, do you have a pen?
Caller: Just a second, please … ok, go ahead.
Christoph: The number is 0049-170 557624.
Caller: Sorry, I didn't catch that. Could you speak up a bit?
Christoph: Yes, of course. The number is 0049-170 557624.
Caller: Thank you very much.
Christoph: You're welcome. Maybe you can give me your phone number.
Caller: Certainly. It's 0045, that's the country code for Denmark, 32, the area code for Copenhagen, and then 54 58 11. Oh, and my extension number is 944.
Christoph: 0045-32 54 58 11, extension 944. Thank you very much. Goodbye.
Caller: Goodbye.

WORD BANK

breakdown – Störung, Ausfall
crash – Absturz
leak – Leck

INTERCULTURAL BOX

Intercultural awareness – Telephoning in English-speaking countries

When talking on the phone in English it is important that you use suitable and polite phrases. For example, if you know the person you are calling, it is common to make a little small talk before getting down to business. One thing to remember: Although it is common for English people to quickly switch to first names, it is still important to remain polite and remember that you are talking to a customer or a colleague, and not your best friend.

Example: *How are you? I haven't spoken to you for a while.*

If you have to give bad news or talk about a problem, then you should begin with *I'm afraid* … or *Unfortunately* … .

Example: *I'm afraid we cannot install your wireless internet connection this week.*

A request often begins with *Could you possibly* … or *I would be grateful if you would / could* … .

Example: *I would be grateful if you would call me back later.*

When someone thanks you for your help, or for a job well done, you can simply say *You're welcome*. And be careful! Whereas in German, just saying *yes* or *no* may be fine, this is considered to be quite impolite in England. Instead, just say *Yes, I think so*, or *No, I'm afraid not*. If you call somebody, you should give your name, where you are calling from, and say who you would like to speak to.

Example: *Hello, my name is Felix Hirschbach, calling from Crown Electronics. Could I speak to Ms Cameron, please?*

P **3** **How would you say the following things more politely?** → **PHRASES:** Telephoning

1. Eh? Say it again!
2. Give me your number!
3. What do you want?
4. What's your name?
5. I can't hear you!
6. What?
7. He's not here!
8. Give me Ms Bauer!

I **4** **Sie arbeiten im International Calls Service Center von Smart EDV in Kiel und erhalten**
KMK I **einen Anruf. Führen Sie das folgende Telefongespräch mit einem Partner auf Englisch.**

Smart EDV GmbH, Kiel.	Stefanie Berg, dänische Kundin
Nehmen Sie den Anruf entgegen.	Nennen Sie Ihren Namen. Sie möchten mit Herrn Gebhardt sprechen.
Sagen Sie, dass Sie die Anruferin schlecht verstehen und bitten Sie sie, etwas lauter zu sprechen.	Sprechen Sie etwas lauter und fragen Sie, ob Sie jetzt besser zu verstehen sind.
Bejahen Sie und fragen Sie, worum es geht.	Erklären Sie, dass die Firma Smart EDV gestern in Ihrer Firma neue Hardware und Software installiert hat, und dass heute Morgen der Server abgestürzt ist. Es ist dringend!
Sagen Sie höflich, dass Herr Gebhardt in einer Sitzung ist und sich später melden wird. Fragen Sie, ob Herr Gebhardt die Nummer der Anruferin hat.	
	Bejahen Sie. Bedanken Sie sich und beenden Sie das
Bedanken Sie sich auch und verabschieden Sie sich.	Gespräch.

B | Giving information over the phone

Making a quick call is often the fastest and easiest way of passing on valuable information, such as measurements or figures. However, misunderstandings can happen very quickly, so it is important to make sure any information is delivered clearly and correctly.

1   Match the English word to the German translation.

1.	height	a.	Breite
2.	length	b.	Gewicht
3.	width	c.	Höhe
4.	weight	d.	Tiefe
5.	depth	e.	Länge

INFO BOX: Saying weights and measurements

nine **point** five milimetres (9.5 mm)	100 **by** 30 **by** 15 (100 x 30 x 15)
thirty one **square** metres (31 m²)	twenty **cubic** metres (20 m³)
one **point** two five litre engine (1.25 l)	6000 revolutions **per** minute (6000 rpm)
170 kilometers **per** hour (170 kph)	two hundred **and** twenty volts (220 V)

2   What are the adjectives for the nouns in exercise 1?

3   Sit back to back with a partner. Take turns in giving each other different information over the phone. Partner A uses role card A, Partner B uses role card B (see Appendix).

4   Sit back to back and spell your name, the name and address of your company, and your email address. Use the table below to help you.

Symbol	Name	Example
@	at	info@
B / b	capital letter / lower case	NYC / asap
-	hyphen / dash	t-online
ö	o-umlaut / oe / o with two dots	Schönberg
:	colon	http:
/	slash / stroke / forward slash	org/news
\	backslash	\docs
.	dot	.de
_	underscore	customer_info

R 5
KMK I
⊙ A 1.3

Alex Bauder works for Fertighaus Henke in Magdeburg and is called by Mr. Reid, an English customer who lives in Germany and who is currently building a house near Magdeburg. Listen to the conversation and answer the following questions in German.

1. Who is Mr Deschler?
2. Why can't Mr Reid speak to him personally?
3. Why does Mr Reid want to speak to Mr Deschler?
4. When will Fertighaus Henke begin building Mr Reid's cellar?
5. Why does the extractor fan need to be moved to the left?
6. Which changes is Mr Deschler not responsible for?
7. What should Mr Deschler do next?

R 6
⊙ A 1.3

Now listen to the conversation again and make notes of the changes Mr Reid wants, where he wants them, and details about the measurements, where given.

WORD BANK

cubic metre – Kubikmeter
revolutions per minute – Drehzahl
socket – Steckdose
square metre – Quadratmeter

WORD BANK ⊙

construction manager – Bauleiter
diameter – Durchmesser
extractor fan – Dunstabzugshaube
foundation pit – Baugrube
hob – Kochfeld

04

NACH DIESEM MODUL:

√ kann ich wichtige Elemente der Automatisierung auf Englisch nennen,

√ kann ich einen automatisierten Arbeitsablauf auf Englisch beschreiben.

Automation systems

Automation systems are applied in all areas of manufacturing and services. These systems are based on pneumatic, hydraulic, electrical and mechanical systems, which are usually computer-controlled. Human operators are replaced to a great extent by automated process technologies. As a result of automation, processes are more reliable and hygienic as well as being safer. Production and quality are also greatly increased and delivery times are shortened significantly.

1   Describe the automation systems in the photos. Use the words in the box.

> warehouse · bottling · assembly · automobile · line · management · CNC · plant · machine tools · factory · system

2   Describe the automated processes in the photos using the verbs.

> control · assemble · operate · transport · fill · manufacture

3   List the advantages of the automated processes shown in the photos for the companies and employees involved.

4   Think of examples of automated processes that you find either in manufacturing or service industries.

A | Automated working processes

Automated working processes can be broken down into a series of single tasks. Elements such as feeding and monitoring systems, computer panels, control units and conveyor belts are the parts we usually recognise in a production line. These devices are controlled by software that is loaded on the PLC (programmable logic controller). The parts that do the actual work, and which we do not normally see, include sensors, actuators, motors, transmitters, pistons and switches. These parts are linked to the PLC by a digital, bi-directional control network called the fieldbus system.

P **1** Label the diagram of the fieldbus system using words from the text.

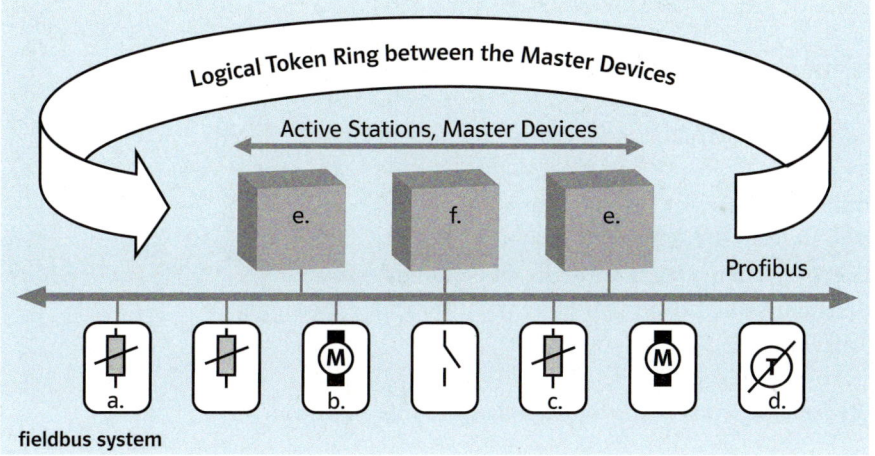

2 Complete the text about fieldbus systems using the words in the box.

> reliable · redundancy · PLC control systems · smaller · personnel ·
> I/O cards · installation · fault · distributors · cables · bus cable

A fieldbus connects different levels in an automated process. The fieldbus replaces several parallel cables with one single **1** . Whether you use **2** or PC-based controls, the transmission medium of the fieldbus transmits all necessary information. Interface cards replace traditional **3** . Thus
5   switch cabinets can be much **4** units than they used to be. Savings on
5 and wiring are another positive effect. Fieldbus systems are able to diagnose themselves as well as being highly **6** and easy to maintain. A service person no longer needs to search for a **7** among lots of cables. Open fieldbus systems allow the easy transfer between components from
10 other **8** on the market, at least when it comes to basic communication between the systems. If you need to exchange or alter your **9** , a quick and flexible replacement is possible. On the other hand, you need more qualified **10** to handle the complex system of fieldbuses. Components are more complicated and a certain **11** is necessary to make sure the
15 production line continues working even if one bus system breaks down.

P **3** Use the Internet to find out about fieldbus systems that are currently available on the market. Present your results in class.

→ **PHRASES**: Presentations

WORD BANK

automation system – Automatisierungssystem
bi-directional – in zwei Richtungen
cable – Kabel
computer-controlled – computergesteuert
control unit – Steuerung
conveyor belt – Förder-, Montageband
device – Gerät, Vorrichtung
diagnose itself (v) – selbstständig Fehler erkennen
feed (v) – zuführen, bestücken
fieldbus system – Feldbussystem
interface – Schnittstelle, Interface
load (v) – laden, aufladen
maintain (v) – warten, in Stand halten
monitor (v) – überwachen
operate (v) – bedienen
operator – Bediener(in)
piston – Kolben
switch cabinet – Verteilerkasten, Schaltschrank
transfer – Übertragung, Übermittlung
transmission – Übertragung
transmit (v) – übertragen
wiring – elektrische Verdrahtung

B | Planning an automated system

The key to an effective automated system is good planning and documentation. Each part of the operation or sequence must be examined and integrated in the design of the system. The most important planning tools are a sequence description, a positional sketch, a circuit diagram and a displacement-step diagram. These tools describe the whole system or parts of it, either verbally or in a diagram.

1 Find the English words for the planning tools in the text above.

1. Ablaufbeschreibung
2. Schaltplan
3. Wegschrittdiagramm
4. Technologieschema

2 Match the definitions with the words in exercise 1.

1. It defines the position of the actuators and shows how the machine devices are connected.
2. It explains the motion sequences of the actuators.
3. It describes all of the steps in the operating sequence.
4. It shows the position of elements such as the input elements, processing elements, control elements and power components. It indicates the signal flow between these elements.

3 Say which planning tools you have worked with and mention any difficulties you may have had.

4 Look at the diagram and identify the parts of the piston using the words below.

> outlet port (exhaust) · retracted-end position · cylinder ·
> inlet port (supply port) · forward-end position

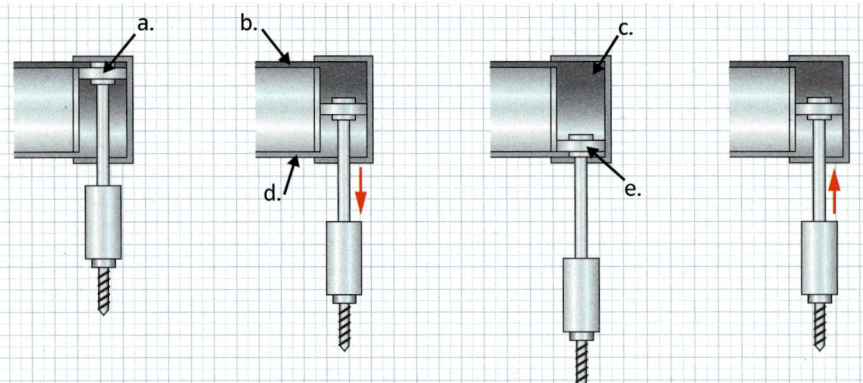

5 Explain how the piston valve in exercise 4 works.

6 UNDERSTANDING TECHNICAL ENGLISH
Give the general and technical meanings of the words. Use an online dictionary.

a. operation
b. feed
c. power

C | Automated processes

R/M **1**
KMK II
◎ **A 2.4**

Sie haben von einer internationalen Fachmesse in München einen Podcast über eine Forumsdiskussion zum Thema „Automatisierung technischer Prozesse" gefunden. Ihr Ausbilder bittet Sie, die wichtigsten Infos auf Deutsch für die anderen Auszubildenden zusammenzustellen. Zunächst stellen Sie die wichtigsten Stichwörter in der untenstehenden Tabelle auf Deutsch zusammen.

Rationalisierung des Arbeitsablaufs	Mechanik	Automatisierung technischer Prozesse

R/M **2**
KMK II
◎ **A 2.4**

Hören Sie das Gespräch ein zweites Mal an und ergänzen Sie fehlende Punkte anschließend zusammen mit Ihrem Partner. Fassen Sie die Punkte in ganzen Sätzen auf Deutsch zusammen.

M **3**
KMK II

In den Materialien von der Messe in München finden Sie einen Artikel über Materialzuführung bei automatisierten Produktionsstraßen. Damit die spanischen Studenten, die gerade ein Praktikum in Ihrer Firma machen, den Artikel verstehen, fassen Sie den Text auf Englisch zusammen. Die Wörter in der Sprachbox können Ihnen dabei helfen.

> feed system · robot arm · pick and place application · machine vision system · precise · high quality · standstill · quantity

Materialzuführung

Automatisierte Produktionsstraßen benötigen eine reibungslose Zuführung der für die Produktion notwendigen Materialien oder erforderlichen
5 Bauteile. Deshalb sind automatisch gesteuerte Zuführungssysteme oder Pick-and-Place-Anwendungen aus vielen Industriebranchen nicht mehr wegzudenken. Sie stehen bei Fertigungs- oder Montagevorgängen nicht nur am Anfang
10 des Produktionsprozesses, sondern sind auch Bestandteile innerhalb des Fertigungsvorgangs, um Bauteile zum nächsten Arbeitsschritt zu befördern. Moderne Zuführungssysteme kommen insbesondere dann zum Einsatz, wenn hohe
15 Stückzahlen produziert werden und eine sichere, schnelle und kontinuierlich präzise Beschickung ein absolutes Muss für qualitativ hochwertige Endprodukte ist. Bei den Unternehmen sind insbesondere Standardsysteme gefragt, die
20 sich bei Bedarf ohne großen Kostenaufwand und Produktionsstillstand umrüsten lassen.

Besonderer Beliebtheit erfreut sich in diesem Zusammenhang der Pick-and-Place-Roboter, der in der Lage ist, Bauteile in Sekundenschnelle aufzugreifen und so zu platzieren, dass der folgende Arbeitsschritt unmittelbar anschließen 25 kann. Bildverarbeitungssysteme erkennen dabei verwirbelte Teile und geben die Informationen an den Roboterarm weiter, der die richtigen Teile exakt aufgreift und transportiert. 30

D

NACH DIESEM MODUL:

✓ kann ich auf Englisch kurze Anfragen, Angebote und Bestellungen als Brief, E-Mail oder Fax erstellen,

✓ kann ich englische Briefe, E-Mails und Faxe beantworten.

Written communication

Written communication such as emails, faxes and business letters play an essential role in business, both in the office and the workshop. For any company to run efficiently, it is necessary to have an effective communication system – making sure that enquiries are answered promptly, offers are made on time, and orders are placed and processed correctly. The standard business letter has been replaced in recent years by the faster email, and to a lesser extent, the fax. In all areas of business today it is common to have dealings with countries across the globe, meaning you need to be able to understand written communication in English.

P **1** Look at the pictures above and describe them in your own words.

P **2** What are the advantages and disadvantages of the forms of written communication shown in the pictures? Create a list. Use these words to help you:

confidential · instant · easy · time-consuming · reliable · signal · misunderstanding · slow · personal · formal · informal

3 Compare your lists with a partner and come up with a final list for each form of communication. Share your final list with the class.

A | Enquiries

Business transactions generally begin with an enquiry. In the example below, a car garage is looking for a new supplier of tools.

M **1** Stephen Bains from City Garage in Wolverhampton, England is interested in buying some tools from Hauch Werkzeuge KG in Gelsenkirchen, a toolmaking company specializing in tools for car mechanics. Read Stephen's enquiry and sum up the main information in German.

Dear Sir/Madam,

Automotive mechanic tool supplier

We saw your advertisement in this month's edition of *Under the Bonnet* magazine regarding your selection of tools for car mechanics.

We are a family-run car mechanic company in Wolverhampton, England, with over 20 employees.

We have recently expanded and are looking for a new supplier of quality tools for our new workshops. Therefore we would ask you to send us a copy of your latest catalogue and price list.

Please also inform us about your export prices and possible discounts as well as terms of payment and delivery and delivery times.

As we would like to test your tools, we would appreciate it if you could send us some samples.

Thank you for your attention to this enquiry and we look forward to hearing from you.

Yours sincerely,

a. appropriate salutation

b. subject line

c. source of address

d. introduction of your firm

e. reason for enquiry

f. request to send catalogue and price list

g. request for information on prices and discounts and terms of payment and delivery

h. further requests

i. closing phrase

j. complimentary close

R **2** Match these parts of an enquiry with the descriptions (a.–j.) above.

1. Best wishes.
2. Your company was recommended to me by a colleague.
3. We are a large production company, specialising in machine components.
4. Please let us have a detailed cost estimate for configuring our IT network.
5. We hope to hear from you soon.
6. What are your terms of payment for regular customers?
7. As we are convinced that your products will sell well on the American market …
8. A visit by your representative would be greatly appreciated.
9. Please let us know whether you can supply from stock.
10. Machine component supplier

WORD BANK

bonnet – Motorhaube
car mechanic – KFZ-Mechaniker(in)
toolmaking company – Werkzeug-macher
workshop – Werkstatt

B | Offers

P **1** Read the offer email below and complete it using the words from the box.

> bank transfer · discount · interest · business · working days · sample ·
> attachment · delivery period · stock · orders

From:	mailto:t.wolf@hauch…de	Sent:	201_-05-30 14:52
To:	mailto:info@citygarage.co…uk		
Cc:	mailto:k.mueller@hauch…de		

Subject: Your enquiry

📎 **Attachments** Hauptkatalog_2012.pdf

Dear Mr Bains

Thank you for your enquiry and your **1** in our products.

We are sending you our latest brochure and price list as an **2** .
For **3** of 200 units or more we are able to grant a quantity **4** of five per cent.
For large orders (over 250 units) we require a **5** of 10 – 14 **6** .
Smaller orders can be delivered from **7** and within 3 – 5 working days.

Our usual terms of payment are by **8** to our account with the GDB Bank in
Gelsenkirchen.

One **9** case of ratchets, sockets, wrenches and screwdrivers has been dispatched
to you this morning and should reach you in the next few days.

Thank you again for your enquiry. We look forward to establishing regular **10** with you.

Yours sincerely

Tim Wolf

P **2** Use the following notes to write an enquiry and an offer in English.

→ **PHRASES:**
Written communication

Enquiry
(You work at Construct World.)

- large DIY store in Poland (Construct World), looking to buy quality German-made tools
- saw your company (Hauch Werkzeuge KG) at a trade show in Hannover
- would like information about delivery times, discounts, copy of catalogue
- would like some samples to inspect
- polite ending

Angebot
(Sie arbeiten bei Hauch Werkzeuge.)

- Bedanken Sie sich für die Anfrage.
- Gerne schicken Sie Ihren aktuellen Prospekt inklusive Preisliste zu.
- Lieferzeit (nach Polen): große Bestellungen (über 500 Stück): 5 – 10 Werktage, kleine Bestellungen: 2 – 4 Werktage
- Preisnachlass ab Bestellwert von 2.500 € möglich (5 %)
- Sie würden sich freuen, mit Construct World zusammenarbeiten zu dürfen.
- höflicher Schluss

C | Orders

1 Read the order fax below and complete it using the prepositions in the box below.

for (2x) • by • of • to (3x) • with

TELEFAX Message

City Garage
17 Gorsebrook Rd.
Wolverhampton WV6 5PI
Tel.: 0044 (0)1902 554997… • Fax: 0044 (0)1902 554998…

To: Hauch Werkzeuge KG   Attention: Mr Tim Wolf
Schmiedstrasse 44
45879 Gelsenkirchen   Fax: 0049 209 721965…
Germany

From: Stephen Bains

Subject: Order

Dear Mr Wolf

Thank you very much **1** your email **2** 30 May.

Thank you also for sending us your catalogue and price list.
We were very impressed **3** your range of tools for car mechanics and
would like to place a trial order **4** 16 socket sets, 16 screwdriver sets,
30 adjustable wrenches and 16 torque wrenches.

Please confirm this order indicating the bank account **5** which you wish
to have the sum in question transferred.

Please deliver the tools **6** our workshop at 17 Gorsebrook Rd.,
Wolverhampton, WV6 5PI.

We look forward **7** receiving the consignment soon and to placing
further orders **8** you.

Best regards

S. Bains

Stephen Bains

M **2** Sie arbeiten bei Hauch Werkzeuge KG in Gelsenkirchen. Ihr Chef bittet Sie, das

obige Fax für ihn auf Deutsch zusammenzufassen, damit er über den Auftrag
informiert ist.

WORD BANK

ratchet – Knarre
screwdriver – Schraubenzieher /
-dreher
socket – Steckdose, Stecknuss
torque wrench – Drehmomentschlüssel
(adjustable) wrench – (verstellbarer)
Schraubenschlüssel

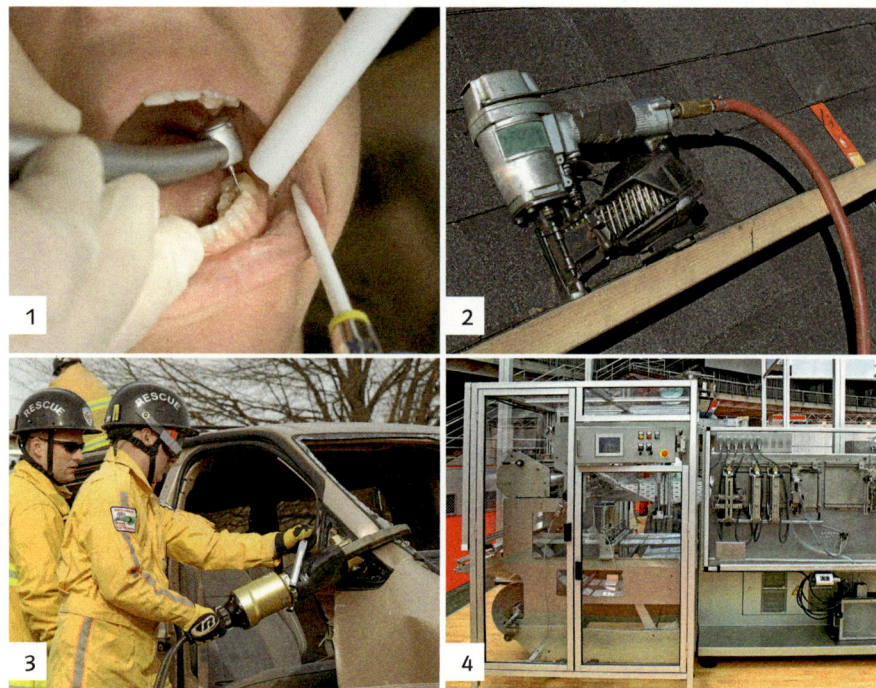

NACH DIESEM MODUL:

√ kenne ich die englischen Bezeich-
nungen für wichtige pneumatische
Bauteile, sowie deren Bestandteile,

√ kann ich den Aufbau einfacher
pneumatischer Schaltkreise und
die Funktionsweise einer pneuma-
tischen Anwendung auf Englisch
beschreiben.

Pneumatic control and components

In order to compete successfully on global markets, manufacturers have to reduce machine costs, improve quality and react quickly to demand. These goals are achieved by automation, a process which replaces manpower. Pneumatics plays a major role in automation and its use in industry is constantly expanding.

R **1** **Match the English terms in the box with the pneumatic applications in the photos.**

> packaging machine · pneumatic bus doors · pneumatic metal cutting shears ·
> pneumatic screwdriver · dentist's drill · tyre fitting machine ·
> pneumatic nail gun

I/P **2** **Make a list of pneumatic applications you know. Describe briefly how they work.**
Use a dictionary if necessary. Present your results to the class.

→ **PHRASES:** Presentations

Example:

Pneumatic applications	Description
air brakes	When the brake pedal is pushed, the brake chamber is supplied with compressed air and the wheels turn more slowly.

A | Pneumatics and pneumatic components

Pneumatic components have many industrial applications, e.g. in automation and robotics. They require less power than hydraulic components. Various pneumatic components are needed to install a pneumatic system where compressed air transmits power, force and motion. These components include pneumatic hoses, pressure regulators, air valves, e.g. pilot valves, pneumatic relays and pneumatic cylinders (actuators). The double-acting cylinder is the most common piston cylinder in use.

WORD BANK

actuator – Aktuator
compressed air – Druckluft
double-acting cylinder – doppelt wirkender Zylinder
hose – Schlauch
pilot valve – Steuerventil
piston cylinder – Kolbenzylinder
relay – Relais
valve – Ventil

1 The compound English words are all parts of the double-acting cylinder. Match them with their functions and give the German meanings.

1. inlet port	it prevents damage to the cylinder	Dämpfungsschraube
2. outlet port		Zylinderrohr
3. cylinder barrel	it is connected to the pressure port	Lagerdeckel
4. piston rod		Abstreifring
5. cushioning screw	it seals the cylinder and cleans the piston rod	Kolbenstange
6. scraper ring		Druckanschluss
7. bearing cap	it covers the piston rod	Lagerbuchse
8. bearing bush	it is used as an air exhaust	Entlüftungsanschluss
	it guides the piston rod	
	it performs forward and return strokes	
	it houses the cylinder	

2 Find the parts mentioned in exercise 1 in the drawing. Compare your solution with your partner's.

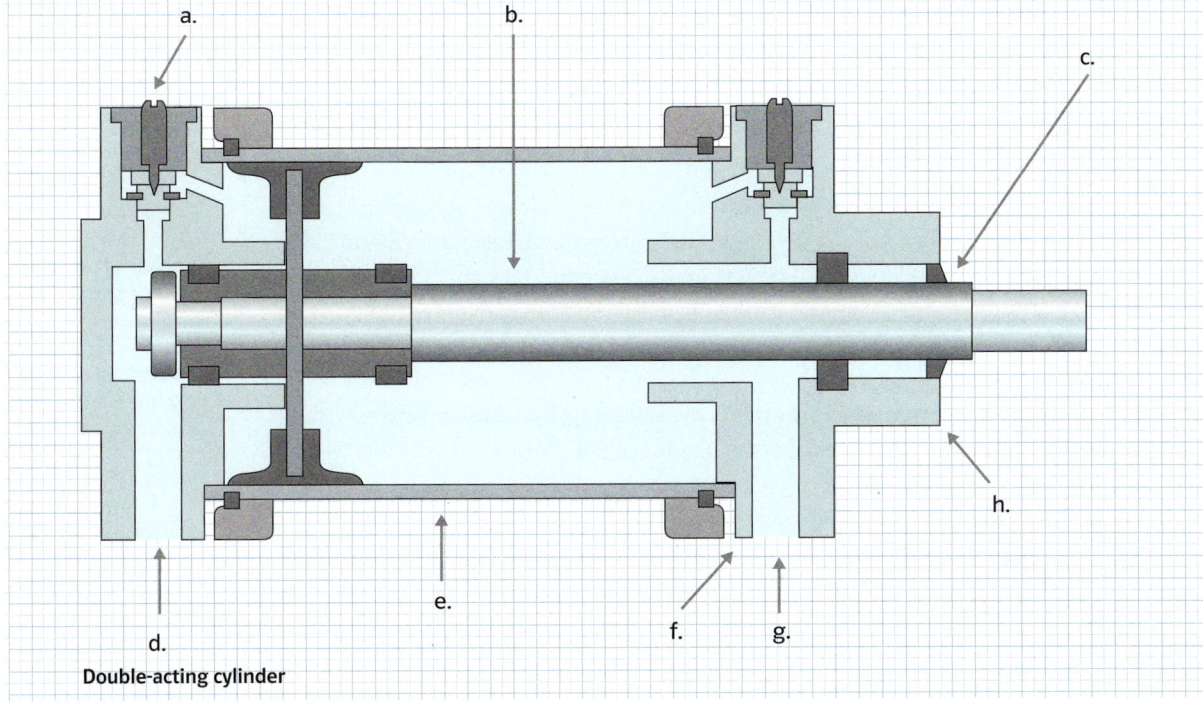

Double-acting cylinder

3 Directional air control valves control pneumatic cylinders. Pneumatic symbols show how a pneumatic component is actuated, the number of positions, the flow paths and the number of ports. Complete the text using the words in the diagram.

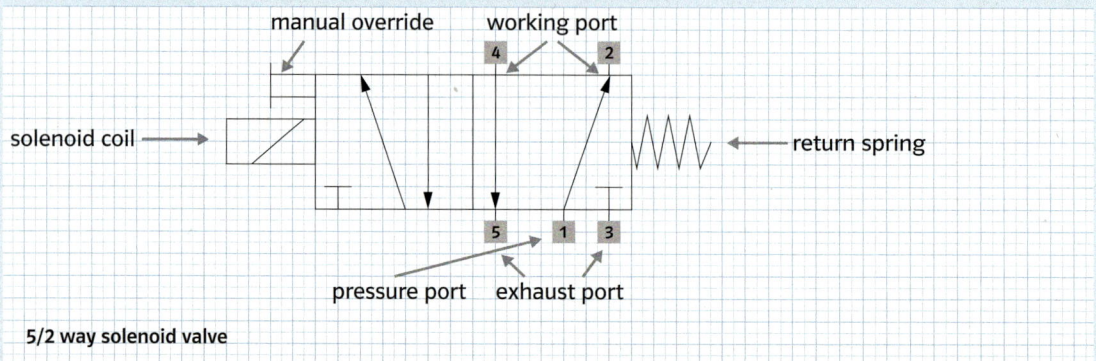

manual override   working port

solenoid coil ⟶

return spring

pressure port   exhaust port

5/2 way solenoid valve

Directional control valves influence the path of the air flow in the pneumatic cylinder. Every valve has at least two positions and each position has one or more flow paths. A 5/2-way
5 solenoid valve, for example, has separate **1** for each cylinder port, which allow the air to come out. In the initial position, the **2** is not activated. The **3** holds the valve in this position.

When actuated, the valve switches into flow position. The **4** is then connected with the **5** . 10 The **6** is indicated by the arrows in each box when the valve is in that position. A **7** allows the user to actuate the valve without using the switches that would normally be used. In this way, a circuit may be 15 tested without moving the machine elements.

P **4** Identify the components of the valve and describe how it is actuated.

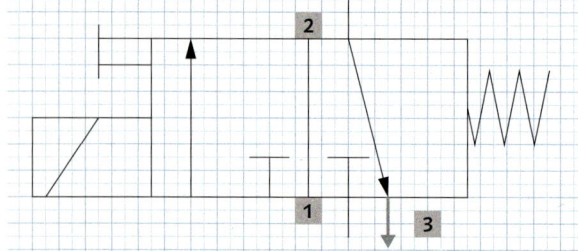

R/P **5** Electro-pneumatic control elements combine the advantages of electrical compo-
⊙ A 2.5 nents (highly efficient, relatively high safety levels) and pneumatic components (cheap, light, fast). Heiner is a trainee in the first year of his apprenticeship. He has to install an electro-pneumatic circuit. Chad, an American exchange student, is helping him. Listen to the dialogue. Make a list of the valves and cylinders in the circuit.

R **6** Listen to the dialogue again. Decide if the statements are true or false.
⊙ A 2.5 Correct the false statements.

1. Double-acting cylinders have two ports.
2. Single-acting cylinders provide power on the push and the return stroke.
3. Reed contacts are used to adjust end-position cushioning.
4. End-position cushioning helps to prevent damage to the components.
5. Silencers reduce the noise level of pneumatic pistons.
6. The solenoid coils on the valves are powered with 230 volts.

WORD BANK

actuate (v) – betätigen
circuit – Schaltkreis
control valve – Steuerventil
feed (v) – zustellen
production line – Fertigungsstraße
5/2 way solenoid valve – 5/2 Wege Elektromagnetventil

WORD BANK ⊙

end-position cushioning – Endlagen-dämpfung
impact – Anschlag
piston – Kolben
plug (v) – stecken
reed contact – Reedkontakt
silencer – Schalldämpfer

B | Pneumatic solutions

Pneumatic actuators feed parts in production processes. This is why they are important when it comes to finding solutions for pneumatic problems, e.g. improving automation processes.

 M 1
KMK II

Ihre Firma ist Zulieferer einer großen Automobilfirma und möchte einen Auftrag zur Produktion von Fahrzeugtüren erhalten, in welche eine Komponente eingeklebt werden soll. Geplant ist der Einsatz eines verbesserten Zuführungssystems, um hohe Stückzahlen zu erzielen. Ihr Chef hat einen Lösungsansatz gefunden. Er spricht nicht sehr gut Englisch und bittet Sie, die Funktionsweise einer möglichen Vorrichtung auf Deutsch zusammen zu fassen.

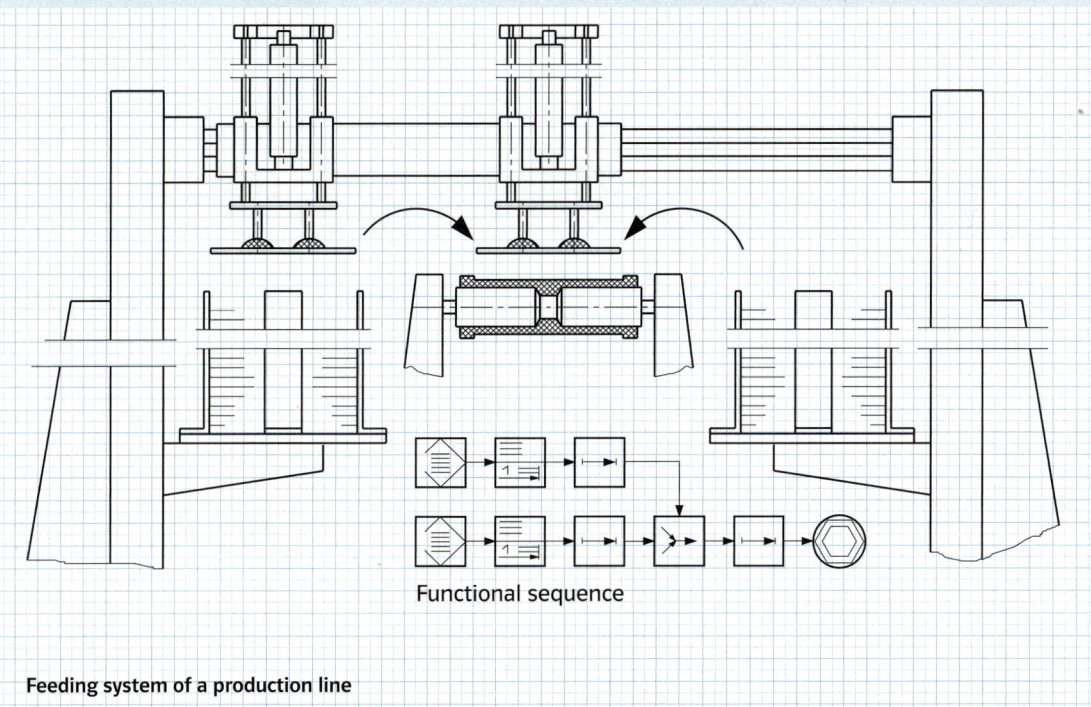

Functional sequence

Feeding system of a production line

By using this pneumatic solution, it is possible to put adhesives on the surface of car doors, for example. In order to feed the workpieces in quick succession, they have to be placed
5 on a conveyor belt. It is often not possible to achieve such a high frequency with a normal pick-and-place machine.
   One solution to this problem is the installation of a two-magazine solution. This means that
10 the workpieces are fed alternately from two different magazines. One unit sets down the workpiece while the second unit picks up another one at the same time. Both units are mounted on a slide. This kind of feed system saves significant amounts of time compared 15 with an ordinary pneumatic drive system. The workpieces are normally placed on carriers located on the conveyor belt. Then it is necessary to synchronise the motion sequences of the conveyor belt and the feeding system. 20

 P 2
KMK II

SAFETY FIRST ⚠
Use the Internet to make a list of the safety rules for the installation and operation of the application in exercise 1. Present your findings to the class.
→ **PHRASES:** Presentations

E

NACH DIESEM MODUL:

√ kann ich eine Stellenanzeige auf Englisch verstehen,

√ kann ich meine Fähigkeiten und Qualifikationen auf Englisch beschreiben,

√ kann ich eine Bewerbung auf Englisch schreiben.

Applications

The world today is full of opportunities. You might decide to work in your hometown, a big city, or even another country. Maybe you want to work for a small family-run company or a major corporation with branches across the globe. Whatever you decide, the opportunities are out there, but it is up to you to take them.

1 **Look at the pictures above and describe them using the words below.**

> to apply · job advertisement · letter of application · CV · to search · job interview · employment contract · to invite · newspaper · to write

2 **Put the steps of the application process shown in the pictures above into the correct order.**

P **3** **Work on your own. What skills and qualifications do you need for a job in your industry? Make a list. Use these words to help you:**

> hard-working · motivated · logical · good with numbers · good with your hands · communicative · good team player · technical skills · able to understand plans and diagrams · attention to detail · computer skills

4 **Work with a partner and decide upon a final list. Share it with the class.**

A | Job advertisements

Read the three online job advertisements below and find the English translations for the following German words and expressions.

1. verantwortungsbewusst
2. aktiv, praktisch
3. Bewerber
4. Störungssuche
5. pünktlich
6. lernbereit
7. begeistert
8. gültige Fahrerlaubnis
9. Erfahrung
10. abgeschlossene Ausbildung
11. gute Bezahlung
12. fließendes Englisch
13. teamfähig
14. Montage
15. Grundkenntnisse in CAD
16. freie Stelle

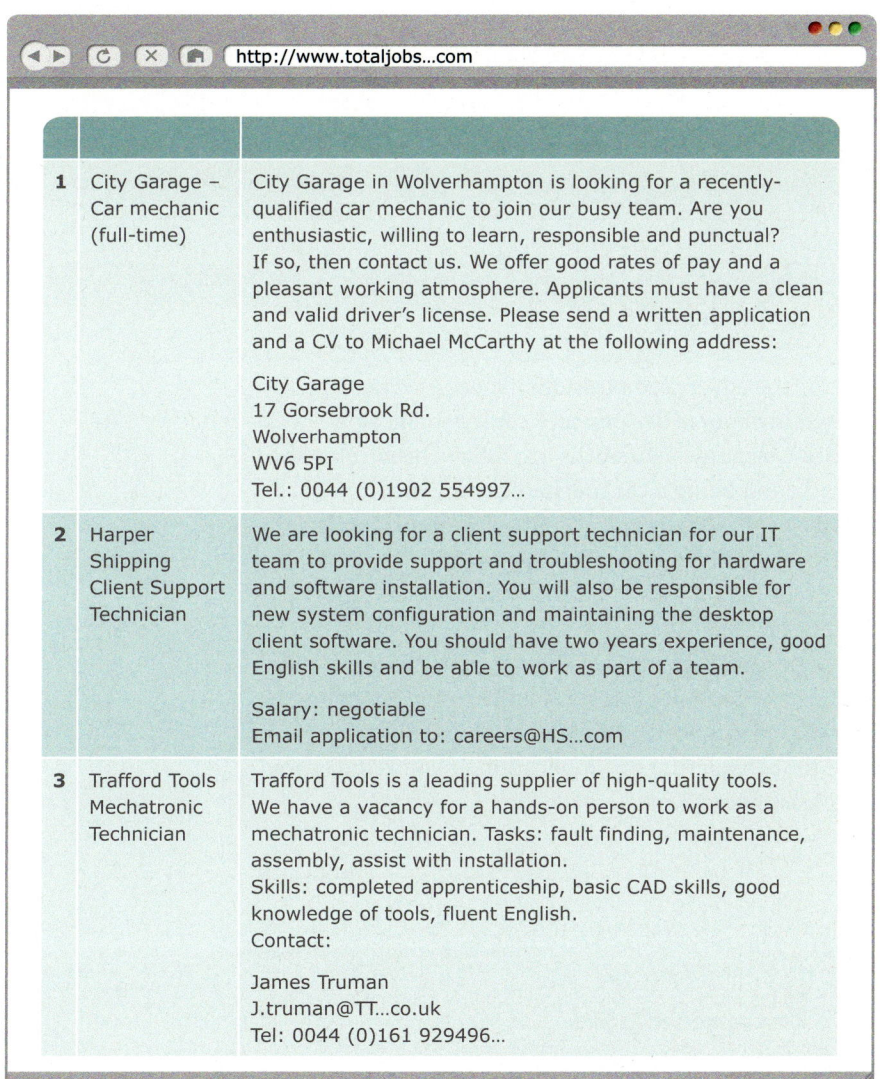

1	City Garage – Car mechanic (full-time)	City Garage in Wolverhampton is looking for a recently-qualified car mechanic to join our busy team. Are you enthusiastic, willing to learn, responsible and punctual? If so, then contact us. We offer good rates of pay and a pleasant working atmosphere. Applicants must have a clean and valid driver's license. Please send a written application and a CV to Michael McCarthy at the following address: City Garage 17 Gorsebrook Rd. Wolverhampton WV6 5PI Tel.: 0044 (0)1902 554997…
2	Harper Shipping Client Support Technician	We are looking for a client support technician for our IT team to provide support and troubleshooting for hardware and software installation. You will also be responsible for new system configuration and maintaining the desktop client software. You should have two years experience, good English skills and be able to work as part of a team. Salary: negotiable Email application to: careers@HS…com
3	Trafford Tools Mechatronic Technician	Trafford Tools is a leading supplier of high-quality tools. We have a vacancy for a hands-on person to work as a mechatronic technician. Tasks: fault finding, maintenance, assembly, assist with installation. Skills: completed apprenticeship, basic CAD skills, good knowledge of tools, fluent English. Contact: James Truman J.truman@TT…co.uk Tel: 0044 (0)161 929496…

http://www.totaljobs…com

I/M 2 **One of your colleagues does not speak English and asks you to tell him about one of the job ads. Choose one of the ads and give him a brief summary in German. Swap roles.**

WORD BANK

branch – Filiale
family-run company – Familienunternehmen
job application – Bewerbung
maintain (v) – warten
opportunities – Möglichkeiten
qualifications – Qualifikationen
skills – Fähigkeiten
troubleshooting – Fehlerbehebung

B | Letter of application

R **1** Read the letter of application and decide whether the following statements are true or false. Give reasons for your decisions.

1. Erkan is in the final year of his apprenticeship as a car mechanic.
2. He has always wanted to be a car mechanic.
3. Erkan had a holiday job at *Werkstatt Kuhn*.
4. He is looking forward to working abroad.
5. Erkan has included his CV in the application.

Erkan Celik • Waldstrasse 48 • 50679 Köln • Germany

Michael McCarthy
City Garage
17 Gorsebrook Rd.
Wolverhampton
WV6 5PI
England

12 June 20_

Dear Mr McCarthy,

Application for job as car mechanic

I am writing to apply for the advertised position of a car mechanic at City Garage. I completed my apprenticeship as a car mechanic at a technical college here in Germany six months ago. I have been interested in cars since I was a child and being a car mechanic is my dream job.
As you will see from my CV, I recently completed a six-month internship at Werskstatt Kuhn. This not only gave me the opportunity to put my theoretical skills into practice, but I also had the chance to gain more experience with customers.
I am a very enthusiastic person. I am also reliable, responsible and willing to learn. Furthermore, I have good English skills and I would welcome the opportunity to gain some experience working in another country.
Thank you in advance for considering my application. If you require any further information, please contact me.

Yours sincerely,   Encl.: CV
Erkan Celik

WATCH OUT!
I am interested ~~for~~ cars.   I am interested <u>in</u> cars.

M **2** Fassen Sie mit Hilfe der unten stehenden Stichworte die wichtigsten Inhalte des Bewerbungsschreibens auf Deutsch zusammen.

KMK I

1. Beruf, für den sich Erkan bewirbt   2. Berufserfahrung   3. Motivation
4. Persönliche Qualifikationen/Fähigkeiten   5. Kontaktperson

C | The CV

R **1**
KMK II
⊙ A 1.4

Andrea Wagner ist Auszubildende bei einer IT-Firma in Nürnberg. Sie möchte sich für eine Praktikumsstelle in der englischen Niederlassung ihrer Firma bewerben und fragt David, einen Praktikanten aus England, ob er ihr ein paar Tipps geben kann. Hören Sie das Gespräch an und vervollständigen Sie die folgenden Sätze auf Deutsch.

1. Andrea möchte sich für eine Praktikumsstelle in `?` bewerben.
2. Sie bringt am Montag `?` mit ins Büro.
3. Der Lebenslauf sollte nicht länger sein als `?` .
4. Man sollte niemals einen Lebenslauf ohne `?` senden.
5. Man sollte den Lebenslauf dazu benutzen, seine `?` und `?` hervorzuheben.
6. Wenn man seine Arbeitserfahrung auflistet, sollte man mit `?` anfangen.
7. In England muss ein Lebenslauf kein `?` enthalten.
8. Man sollte sicherstellen, dass man zwei `?` nennt.
9. Man sollte niemals `?` .
10. Wenn der Lebenslauf fertig ist, sollte man ihn auf `?` und `?` überprüfen.
11. Es ist eine gute Idee, den Lebenslauf `?` zu geben.
12. Wenn man den Lebenslauf abschickt, sollte man `?` behalten.

P **2**
KMK II

Verfassen Sie ein Anschreiben für eine der in Modulteil A ausgeschriebenen Stellen auf Englisch. Arbeiten Sie dabei die unten aufgeführten Inhalte ein.

→ **PHRASES:** Applications

- Wählen Sie einen geeigneten Betreff.
- Nehmen Sie Bezug auf die Stellenanzeige und bekunden Sie Ihr Interesse an der ausgeschriebenen Stelle.
- Sie werden bald Ihre Ausbildung als … abschließen.
- Bringen Sie zum Ausdruck, dass Sie ein geeigneter Bewerber sind: organisiert, erfahren, hoch motiviert, teamfähig, flexibel, lernbereit, zuverlässig. Sie haben gute Englischkenntnisse.
- Beenden Sie den Brief angemessen und unterschreiben Sie.
- Weisen Sie auf Ihren Lebenslauf hin.

WORD BANK

consider (v) – betrachten
gain (v) – sammeln
internship – Praktikum
letter of application – Bewerbungsschreiben
reliable – zuverlässig
require (v) – benötigen

INFO BOX: Translating German school types and qualifications

It is not always possible to find the equivalent of your school type or qualification in English. However, the following table gives some useful translations.

Schools

Grundschule	Elementary school / Primary school	Berufsschule (Duales System)	Part-time vocational school (dual system)
Hauptschule	General secondary school	Berufsfachschule	Full-time vocational school
Realschule	Intermediate secondary school	Fachschule für technische Berufe	Technical college
Gymnasium	Upper secondary school	Fachoberschule	Upper secondary vocational school
Gesamtschule	Comprehensive school	Fachgymnasium	Specialized upper secondary school

Qualifications

Hauptschulabschluss	secondary modern school qualification	Fachabitur	advanced vocational certificate of education
Mittlere Reife	secondary school leaving certificate	Zusatzqualifikation	additional qualification
Abitur	A level/high school diploma		

06

NACH DIESEM MODUL:

✓ kann ich verschiedene Arten von Sensoren benennen und deren Einsatz auf Englisch beschreiben,

✓ kann ich ein englisches Datenblatt lesen und die erforderlichen Angaben für eine Sensoranwendung finden.

Sensors

Sensors are devices that can measure a physical value and convert it into an electrical signal. Many technical systems include sensory devices which record data: gas sensors warn of the presence of toxic gases; temperature sensors detect increases in temperature which may in turn indicate that a machine or a motor is overheating. Other applications of sensors include measuring pressure and liquid levels in production lines in the chemical industry. In private homes, sensors attached to the heating system are used as an input for a control loop to regulate values such as room temperature.

1 Identify the applications of sensors in the photos using the words below.

> machines · belt · screen · validation · touch · detector · smoke · conveyor · ticket

2 Match the types of sensors with the applications in the photos. You will not need all of the words.

> gas sensor · pressure sensor · temperature sensor · liquid level sensor · optical sensor · proximity sensor

3 Think of other possible applications of the sensors in exercise 2.

A | The working principles of sensors

Sensors are like 'feelers' that monitor and control aspects of their surroundings.
For this reason sensors are typical components in both measurement and control
systems.

1 Find the English terms for the verbs in the text.

1. erkennen
2. anzeigen
3. verstärken
4. abgleichen
5. umwandeln
6. verarbeiten

How sensors work

The working principles and components of
sensors vary according to the value to be
measured. Capacitive proximity sensors contain
a capacitor to hold an electric charge. The coil
and oscillator in an inductive proximity sensor
creates an electromagnetic field to detect metallic
objects. Optical sensors in mobile phones and
tablets react to the presence of light by regulating
the backlighting of the device. Magnetic sensors
detect speed, rotation and position. They are
often used in car production and other industrial
applications. Acoustic sensors register inaudible,
high-frequency sound waves.

In all cases an input measure is necessary before
the sensor starts working. In a second step, the
sensor signal is transformed or amplified. In
addition, many sensors need to be calibrated with
a reference signal. Analogue voltage or current
signals are often converted into digital signals.
A microcontroller, which is a small computer
embedded in the device, processes the signal.
The third part of the measurement unit is the
signal output. This can be shown on a display.
In the case of a control loop, the signal is
connected to the control unit. Graphically you
can illustrate this procedure as follows.

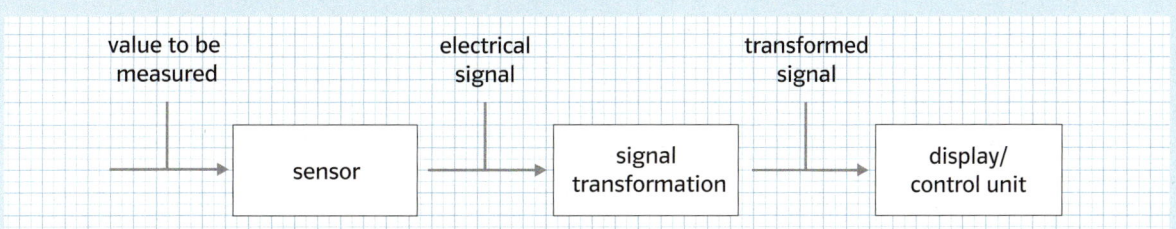

2 Read the text again and match the parts of the sentences about sensors.

1. Objects made of metal are
2. Acoustic sensors make it possible
3. If the sensor does not start working,
4. A reference signal is necessary
5. The signal is processed

a. the sensor signal cannot be amplified.
b. by a microcomputer.
c. to register inaudible sound waves.
d. detected using inductive proximity sensors.
e. to calibrate the sensors.

M **3** Summarize the main points of the text in German.

4 Find out how one of the sensors in the text in exercise 1 operates. Present your findings in English to your class.

→ **PHRASES:** Presentations

WORD BANK

analogue voltage signal – analoges Spannungssignal
capacitive proximity sensor – kapazitiver Näherungssensor
capacitor – Kondensator
component – Bauteil
control (v) – steuern
control loop – Regelkreis
control unit – Steuerungseinheit
current signal – Stromsignal
feeler – Fühler
inductive proximity sensor – induktiver Näherungssensor
input – Eingabe
monitor (v) – überwachen
optical – optisch
oscillator – Oszillator
reference signal – Referenzsignal

B | Choosing a suitable sensor

R **1** A conveyor belt system was installed in your company last year. Recently the motor
⊙ A 2.6 has been overheating slightly and the maintenance technician calls the installation
company ModTranSys in England. Listen to the phone call and make notes about the
solution they agree on.

R **2** Listen to the phone call again and complete the missing information in the data sheet.
⊙ A 2.6

SENTEMP
Europe Ltd

STE 40120
Temperature Sensor

Features
- calibrated in **a**
- low **b**
- resistance 30 kΩ
- suitable for remote installations
- highly **c** ±0.6 °C
- linear output within 0.3 °C
- measuring range between −40 °C and 120 °C
- optimal resolution < 0.05 °C

Applications
- thermal **d**
- measuring instruments
- check / prevent overheating of motors
- household appliances
- environmental control systems
- fire alarms
- CPU **e**

Description

Our new STE 40120 temperature sensor is a sophisticated new component that makes it easier than ever before to monitor and record temperatures in heating systems. The **f** allows you to check and compare signals. The sensor works in a temperature range of -40 °C to +120 °C. Its <0.05 °C resolution is fantastic and can be used for high precision applications. The sensor is available in any housing you might need. Please contact us for details and prices.

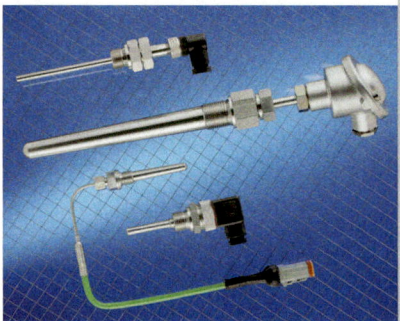

I **3** 🔺 Sean Miller orders the sensors for his trip to Germany from Sentemp Europe Ltd.
👥 Later that day he receives a phone call from the manufacturer. Prepare and act out
the call using the role card below and in the Appendix (Speaker B). → **PHRASES:** Telephoning

Speaker A

You work for Sentemp Europe Ltd. Do the following:
1. Explain that temperature sensor number STE 40120 is not available for delivery at the moment. Give a reason. Apologise.
2. Ask about the required specifications of the sensor.
3. Suggest an alternative product: STE 44220.
4. Ask for delivery address, quantities.
5. Tell the caller confirmation will follow.
6. Thank the caller.

C | Intelligent sensors

M   1
KMK II
Ihr Ausbilder hat einen Artikel in der Fachzeitschrift "Sensor Highlights" gefunden. Er bittet Sie, anhand des Artikels ein Eingangsreferat für das nächste Lernfeld vorzubereiten. Stellen Sie die wichtigsten Informationen im Artikel auf Deutsch zusammen. Schreiben Sie vollständige Sätze.

How intelligent sensors were developed

The combination of a sensor and a microcontroller in one device is known as an intelligent sensor. This development only became
5 possible as switches became smaller and smaller. It also became possible to combine sensory elements and evaluating switches, sensors, actuators and bus systems. Microcontrollers were added to compensate for any differences
10 between traditional 'feelers' and modern sensors. When producers finally agreed on standardised interfaces between sensors and microcontrollers, sensors became easily interchangeable. As a result, they could be produced, distributed and
15 applied more easily and in larger numbers. Customised technologies now use bus lines to reduce the necessity for long cables for the installation of sensors and actuators. As a result input und output components can be connected
20 more easily with processing controllers. An exact protocol ensures that the correct flow of information addresses each participating component individually. Of course this also means that sensors must be equipped with
25 microcontrollers to digitalise analogue impulses. A bus coupler allows communication between the sensors and the microcontroller. A teach-in-mode enables sensors to change their own configuration or to recognise the configurations of other sensors. These 'intelligent' sensors also 30 provide information on leakage, short-circuits, defaults and gradual contamination. This means that it is possible to react before production machinery comes to a complete standstill, thus saving the company a lot of money. When 35 a defective sensor is replaced with a new one, it adopts existing parameters. Electrical engineering has refined intelligent sensors in such a way that they can communicate with each other via bus systems. These systems keep 40 a manufacturing process running even if single system elements such as sensors or cables do not function properly.

M   2
KMK II
Entscheiden Sie, ob die Aussagen richtig oder falsch sind. Begründen Sie Ihre Entscheidung jeweils mit einem ganzen deutschen Satz.

1. Die Normierung der Schnittstellen erleichtert die Produktion und Anwendung der Sensoren.
2. Sogenannte „intelligente" Sensoren sind außerordentlich teuer und werden deshalb selten eingesetzt.
3. Das Produktionssystem kann über die Kommunikation der Sensoren miteinander weiterarbeiten, auch wenn Fehler auftreten.

 UNDERSTANDING TECHNICAL ENGLISH
Find the general and technical meanings of the words.

1. application   2. bus line   3. installation   4. field

WORD BANK

resistance – elektrischer Widerstand

WORD BANK ◉

data sheet – Datenblatt
output – Ausgabe
self-heating – Eigenerwärmung
short-circuit – Kurzschluss
thermal management – Wärme-management
thermal protection – Wärmeschutz

NACH DIESEM MODUL:

✓ kann ich *Small Talk* auf Englisch machen,

✓ kenne ich die Regeln des *Small Talk*,

✓ kann ich auf Englisch Essen erklären und bestellen.

Socialising

Socialising is very important. It can strengthen relationships with your colleagues and improve the working atmosphere in a company. It can also be a good way of getting to know your customers or potential customers a little better. And in today's global world, English has become the world's language. So although the people you meet and work with are likely to come from a wide range of cultural backgrounds, you will often be required to communicate in English. That means that it is important to not only have the necessary language skills, but also the intercultural knowledge so that you can make a good first impression and develop professional and personal relationships.

I **1** Look at the pictures above. What relationship do you think these people might have to each other? Discuss with your partner.

2 Brainstorm a list of topics these people might be talking about.

P **3** Choose one of the pictures and create a small dialogue.

4 Look at photo 1. Brainstorm what cultural misunderstandings could take place when a German employee meets a person from another country.

P **5** Make a list of situations when a German technician might have contact with foreign colleagues – for example, customers, suppliers, manufacturers, etc.

A | Small talk

Your company has visitors from a subsidiary in Poland. Fabian, a German trainee, has been asked to show Jan, a Polish trainee, around the company.

R **1** Listen to the dialogue between Jan and Fabian. Take notes of the topics the two
⊙ A 1.5 are talking about. Then listen again and make a list of the phrases they use.

2 Name other topics that Jan and Fabian could also talk about.

3 Which of the following topics would / wouldn't you talk about? Why? Discuss in class.

> free-time activities · films you have recently seen · sex · your job or school
> course · politics · money · personal problems · fashion · sports · food ·
> the boss's wife · the weather · your favourite music · religion

P **4** Small talk is not that difficult. All that is needed is an 'ice breaker' to get things
going. Look at the following examples and come up with appropriate answers.

→ **PHRASES:** Socialising

In the workshop:
a. Did you see the game last night?
b. How was your weekend?
c. It's warm today, isn't it?

In the car:
a. How was your trip / flight?
b. Is this your first time in Germany?
c. How's the weather in Sao Paolo?

At a trade fair:
a. Did you have any problems
   finding our stand?
b. Would you like a brochure?
c. If you like, I could give you a
   demonstration.

In the canteen:
a. Have you tried the tiramisu?
   It's amazing!
b. Is anybody sitting here?
c. Ah! I see you like spicy food.

P **5** Now it's your turn to break the ice! Think of at least three ice breakers for each of
the following situations:

→ **PHRASES:** Socialising

1. You are at a bar with colleagues on Friday evening.
2. You work with a new colleague one afternoon.
3. You are at the "Green Technology" conference. It's time for a coffee break.
4. You've just arrived at work and you're in the lift. A person you don't know
   enters.

I **6** Choose one of the four situations above. Start a conversation and try to keep it
going for as long as possible. Then end the conversation politely and act it out in
front of the class.

→ **PHRASES:** Socialising

P **7** Check the Internet and create your own 'Dos & Don'ts' guide to making small talk
and present it to your class. Also include some intercultural aspects.

WORD BANK

subsidiary – Tochtergesellchaft
trainee – Auszubildende(r)

Dos	Don'ts
Make eye contact.	Ask personal questions.

B | Small talk in business

Ihr Arbeitgeber hat im Internet folgenden Artikel gefunden. Da er nur wenig Englisch kann, bittet er Sie, die folgenden Fragen auf Deutsch zu beantworten.

1. Was wird oft in abwertender Weise über Small Talk gesagt?
2. Was passiert, wenn man sich nicht am Small Talk beteiligt?
3. Was sind die positiven Auswirkungen von Small Talk?

Small talk in business

Small talk is often dismissed as a waste of time, or as the art of saying nothing with a lot of words. Some people say it has no place in the business world, since the subjects discussed are often
5 'unimportant' – i.e. the weather, sports, fashion or other trivial matters. However, if you don't take part in small talk, your business partners might feel that you are being unfriendly or antisocial. When people just stand next to one another,
10 without any signs of communication between them, it can lead to a feeling of uneasiness, and even tension. And this is certainly not good for future business or private relations. Small talk is in fact a very important and effective tool for avoiding an
15 awkward silence between people who don't know each other, especially business partners who may want to form a relationship. Making small talk with strangers helps to break the ice; you discover what they like or dislike, so you can find a common ground of some sort. It helps, for example, if you 20 support the same football team, like the same kind of car, or read the same kinds of books. However, it is also important to know who you are making small talk with. The rules of small talk are not international and different cultures have their own 25 dos and don'ts. For example, you may have been told to always make eye contact when talking to your counterpart – but this may offend a material supplier in China. If you are going to have contact with someone from a different cultural background, 30 it is a good idea to do a little research to avoid any embarassing mistakes.

Ihr Arbeitgeber bittet Sie, für die Mitarbeiter stichwortartig ein kurzes Merkblatt anhand dieses Textes auf Deutsch zu erstellen.

Sind Sie ein guter Smalltalker? Bewerten Sie die Aussagen zum Small Talk in einem Online-Test mit „Yes" oder „No". Notieren Sie die entsprechenden Buchstaben.

Statements	Yes	No
1. Small talk deals with rather unimportant topics. Another word for it is chitchat.	a	c
2. Religion always makes a good topic, because it is controversial.	d	e
3. Answering questions with 'yes' or 'no' during small talk is appropriate.	i	e
4. A good answer when asked if you'd like something to drink is: "I'd love a cup of coffee, thank you."	g	h
5. "That's great" is an acceptable answer to the statement: "I got the job!"	b	i
6. The noun "talk" can also mean speech.	a	c
7. Small talk is an icebreaker.	b	f

Wer hat die höchste Zahl? (Maximum 21)

Addieren Sie die Buchstabenwerte a = 3, b = 3, c = 1, d = 0, e = 3, f = 3, g = 1, h = 1, i = 1.

C | Eating out

1 Look at the German words (1.–16.) below and match them with the English
equivalent (a.–p.).

1.	Speisekarte	a.	well-done
2.	Rechnung	b.	pork
3.	Rind	c.	side order
4.	Vorspeise	d.	bill
5.	Schweinefleisch	e.	game
6.	Wild	f.	dessert
7.	durchgebraten	g.	savoury
8.	Hauptgericht	h.	fork
9.	Geflügel	i.	menu
10.	Kellner(in)	j.	main dish
11.	Nachtisch	k.	beef
12.	Trinkgeld	l.	poultry
13.	Beilage	m.	starter
14.	vegetarisch	n.	waiter/waitress
15.	herzhaft	o.	vegetarian
16.	Gabel	p.	tip

I/M **2** Partner 1: You are taking a foreign colleague out to dinner in a traditional German
restaurant. Study the menu below and explain the dishes to him/her.
Partner 2: Take the role of the foreign colleague and ask questions about the menu.

Gasthaus Sonne

Tagesmenu (10,95 €)

Vorspeisen
Lauchcremesuppe **oder** *kleiner gemischter Salat*
★★★
Hauptgerichte
Rinderrouladen mit Kartoffelklößen & Sauerkraut
oder
Putenschnitzel mit Pommes Frites
oder
Forelle Müllerin mit Salzkartoffeln
★★★
Nachtisch
Rote Grütze mit Sahne **oder** *Gemischtes Eis*
(Vanille/Erdbeere/Schoko)

Inklusive ein alkoholfreies Getränk (0,3l)

WORD BANK

avoid (v) – vermeiden
awkward – unangenehm
common ground – gemeinsame
Basis
dismiss (v) sth. as – etwas abtun als
tension – Spannung
trivial – unbedeutend
uneasiness – Unbehagen

I **3** Now the two of you are ready to order. The young German waitress/waiter doesn't
mind taking the order in English. Study the eating out phrases at the end of the
book and create a role play. Practise, and perform it in front of the class.

→ **PHRASES:** Socialising

07

1
2
3
4

Hydraulics

Hydraulic machinery is used in industry and on construction sites to lift and move heavy objects. This type of machinery is equipped with hydraulic systems that are powered by liquid, also called hydraulic fluid, which is pressurised and transported to hydraulic motors and cylinders. Great care should be taken when working with hydraulic systems as damage to or failure of a system may result in serious injuries to persons working nearby.

R **1** Match the terms in the box with the hydraulic applications in the photos. Not all applications are shown in the photos.

> crane · elevators · hydraulic bike brakes · excavator · hydraulic car lift ·
> hydraulic press · dump truck

I/P **2** Make a list of other hydraulic applications that you know and describe briefly how they work. Use a dictionary if necessary. Then present your results to the class.

→ **PHRASES:** Presentations

Example:

hydraulic application	description
forklift truck	It is used in industry to lift and transport material.

A | Installing a hydraulic hose

A hydraulic system basically consists of a drive unit, a hydraulic motor and a control circuit. The drive unit can either be an electric motor, a conventional diesel engine or an air-driven motor.

The drive unit is connected to the hydraulic motor with hoses and fittings to transmit high-pressure hydraulic fluid. This makes a hydraulic system the ideal means of performing heavy-duty work.

When working with a hydraulic system, the most basic task is to install a hydraulic hose.

R **1** Put the instructions for replacing a hydraulic hose into the correct order.

a. Start the engine and check the system for leaks.
b. If there is an o-ring, you have to replace it with a new one.
c. Relieve any pressure that might be present in the hydraulic system.
d. Check the level of the hydraulic fluid; if necessary, add more fluid until it reaches a proper level.
e. Put a drain pan under the fitting you want to open first.
f. Loosen the fitting by holding a spanner on one side of the fitting, then use a second spanner to turn the fitting counterclockwise.
g. Clean the inside and outside of the fitting. Align the hoses and tighten the fitting again.

M **2** Explain the steps which you should follow when replacing a hydraulic hose in German.

R **3** Look at the sentences in exercise 1 again and rewrite them using the passive voice.

Example:
The engine is started and the system is checked for leaks.

R/P **4** **SAFETY FIRST** ⚠

1. Hydraulic systems work with high pressures. Use the Internet to find the most important safety rules for installing a hydraulic system. Compare your lists of rules in groups of four and create one list per group. Present your list in class.

⊙ A 2.7 2. Listen to the dialogue and answer the questions.

a. Who is talking?
b. What has happened?

⊙ A 2.7 3. Listen to the dialogue again and write down what steps will be taken.

I/M 4. Prepare and act out a telephone call to emergency services using the role cards for Speaker A and Speaker B in the Appendix. → **PHRASES:** Telephoning

WORD BANK

align (v) – fluchten, ausrichten
drain pan – Ablaufwanne
drive unit – Antriebseinheit
fitting – Verschraubung
hose – Schlauch
leak, leakage – Leckage

P **5** **UNDERSTANDING TECHNICAL ENGLISH**

1. Check the words in an English-German dictionary or an online dictionary and
   list all of their meanings.

   a. hose   b. pipe   c. tube

2. Translate the sentences into English.

   a. Der Hydraulikschlauch hat ein Leck.
   b. Der Pneumatikzylinder wird mit einem Schlauch an das Ventil
      angeschlossen.
   c. Die Straßenarbeiter wurden aus einem Rohr gerettet.

P **6** Look at the block diagram and describe how a hydraulic system works in English.
Use the phrases in the table and form passive sentences.

Example:
The hydraulic system is put into operation by an input signal, e.g. the
operator activates a lever in an excavator.

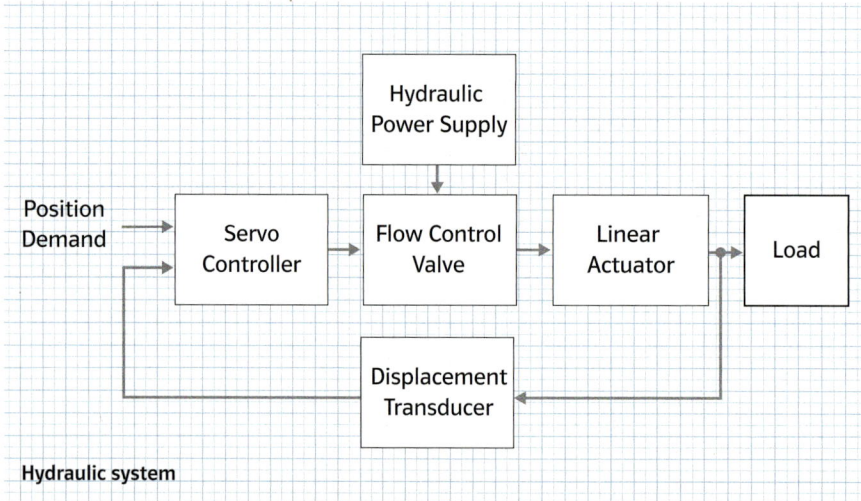

Hydraulic system

Phrases		
1. hydraulic system	to put into operation	input signal
2. input signal	to give	–
3. load	to move	to a different position
4. signal	to compare	with signal from the transducer
5. position errors	to determine, to correct	servo controller
6. signal	to give	switch flow-control valve
7. pressurised oil	to supply to the valve	piston pump
8. control valve	to switch	to flow position
9. forward stroke	to perform	actuator
10. particular mechanism	to move	actuator

B | Troubleshooting and hydraulic systems

I/M **1**
KMK III

Ordnen Sie jedem Problem einen Test zu. Achtung, nicht für alle Probleme sind Tests beschrieben! Suchen Sie in Partnerarbeit nach Ihnen bekannten Tests für die Probleme, denen kein Test zugeordnet werden kann. Übertragen Sie dann Ihre Lösungen ins Deutsche und stellen Sie sie der Klasse vor.

The most important causes of faults in a hydraulic system are:
1. Not enough hydraulic fluid
2. Air in the system
3. Dirt in the hydraulic system
5. 4. Components are not adjusted properly.
5. Leakage of hydraulic fluid
6. Components have been damaged.
7. Wrong hydraulic fluid
8. Temperatures were too high.

10. The following tests can be carried out to solve a problem:
1. The contaminant test: Pour a small amount of hydraulic fluid into a glass. Then wait for several hours. Any dirt will sink to the bottom.
2. The crackle test: Place two or three drops of the oil on a hot plate. The drops will crackle if there is water in the oil.
15. 3. The particle count: Inspect the filter in the machine. Open the filter and pour the substance in it onto a workbench. Check the filter for particles with a microscope. You can also detect any ferrous material with a magnet.
4. The colour test: check the colour of the hydraulic oil. If it has
20. become darker or changed colour, take a sample and analyse it. The darker colour could also be a result of high temperatures. Check the oil temperature with an infrared thermometer.
5. The leakage test: In the case of a hot spot, e.g. on a cylinder barrel, use an ultrasonic tester to find the leak. External leaks can be very
25. dangerous, so be careful when trying to solve high-temperature problems.
6. The noise test: Use an ultrasonic tester to control cavitation or aeration at hydraulic pump inlet ports or other components.
7. The foam and air entrainment inspection: Darker hydraulic fluid
30. tells you that oxidation is taking place. When there is air in the system and the pressure is released, foam is produced and the air escapes. This air now gets inside other components, which results in irregular movements and higher temperatures. Hydraulic systems are constantly being improved and as a result, operating pressures
35. are also rising. Therefore, companies have to carry out much more predictive maintenance in order to reach high degrees of safety and reliability.

WORD BANK

control valve – Steuerventil
flow position – Durchflussstellung
flow-control valve – Stromventil
forward stroke – Vorwärtshub
piston pump – Kolbenpumpe
servo controller – Stellantrieb
transducer – Meßwertgeber

M **2**
KMK II

Ihr Ausbilder bittet Sie, für die anderen Auszubildenden ein Poster mit den häufigsten Ursachen von Fehlern in hydraulischen Systemen sowie gängigen Tests zur Fehlersuche auf Deutsch zu erstellen. Erstellen Sie dieses Poster in Partnerarbeit.

 3b9c4h

G

NACH DIESEM MODUL:

✓ kann ich eine englische Präsentation vorbereiten,

✓ kann ich auf Englisch präsentieren.

Presentations

At some point in your career you may be required to present your company, or their products or services, either informally or on a more formal level. This could mean presenting a new product to a potential customer, or presenting the company as a whole, or something more specific, such as assembly instructions or a positional sketch. Whatever you may be presenting, the ability to give an oral presentation is a key skill. It is also a skill that can be developed and improved.

P **1** **Look at the pictures above and describe them using the words below.**

> to present · meeting · flipchart · graph · chart · laptop · preparation ·
> to explain · sales pitch · audience · projector

P **2** **For what reasons might you have to give a presentation? Write a list.**

3 **With a partner, decide upon a final list and share it with the class.**

4 **With the same partner brainstorm what you think is important to remember when giving a presentation. Write your answers in a word web like the one below.**

presentations — be well prepared

A | Preparing a presentation

1 In the following table are words which are linked to presentations.
Match the English words (1.–10.) with the appropriate German words (a.–j.).

1. audience	a. Augenkontakt		
2. prompt cards	b. beschreiben		
3. body language	c. Zusammenfassung		
4. eye contact	d. visuelle Hilfsmittel		
5. handout	e. Publikum		
6. to prepare	f. Schaubild		
7. graph	g. Stichwortkarten		
8. visual aids	h. Körpersprache		
9. to describe	i. vorbereiten		
10. summary	j. Informationsblatt		

M **2** **Fassen Sie den folgenden Text über die Vorbereitung einer Präsentation unter**
KMK II **Beantwortung folgender Fragen auf Deutsch zusammen.**

1. Warum soll eine Präsentation nicht schriftlich ausformuliert werden?
2. Wie soll eine Präsentation gegliedert sein?
3. Was ist „signposting"?
4. Welche Vorteile bieten visuelle Hilfsmittel?
5. Wie müssen Präsentationsfolien aussehen, damit sie wirken?

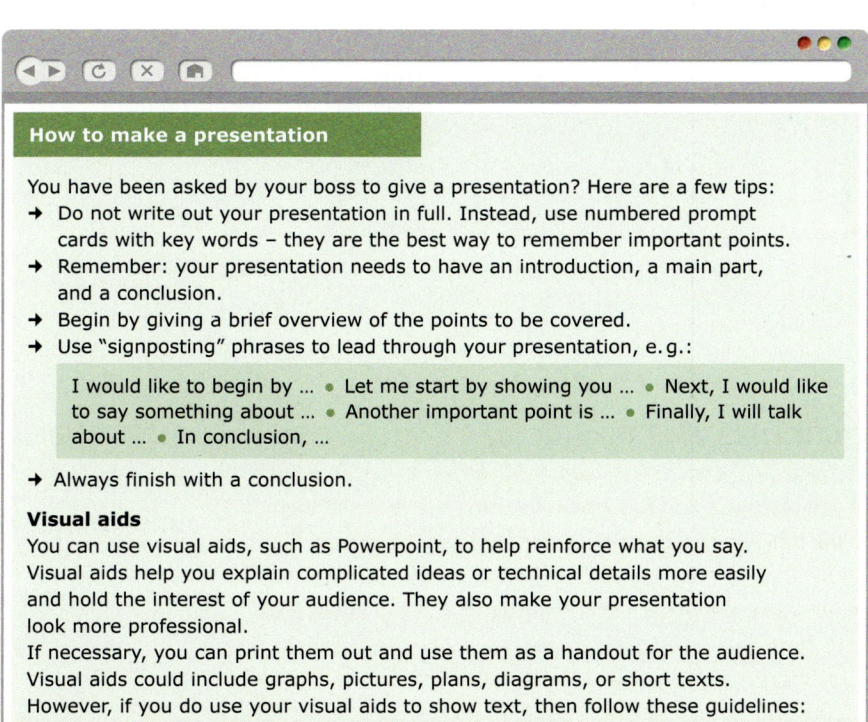

How to make a presentation

You have been asked by your boss to give a presentation? Here are a few tips:
→ Do not write out your presentation in full. Instead, use numbered prompt cards with key words – they are the best way to remember important points.
→ Remember: your presentation needs to have an introduction, a main part, and a conclusion.
→ Begin by giving a brief overview of the points to be covered.
→ Use "signposting" phrases to lead through your presentation, e.g.:

> I would like to begin by … • Let me start by showing you … • Next, I would like to say something about … • Another important point is … • Finally, I will talk about … • In conclusion, …

→ Always finish with a conclusion.

Visual aids
You can use visual aids, such as Powerpoint, to help reinforce what you say. Visual aids help you explain complicated ideas or technical details more easily and hold the interest of your audience. They also make your presentation look more professional.
If necessary, you can print them out and use them as a handout for the audience. Visual aids could include graphs, pictures, plans, diagrams, or short texts. However, if you do use your visual aids to show text, then follow these guidelines:

→ Limit the text to six lines.
→ Try to use no more than six words per line.
→ Print the text in large letters, using upper and lower case letters.
→ Use dark colours, such as black, red, blue, or green. Light colours are difficult to read.

WORD BANK

assembly – Montage
positional sketch – Technologie-schema

3 Match the visual aids (1.–6.) with the pictures below (a.–e.).

1. plan   2. pie chart   3. line graph   4. bar chart   5. diagram   6. table

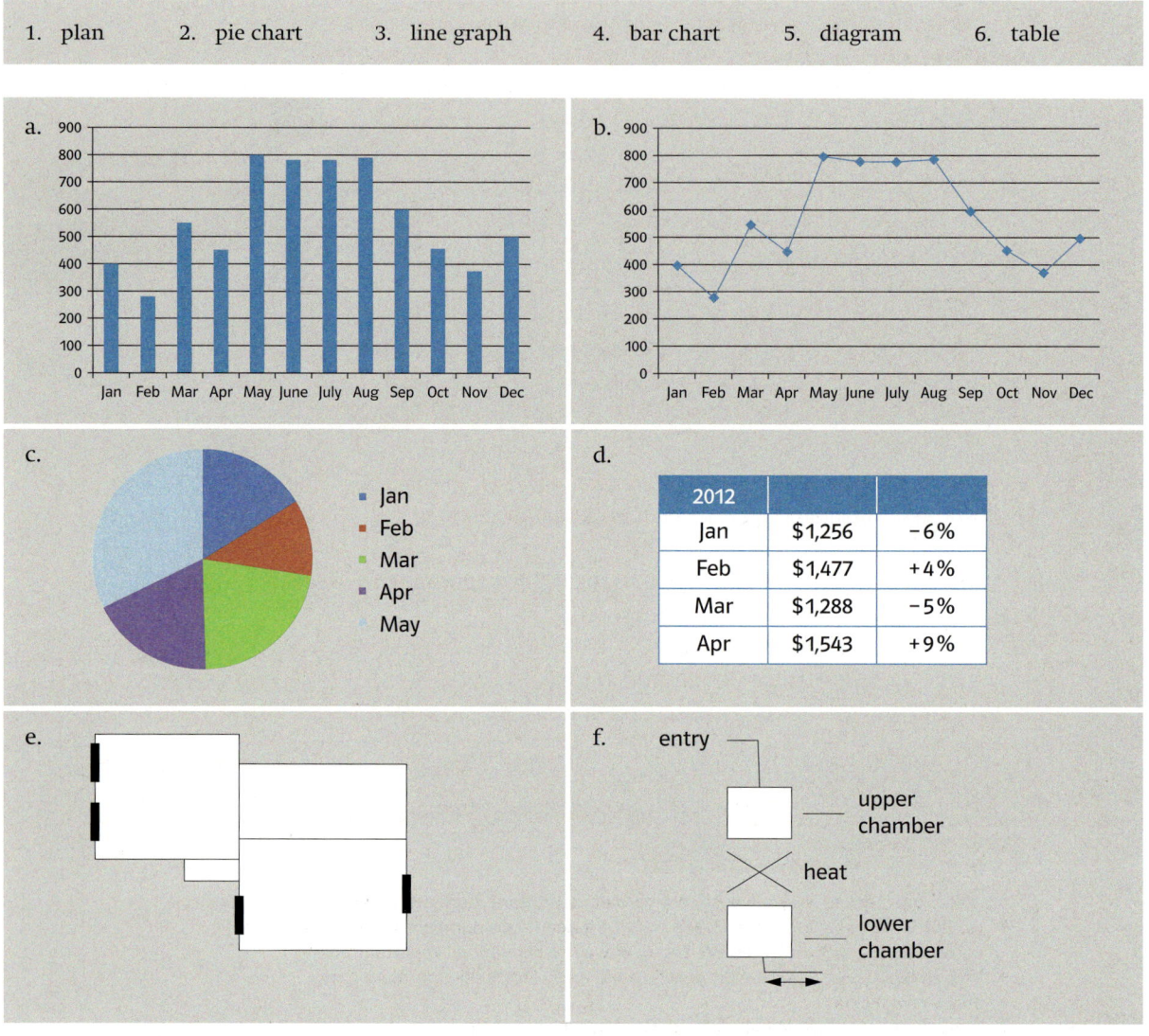

B | Describing materials and products

P **1** Think of something that you often use and describe it by using the terms in the box to help you. Don't name the item you are describing. Try and write 3 to 5 sentences.

I **2** Take it in turns to read your sentences to each other and see if you can guess what your partner is describing.

INFO BOX: Useful phrases for describing materials and products
It is a | strong · sturdy · rigid · flexible · lightweight · shiny · robust · matt | material.
The design is | modern · state-of-the-art · classic · elegant · old-fashioned.
It is | user-friendly · difficult to operate · reliable · innovative · hand-crafted.

C | Delivering a presentation

R **1** Max Wiesinger, a trained carpenter who works for a furniture design company,
⊙ A 1.6 is presenting a new line of furniture at a trade show. Listen to the presentation
and complete the following text.

Good morning ladies and gentleman. Today **1** our new range
of **2** , *Simply Wood*. The range, which is shown here on the first
slide, includes chairs, a large table, a lounger, and benches.
I would like to start by talking about the **3** used in the
5 furniture. All of the *Simply Wood* range is made from single
softwood timber and has been **4** by our highly-skilled
carpenters and joiners.
If you look at this picture, you can see that the benches and the
seats are designed with a low back, deep seats and long arms
10 to offer a great deal of comfort and convenience. Thanks to a
special varnish, the furniture is 100 % **5** and will not suffer from discolouring.
6 from this final slide, the furniture is also available in white, to give it
a classic, timeless look. And do not worry, we have used a durable white
polyurethane coating that is suitable for every environment.
15 On your handout you will see more details about each piece, including the
measurements. **7** this morning. Are there any questions? Yes …

P **2** Now it's your turn. Work in small groups and design a chair, a pocket torch, or any
other object of your choice. Present your ideas in class. Use the following words and
phrases to help you:

→ **PHRASES:** Presentations

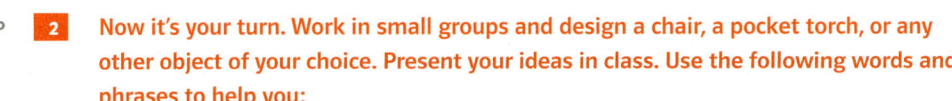
We have designed a … • Our idea was to … • Our design is made of … •
The advantage of the material we used is … • Its measurements are … •
length • diameter • weight • width • height • rectangular • circle •
circular • square • smooth edges • glued/screwed together • made out of
one piece

M **3** Ihre Kollegin muss nächste Woche eine wichtige Präsentation halten und bittet Sie
 um Ihre Hilfe. Sie hat den folgenden Text gefunden, versteht aber leider nur wenig
Englisch. Übertragen Sie den Text für sie sinngemäß ins Deutsche.

7 Ways to Do it Right: Presentations

1. Keep it short and simple (KISS).
2. Do not use too many visual aids.
3. If you are presenting in a group, decide beforehand who will say what.
4. Practice at least once in front of an audience.
5. Do not read from your notes. Look at your audience.
6. Structure your presentation with phrases so your audience can follow more easily.
7. Tell the audience when they can ask questions – either during the presentation,
   or at the end.

WORD BANK

carpenter – Tischler(in) /
Schreiner(in)
circle – Kreis
circular – kreisförmig
diameter – Dicke
furniture – Möbel
height – Höhe
length – Länge
rectangular – rechteckig
smooth – glatt
square – quadratisch
trade show – Messe
weight – Gewicht
width – Breite

WORD BANK ⊙

durable – haltbar
joiner – Tischler(in) / Schreiner(in)
polyurethane coating – Polyurethan-
beschichtung
softwood – Weichholz
timber – Holz
varnish – Lack

08

NACH DIESEM MODUL:

√ kann ich gängige Montage-
verbindungen auf Englisch
benennen und beschreiben,

√ kann ich Montage- und
Demontagevorgänge auf
Englisch beschreiben.

Assembly

When joining two materials or components, the joint you use may be permanent or non-permanent. Joints made using screws and nails are non-permanent. The fasteners can be loosened or unscrewed and the components taken apart for maintenance or repair work. Non-permanent joints make it easier to replace components that break down or wear out. Welding, brazing, soldering and riveting all produce permanent joints. When the welded parts of automated systems are taken apart, the welded seams are completely destroyed.

1 Describe what the people are doing in the photos.

2 Make a table with the verbs in the above text: one list describes assembling processes, the other describes dismantling processes.

3 Complete the sentences using verbs from your table in exercise 2.

1. That container needs a base plate, let's ❓ a sheet of metal to the bottom of it.
2. I must ❓ the bolts at the back of the column drill before I can repair it.
3. There is a hole in the metal staircase. Let's ❓ a small sheet of metal over the hole.
4. Look, that wire is loose, we have to ❓ it back to the terminal.
5. I have to repair my bike. First I have to ❓ those big butterfly screws.

A | Assembling processes

Assembling processes include both joining and dismantling techniques. Sometimes the same tool is used for both jobs. For example, you can loosen and tighten screws with a screwdriver or a power drill.

R **1**
A 2.8
Andreas Thiel and Marie Binoche, an exchange student from France, are doing their apprenticeship in a car factory. Listen to them while they talk to technician Herbert Lang and say whether the statements are true or false. Correct the false statements.

1. Marie checked the ball bearings and found that they were faulty.
2. Andreas and Marie have to loosen the wires in order to remove the housing of the machine.
3. Andreas offers to fasten the bolts with a screwdriver.
4. Herbert Lang is happy that there are no rivets because they must be destroyed to undo them.

R **2**
A 2.8
Listen to the dialogue again and then complete Marie's notes about the maintenance job.

Maintenance job		
Step 1: Loosen the ...	Step 4: Remove	Step 7: Check
Step 2: Unplug	Step 5: Fit	Step 8: Replace
Step 3: Reopen	Step 6: Tighten	

M **3** Explain the steps of the maintenance job in German.

4 Match the fasteners in the box with the photos. Two terms do not match.

stud bolts · rivets · screws · nuts · washers · nails

 1
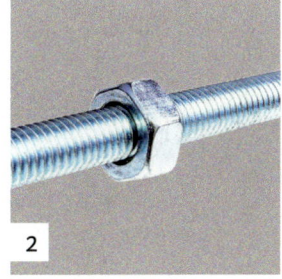 2
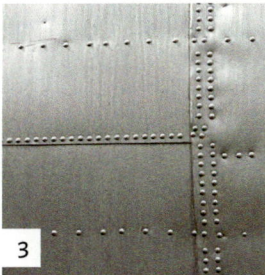 3

P **5** Check the Internet to find the English equivalent of and an explanation for each joining method.

Joining methods
1. Stiftverbindung
2. Welle-Nabe-Verbindung
3. Pressverbindung
4. Federverbindung

WORD BANK

assembly – Montage
bolt – Bolzen
braze (v) – hartlöten
butterfly screw – Flügelschraube
column drill – Ständerbohrmaschine
fastener – Befestigung
join (v) – verbinden
joint – Verbindung
nail – Nagel
power drill – Schlagbohrmaschine
rivet (v) – nieten, vernieten
screw – Schraube
screwdriver – Schraubenzieher
seam – Naht
solder (v) – löten
terminal – Anschluss
weld (v) – schweißen
wire – Kabel

WORD BANK ☉

ball bearing – Kugellager
electric drive – Antrieb, Motor
housing – Gehäuse
rivet – Gewindeniet

B | Soldering and brazing

Soldering and brazing are joining techniques which are applied at high temperatures, although the temperatures used in welding are higher. Both soldering and brazing are primarily applied in electrical engineering and plumbing work. Electrical engineers solder electric wires and parts to radio and TV boards, and plumbers apply brazing to join pipes in houses and other buildings. In soldering the melting point of the solder is lower than in brazing.

M **1** Give a summary of the text about soldering and brazing in German.

Soldering and brazing

In soldering the parts to be joined are heated to temperatures of up to 450°C. The solder begins to melt when it is pressed against the parts and
5 flows into the joint. When the material has cooled down, the joint is finished. In brazing, the solder works at higher temperatures, i.e. the melting point is between 450°C and 900°C. Brass, silver, copper and steel are all suitable for brazing.

Soldering equipment consists of a soldering 10 station with a soldering iron tip, or a soldering piston tip, and an iron holder, as well as solder paste, solder tin and solder wire. A brazing torch and mixer are used in brazing. Oxygen is taken from a blue cylinder and acetylene from a yellow 15 one through hoses. The oxygen and acetylene regulators control the temperature of the flame.

R/M **2** Identify the labelled parts of the soldering and brazing gear using words from the text in exercise 1.

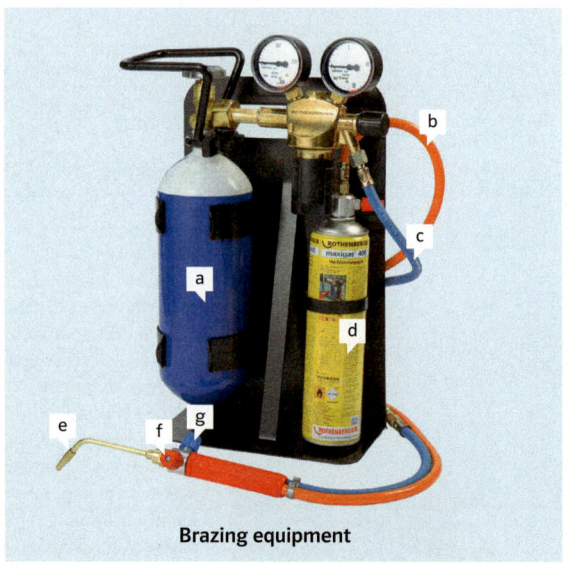

Brazing equipment

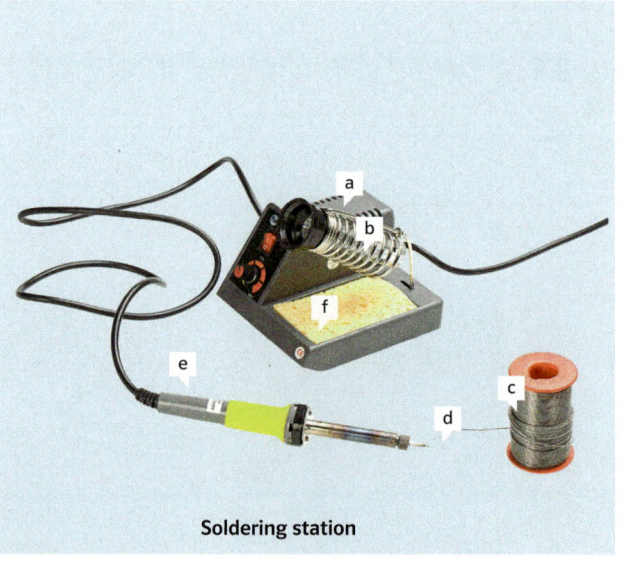

Soldering station

3 Look at exercise 1 again and say if the following statements are true or false. Correct the false ones.

1. When the solder flows into the joint, the joint is then finished.
2. The blue cylinder contains oxygen and acytelene comes from the yellow cylinder.
3. The temperature of the flame is varied by the regulators.
4. Brass and silver are suitable materials to make brazing stations.

Sie haben die Produktbeschreibung einer digitalen Lötstation in einem englischen Katalog gelesen und möchten Ihrem Ausbilder die Leistungsmerkmale auf Deutsch nennen. Fassen Sie die Merkmale auf Deutsch zusammen.

Digital processor-soldering station

The station turns automatically into 'sleep mode' when the soldering iron is left in the iron holder for longer than 15 minutes. In sleep mode, the temperature goes down to 200° C. This function prolongs the life of the soldering tip and saves electricity. When the soldering job is taken up again or any key is pressed, the station automatically goes back to the operating mode and heats up to the preset temperature.

Features

- Integrated automatic "Sleep function"
- Temperature range 150°C – 500°C
- Short warm-up time
- LCD display
- Power 60 W
- Precise, rapid temperature control
- 24 V soldering iron with 1.0 mm tip
- Weight: 2.450 kg

C | Assembly lines

In production processes single parts are assembled to make products. Each stage of production is carried out either manually by a skilled worker or automatically by a robotic system. The stages on the assembly line are planned carefully before production begins. Each stage is broken down into subassemblies. As well as joining and dismantling components, inspection, feeding and secondary operations such as cleaning are also carried out on the assembly line.

1 Complete the plan of an assembly using the correct verbs.

check · make · begin · decide · make sure · remove · clean

WORD BANK

Plan of an assembly
1. ? how to break the assembly into subassemblies.
2. ? an assembly description which includes the sequence of the assembly.
3. ? that the necessary tools are ready to use.
4. ? the components and ? any grease.
5. ? components for faults.
6. ? the assembly process.

P **2** **UNDERSTANDING TECHNICAL ENGLISH**
Use a dictionary to check the general and technical meanings of the English and German words.

a. assembly   b. branch   c. Welle   d. Mutter

acetylene – Azetylen
board – Platine, Leiterplatte
brazing torch – Lötlampe
electrical engineer – Elektroingenieur(in)
feed (v) – zuführen, bestücken
iron holder – Lötkolbenhalter
melting point – Schmelzpunkt
mixer – Mischregler
regulator – Regler
solder – Lot, Lötmetall
solder paste – Lötfett
solder tin – Lötzinn
solder wire – Lötdraht
soldering iron tip – Lötkolbenspitze
soldering piston tip – Lötkolbenspitze
soldering station – Lötstation

H

NACH DIESEM MODUL:

√ kann ich auf Englisch auf Kunden-
beschwerden reagieren,

√ kann ich auf Englisch mit
unzufriedenen Kunden umgehen.

Dealing with customers

The way a company deals with its customers is the key to its success. Whether you
are arranging appointments, handling enquiries, or dealing with complaints, it is
essential that you are able to express yourself clearly, confidently, and politely.
And remember: the customer may not always be right, but they are very important.

1 Brainstorm words that describe what is shown in the photos above.

P **2** Compare your list of words with your partner and work together to describe the
pictures. Use these words to help you:

> complaint · hotline · builder · hard hat · building site · meeting ·
> customer · plans · mechanic · explain · repairs · bonnet · overalls · engine

3 Which of the customers above do you think are happy, and which are unhappy?
Explain your answer.

P **4** In what situations do you deal with customers in your job? Copy and complete the
word web below to brainstorm reasons for talking to customers.

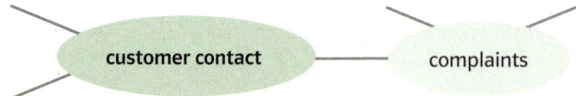

customer contact — complaints

A | Complaints

1 Match the common causes for complaint on the left with the suggested solutions on the right. Several options may be appropriate.

1. delay in delivery	a. offer a price reduction
2. faulty goods	b. improve the service
3. damaged goods	c. repair the goods
4. unsatisfactory services	d. replace the goods
5. wrong goods	e. send the goods by air freight
6. too many/too few goods received	f. send the missing goods
7. too early delivery	g. take the goods back
	h. collect the surplus goods
	i. send a credit note

P **2** What about your industry? Which are the most common reasons for complaints? Make a list and compare it with a partner. Be as specific as possible.

R **3** Which of the following phrases are used for making complaints and which ones for replying to complaints? Make a list.

→ **PHRASES:**
Dealing with customers

1. This is very inconvenient for us because we need the goods urgently.
2. We are sorry for any inconvenience this has caused.
3. We will keep the damaged goods until we hear from you.
4. Please return the damaged goods at our expense.
5. We can assure you that this will not happen again.
6. Some items were badly damaged.
7. We regret to inform you that the order has not yet arrived.
8. We think the damage may have occurred in transit.
9. We are experiencing difficulties with our new logistics software.
10. Could you please look into this problem immediately?
11. Please accept our apologies.
12. The reason for the mistake is that we are extremely busy at this time of the year.
13. Please send us replacements as soon as possible.
14. We hope that this proposal will find your approval.
15. We believe the problem is down to human error.

R **4**  **KMK II** ⊙ A 1.7
You work for *Deutsches Netz*, an IT company in Hamburg. Your boss, Mr Bauder, receives a voicemail message on his mobile phone from Mr Jenkins, owner of *New Wave Marketing*, a subsidiary of an English marketing company based in Hamburg. Listen to the message and answer the following questions.

1. What did the technicians from Deutsches Netz do for New Wave Marketing?
2. What problems are the employees having (three things)?
3. What is the most serious problem?
4. Why is this a serious problem?
5. How should Mr Bauder contact Mr Jenkins?

WORD BANK

bonnet – Motorhaube
builder – Bauarbeiter
building site – Baustelle
hotline – Informationsdienst
repairs – Reparaturen
technician – Techniker(in)

P **5** Mr Bauder asks you to respond to Mr Jenkins' phone call. He sends you the following email and asks you to draft a short email to the customer.

→ **PHRASES:**
Dealing with customers

Von: mailto:s.bauder@DNetz…de
An: mailto:info@DNetz…de
Betreff: Bitte an Herrn Jenkins schreiben (eilt!!)

… diese Firma ist ein sehr wichtiger Kunde von uns und wir wollen ihn **auf keinen Fall** verlieren!! Bitte sagen Sie ihm folgendes:

- Es tut uns sehr leid, dass es diese Probleme gegeben hat.
- Wir verstehen völlig, dass es jetzt sehr ungelegen und ärgerlich ist.
- Wir vermuten, dass das Problem durch menschliches Versagen verursacht wurde.
- Wir werden sofort jemanden schicken, um das Netzwerk zu reparieren. (selbstverständlich auf unsere Kosten!)
- Der Techniker wird spätestens um 17 Uhr dort sein.

Bringen Sie nochmals unser Bedauern für das Problem zum Ausdruck und versichern Sie ihm, dass sich dies nicht wiederholen wird.

Danke,
Bauder

M **6** You work for a plumbing and heating installation company in Leipzig. Your supervisor, Mr Hüber, receives an email about a recent job done for an American family living in the area. Your supervisor does not speak very good English and asks you to read the email and to sum it up in German.

Von: mailto:j.t.levine@kwq…net
An: mailto:info@sippelheizung_sanitaer…net
Betreff: Problems with the heating

Dear Mr Hüber,

I am writing in reference to the heating system installed by your company at my house last week. Unfortunately, my family and I have been having some problems. Firstly, the water in the bathroom takes a long time to warm up – sometimes over 5 minutes!

Secondly, the temperature in the house is too low, and I cannot make it warmer. Also, I cannot find the instruction manual – did your technician take it with him? My final problem is that the underfloor heating does not seem to be working in the bathroom. The tiles on the floor are still cold in the morning. Is something wrong?

As it is winter, and very cold, I would ask you to send someone to my house as soon as possible to find a solution to these problems. Please give me a call, or send me an email to confirm.

Thank you in advance,

John Levine

B | Customer service

P **1** What five tips would you give a colleague about dealing with unhappy customers?

2 Compare your list with a partner.

How to deal with unhappy customers

**No company has happy customers 100 % of the time.
Things can always go wrong and customers can become unhappy – or worse,
upset. Here are some tips on how to avoid making the situation worse.**

Stay calm: The customer may be angry at somebody, but it does not help the
situation if you get just as angry. The last thing you want to do is start an argument –
that is very unprofessional and unhelpful. Try to calm the customer down.

Listen, listen, listen: You will only be able to understand what has upset the
customer if you listen, and listen carefully. Before you start talking, listen actively to
the customer until you fully understand why they are unhappy. If you don't know
what's wrong, you will not be able to do anything about it.

The customer is king: Show the customer that they, and their problem, are important to you. Tell them quickly how sorry you are for their problem and reassure them
that you will do everything you can to help them. And, always be patient and polite.

Stay positive: Do your best to stay positive at all times. Remember that your goal is
to solve the problem and you can do this better if you have a positive frame of mind.
Regardless of how negative and furious the customer gets, it is important that you do
not let it affect your mood.

No excuses: No matter what the problem is, or who you think caused it, do not blame
other people or try to make excuses. Instead, take the initiative and do whatever you
can to solve the problem.

R **3** Find the synonyms in the text for the following words and expressions:

1. to stop sth. from happening
2. disagreement
3. to aim
4. to fix
5. attitude
6. very angry
7. reason
8. to take control

R **4** **Sie lesen den oben stehenden Artikel im Internet. Beantworten Sie die folgenden**
KMK II **Fragen dazu in ganzen Sätzen auf Deutsch.**

1. Warum ist es wichtig zu wissen, wie man mit unzufriedenen Kunden
   umgeht?
2. Was sollte man tun, wenn der Kunde sehr verärgert ist?
3. Warum ist es wichtig, dem Kunden ganz genau zuzuhören?
4. Wie kann man einem Kunden zeigen, dass man sein Problem ernst
   nimmt?
5. Wann ist es gerechtfertigt, jemand anderem die Schuld für das
   vorliegende Problem zu geben?

I **5** **Choose one of the problems you listed in exercise A1 and create a short role play.**
 One of you should play the unhappy / angry customer and the other the employee.
Act out your role play in front of the class.

WORD BANK

instruction manual – Bedienungs-
anleitung
plumbing and heating – Heizung
und Sanitär
underfloor heating – Fußboden-
heizung

09

NACH DIESEM MODUL:

✓ kenne ich die englischen
  Fachbegriffe für gängige
  Messinstrumente und
  kann sie erklären,

✓ kann ich die Bedienung
  der Messinstrumente auf
  Englisch beschreiben.

Measuring instruments

Before working with electricity, it is important to check whether there are still any live wires present and how high the voltage is. Testing equipment like insulated mains testers and voltmeters or oscilloscopes are used to decide whether you are dealing with direct current (DC) or alternating current (AC).

When working with metal in a mechatronics workshop, you use measuring instruments like a micrometer and a vernier calliper. It is important to read the display of the voltmeter or the values on the scales of a micrometer correctly.

1 Identify the tools in the photos and say what you can do with them.

2 Find more measuring tools that are used in a mechatronics workshop.
  Use a dictionary or the Internet.

3 Say which of the following you can measure with the tools in exercise 2.

> weight · height · length · width · depth · voltage · temperature · distance

Measuring tool	What you can measure

A | Using a vernier calliper and a micrometer

WORD BANK

alternating current – Wechselstrom
clamp (v) – einklemmen, festklemmen
direct current – Gleichstrom
insulated – isoliert
live wire – stromführendes Kabel
mains tester – Phasenprüfer
measuring instrument – Messgerät
screw – Schraube
voltage – Spannung

Vernier callipers are the most commonly used measuring instruments for external, internal and depth measurements. Micrometers are used to measure the internal and external dimensions of small objects. Both instruments are easy to use and give precise measurements.

1 Match the English terms with the German parts of the vernier calliper.

1. Lineal	a. metric vernier scale
2. metrische Skala	b. external measuring jaws
3. Zoll-Skala	c. slide or body
4. fester Messschenkel	d. depth gauge rod
5. Schieber	e. inch main scale
6. metrischer Nonius	f. internal measuring jaws
7. Zoll-Nonius	g. clamp screw
8. beweglicher Messschenkel	h. fixed jaw
9. Messschneiden	i. metric main scale
10. Messspitzen	j. moveable jaw
11. Klemmschraube	k. rule
12. Tiefenmaß	l. inch vernier scale

2 Identify the parts of the vernier calliper in the diagram below using the English terms in exercise 1.

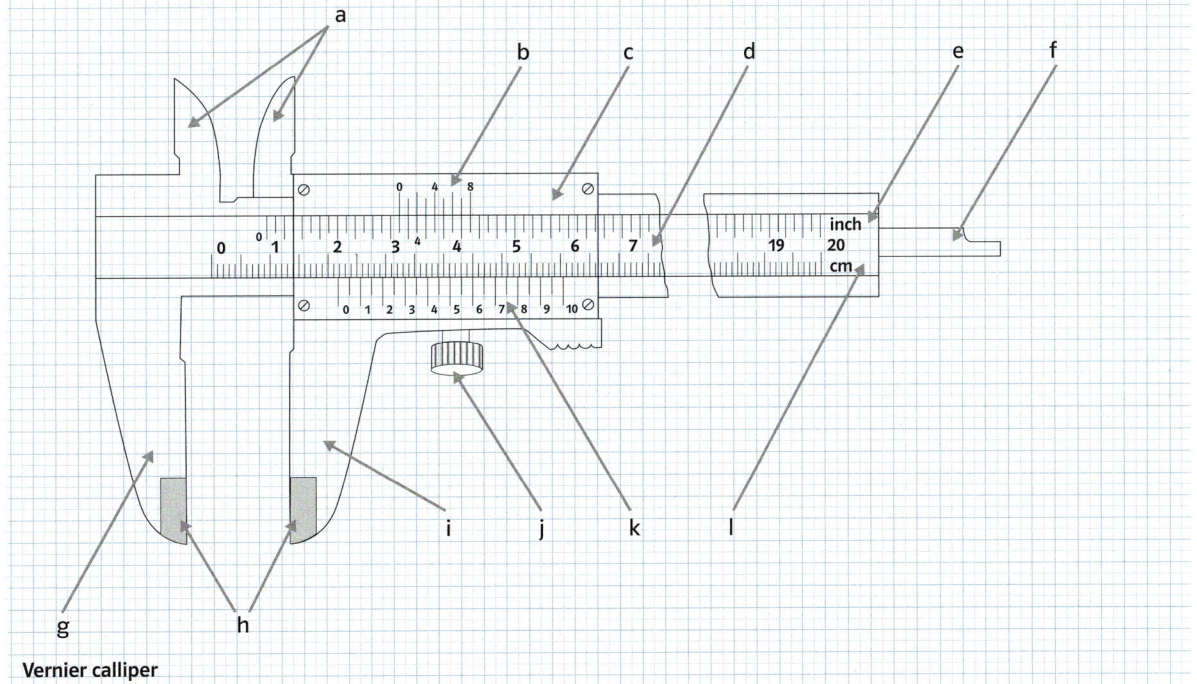

Vernier calliper

P **3** List the rules that are important when working with a vernier calliper.

Example:
The workpiece you want to measure must be clean.

4 Look at the diagram of a micrometer. Then complete the text using the correct form of the words in the diagram.

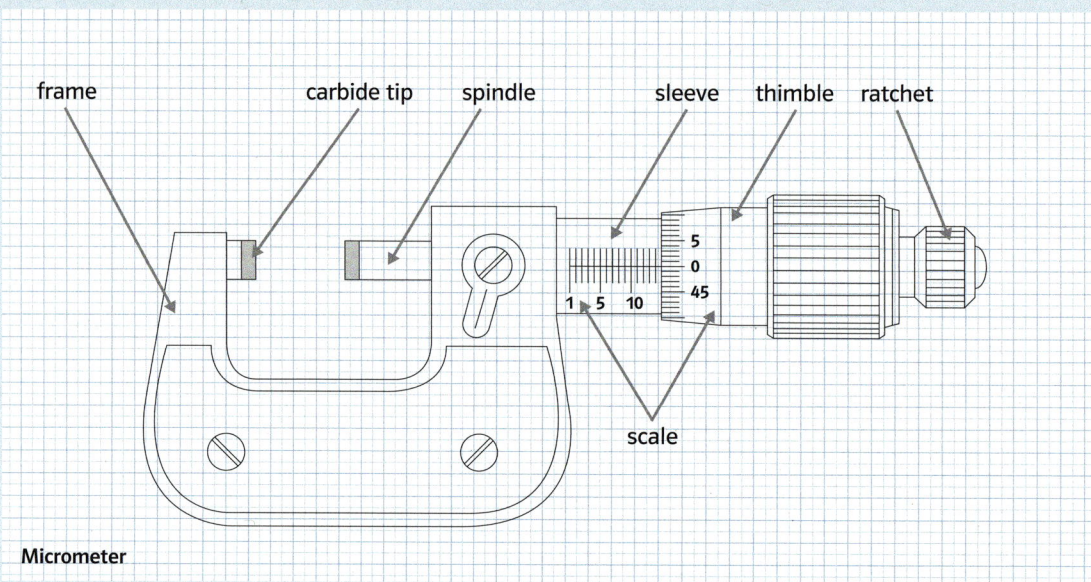

frame   carbide tip   spindle   sleeve   thimble   ratchet

scale

Micrometer

Micrometers

Micrometers can be used to measure wires, shafts, the diameters of holes, the depths of slots, etc. A micrometer consists of a **1** which
5 looks like an arc and has a **2** on the opposite side which looks like a big screw that can be turned. To take precise measurements, you clamp the object between the anvil and the **3** . Both of these parts have **4** . Micrometers
10 typically have a range of 0.5 mm on a **5** marked on a kind of screw. When you rotate the screw, you can see each complete rotation in millimetre steps on the **6** . For incomplete rotations, the values are shown on the **7** , where you can read off hundredth millimetres. 15
This allows readings to a fraction of the smallest scale mark. For the final result, you add the two readings. Nowadays, more modern digital micrometers show the measurement on an electronic display. The two types of 20
micrometers widely used in mechanical engineering and machining are external micrometers and internal micrometers.

 5 Ihr Ausbilder findet im Internet den Text in Aufgabe 4. Er bittet Sie, die wichtigsten
KMK II Informationen auf Deutsch für Ihre Klassenkameraden zusammen zu fassen.

6 UNDERSTANDING TECHNICAL ENGLISH

1. Find the German meanings of the words in a dictionary.

   a. diameter   b. fraction   c. scale

2. Translate the sentences into English.

   a. Mit einem Messschieber werden die Länge und der Durchmesser eines Werkstücks gemessen.
   b. Die Bügelmessschraube misst sehr kleine Abstände, die man durch Ablesen der Teilbereiche auf der Skala ermittelt.

B | Working with an oscilloscope

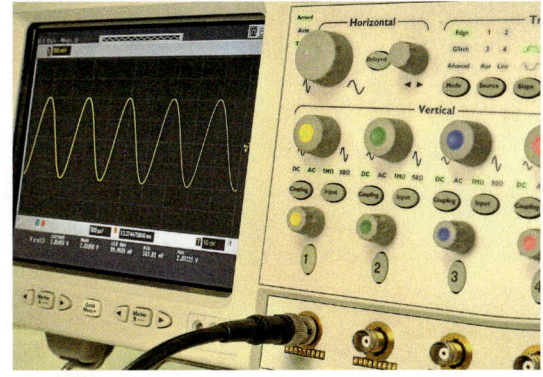

An oscilloscope is also known as a scopemeter or scope. It displays a signal which moves horizontally across the screen from left to right with an adjustable speed. The applied voltage is displayed vertically, from bottom to top. Oscilloscopes are used to observe periodic electrical signals. The frequency, amplitude and shape of the time-dependent electrical signal are analysed. A wide range of frequencies can be displayed, from very slow varying electrical signals up to Gigahertz frequencies.

1 Describe the tasks that can be performed with an oscilloscope in your own words.

R **2**
⊙ A 2.9
Christoph and Ryan, who is from a partner school in Leeds, have to work with an oscilloscope. They ask Lisa, who is a year ahead of them, for help. Listen to the dialogue and make notes about what you can do with an oscilloscope.

R **3**
⊙ A 2.9
Listen to the dialogue again and choose the most suitable options to complete the sentences.

1. An oscilloscope is used for …
   a. measuring amperes.
   b. checking the temperature of a room.
   c. monitoring voltage.

2. In order to draw the behaviour of voltage …
   a. the oscilloscope uses two different diagrams.
   b. the oscilloscope uses an x-axis to show the time and a y-axis to show the voltage.
   c. the oscilloscope uses a straight line.

3. The signal is shown …
   a. as a red line on the screen.
   b. as a straight arrow.
   c. as a dot moving along a wavy line.

4. You can only see the dot when …
   a. it is amplified by the voltage signal knob.
   b. it is dark in the room.
   c. you are wearing 3D-glasses.

P **4**
🌐
Search the Internet for an English description of an oscilloscope. Write a short summary in one column of a table and a German summary in the other.

P **5**
⚠ Both the voltmeter and oscilloscope are used to measure voltage. Explain in which cases you would use these devices.

WORD BANK

amplitude – Amplitude, Ausschlag
anvil – Amboss
frequency – Frequenz
rotation – Umdrehung
shaft – Welle
wire – Draht

WORD BANK ⊙

amplify (v) – verstärken
axis, axes (plural) – Achse
frequency meter – Frequenz-messgerät
input – Eingabe
travel (v) – durchlaufen

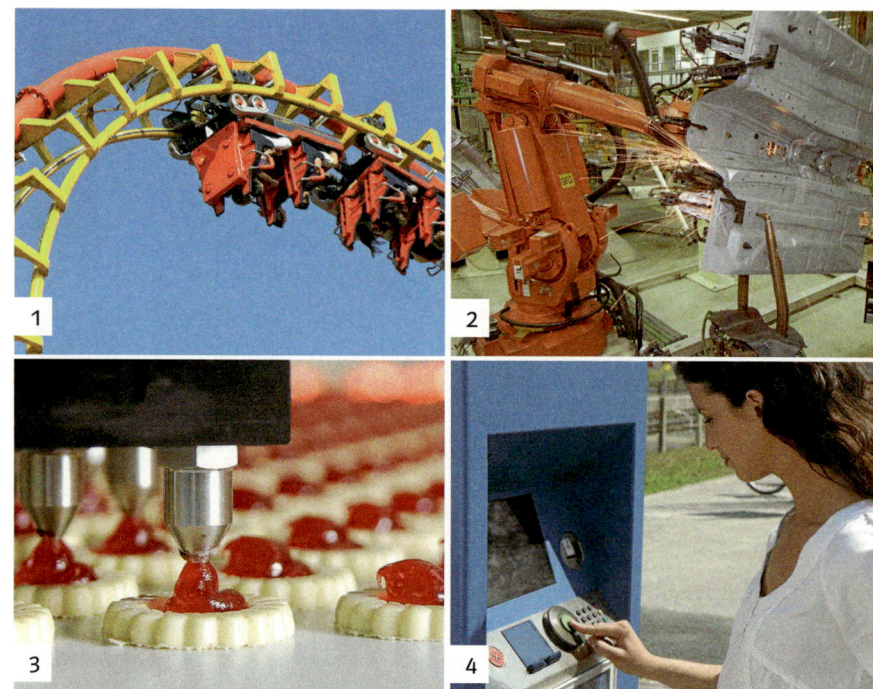

10

NACH DIESEM MODUL:

✓ kann ich mechatronische Systeme und ihre Bauteile auf Englisch benennen und beschreiben.

Mechatronics

Mechatronic systems are a must in manufacturing processes such as the automobile industry, food processing, service and transportation as well as fun parks and the entertainment sector. Mechatronic systems are made up of mechanical, electrical and electronic elements. Software and control systems control the flow of data in the system. Sensors monitor and control how the system works. Actuators are operated by pneumatics, hydraulics or current. They move the parts of the mechatronic system.

R **1** **Describe the photos and decide which sectors they are taken from. Use the words in the box.**

> car body · roller coaster · jam · carriage · ticket request · welding

I **2** **Explain why the machines in the photos are considered to be mechatronic systems. Use the words in the box.**

> transport · detect · monitor · pick · place · process · check · control · complete · read · count

3 **Think of any other examples of mechatronic systems that you know. Describe briefly how the mechatronic parts in these systems work. Use an online dictionary if necessary.**

A | Examples of mechatronic systems

Smart electronic and automated components optimise production processes and the products themselves. Mechatronics engineering is applied by the electronics industry to develop cameras and MP3 players. The car industry requires these systems to produce ABS and automatic drives.

1 Name the elements of a mechatronic system that are found in the machines and devices in the photos.

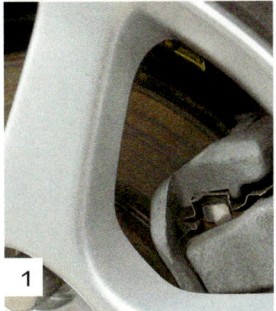
1

ABS brake

2

Automatic drive

3

Digital camera

2 Complete the text using the words in the box. Two words do not fit.

> anti-lock braking system · features · mechatronic · sectors · operate ·
> numerically controlled · hydraulic · handling · peripherals · entertainment

Mechatronic systems

ABS **1** , ESC (electronic stability control) and automatic drives are standard **2** in most modern cars. All three systems are prime examples of **3** systems. ABS systems include sensors, actuators, and a small
5 steering unit that analyses data and influences the application of car brakes. Electronic stability control has electronic, **4** and pneumatic components to keep a car under control when it starts to skid. More and more industrial **5** have discovered the advantages of these systems for their products. Flexible, **6** tools are frequently used
10 to assemble complicated components precisely and rapidly. When combined with accurate **7** systems, the tools allow greater flexibility both in production and logistics processes. Digital CD players, calculators, cameras and MP3 players as well as computer **8** have replaced their analogue predecessors, and revolutionised the **9** sector. Apart from their
15 technological advantages they are easier to **10** and are of a higher quality.

M **3** Write a short summary of the text in German.

4 UNDERSTANDING TECHNICAL ENGLISH
Find the general and technical meanings of the words.

1. read   2. lock   3. mount (v)   4. panel

B | Mechatronic components

Even the simplest mechatronic system contains a lot of electronic and automated components. The everyday example of a CD player includes laser and optical diodes, a beam splitter and a focusing lens. Common tasks in mechatronics are to design photo-optic measuring devices for image processing or window contamination sensors for car windscreens. Complex machines need components like PLC control systems which are programmed to do specific tasks.

1 Define the parts of a PLC system using the words given.

Example:

A laptop is a device which monitors the system that is being controlled.

1. final control elements 2. operating elements 3. electric signals 4. *laptop* 5. control program 6. limit switch	*device(s)* equipment unit program	put a process into motion operate contacts to make or break an electrical connection/determine the presence of an object analyse and process incoming signals change the flow in a process *monitor the system that is being controlled* detect the positions of handling devices

R **2**
⊚ A 2.10
Listen to the two mechatronics students, Moira Ashley from York and Jonas Schulte from Dortmund talking about programmable logic controllers (PLCs). Say which part(s) in exercise 1 they do not talk about.

R **3**
⊚ A 2.10
Listen to the dialogue again and complete the sentences.

1. An example of an operating element is a …
2. This element starts the …
3. Limit switches are used to detect the positions of the …
4. The final control elements regulate cylinders and …
5. A touchscreen panel is a part of a …

4 Match the advantages of PLC systems with their features.

Advantages	Features
1. flexible 2. give reliable results 3. space-saving 4. efficient 5. economical	a. PLC systems save time and analyse received signals quickly and accurately. Thus it is easier to keep a record of output. b. PLCs reduce the costs caused by hardware. c. If you have to change a control task, you only change the control program. You don't have to change the wiring. d. Electronic systems are more accurate and precise than electro-mechanical installations. e. A PLC unit is a single device equipped with lots of contactors and relays. It is useful when you have to install the unit in small machine parts or in narrow passages.

C | A mechatronics project

M **1**
KMK II
Ein Auszubildender an Ihrer Partnerschule in England schickt Ihrem Ausbilder die Dokumentation eines kleinen selbstentwickelten mechatronischen Systems. Ihr Ausbilder bittet Sie, die wichtigsten Informationen auf Deutsch zusammenzufassen. Schreiben Sie ganze Sätze.

Description and summary of our mechatronics project

We have a whole fleet of forklifts in our company. They cruise regularly on shop floors and from time to time there are accidents caused by carelessness,
5 inexperience and overloading. If the load is too heavy, the forklift may tip forwards and the back wheels then lose their grip. At that point the forklift truck cannot be steered anymore and the driver loses control of the vehicle.
10 Our task was to find ways of improving safety when using forklifts, prevent accidents and cut costs caused by damage to goods. We decided to develop a device to monitor the weight of loads. The most important requirements for this device
15 were easy assembly, reasonable costs and it should be easy to replace. The device should not affect officially approved vehicle structures.
We used five components: a load sensor, a steering unit, LEDs, a horn and a vehicle battery. The load
20 sensor was required to monitor loads. The steering unit had a number of functions: it detected the position of the vehicle; it showed when the vehicle had exceeded a safe speed limit; it analysed data. The LEDs were mounted on a panel in the driver's
25 cab. The horn was also installed in the cab.

A vehicle battery provided power for all of the components.
We mounted the load sensor on the rear axle to monitor the load. It sent a signal to the LEDs in the driver's cab to show when the axle load limit had 30 been reached. Different-coloured LEDs indicated various problems: if the front load of the forklift truck was so heavy that the rear wheels lost their grip, a red LED lit up. An orange light showed the battery's current capacity. In addition, the horn 35 warned the driver that the vehicle could not be steered. In this way the device could prevent an accident happening.

P **2**

Make a list of the components necessary for the project in exercise 1.
Use a table like the one below. Some of the components are in the text.

electronic components	electrical components	mechanical components

P **3**
⚠ Make a list of operating instructions for the system in English so that the forklift driver can use it correctly.

Example:

> **Operating instructions**
> When you hear the horn, your vehicle may be in danger of tipping over.
> Stop immediately and …

WORD BANK

beam splitter – Strahlteiler
control task – Steuerungsaufgabe
final control element – Stellglied
focusing lens – Fokussierlinse
handling device – Handhabungsgerät
image processing – Bildverarbeitung
limit switch – Grenztaster
operating element – Bedienelement
PLC control system – SPS-Steuerung
wiring – Verdrahtung

WORD BANK ⊙

control device – Steuerungselement
signal element – Signalgeber
valve – Ventil

11

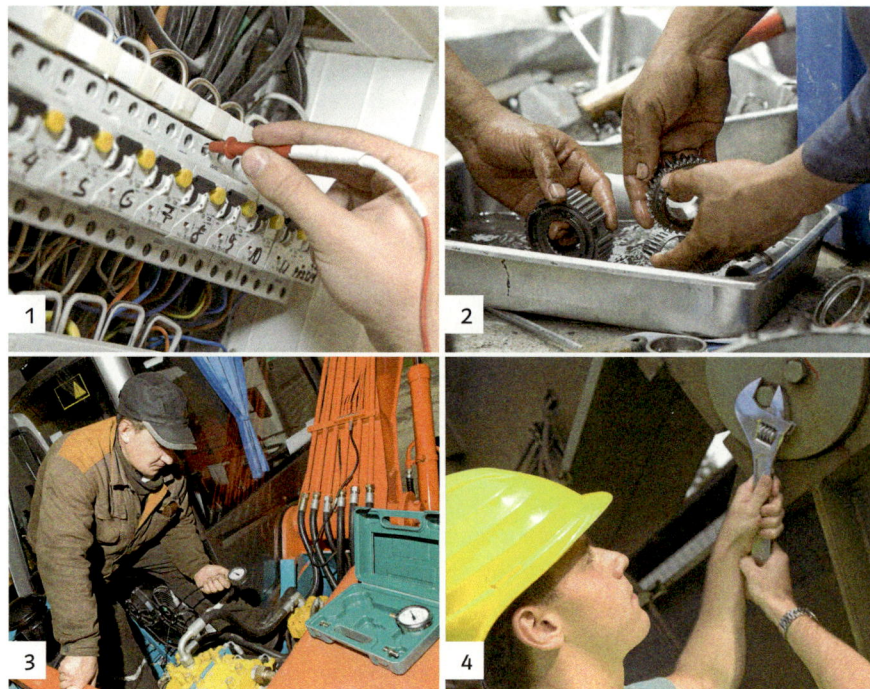

NACH DIESEM MODUL:

✓ verstehe ich einfache Wartungs-
pläne und wichtige Sicherheits-
bestimmungen auf Englisch und
kann diese beschreiben,

✓ kann ich Grundlagen für die
Planung von Wartungsarbeiten
auf Englisch beschreiben.

Maintenance

Complex mechatronic systems require a high standard of maintenance. Certain
routine operations have to be carried out periodically to keep machines running.
This is called scheduled maintenance. Preventive maintenance aims at avoiding
downtimes which might arise from system failures or repairs.

R · 1 Match the maintenance tasks in the box with the photos.

> fix a machine · lubricate a bearing · check the oil level · clean a gearbox ·
> measure the hydraulic pressure · check an electrical installation · replace
> cutting fluid

2 Decide if the tasks in exercise 1 are scheduled or preventive maintenance.

I/P · 3 Make a chart of the maintenance tasks in exercise 1. Then complete the following
aspects. Use a dictionary if necessary.

Example:

maintenance task	time required	maintenance intervals
lubricate a bearing	a few minutes	every 2–3 months

A | Maintaining an electric motor

Mechatronics involves maintaining complex systems, including electrical drives, and pneumatic and hydraulic systems. Maintaining electric motors is an important task because a breakdown could result in dangerous situations for workers, downtimes or damage to other equipment. Service or maintenance plans are important to achieve a good maintenance standard. These plans make it possible to identify and solve specific problems.

1 Explain why it is necessary to maintain mechatronic systems. Give reasons why it is necessary to document maintenance jobs.

M **2** The service plan describes the steps you have to follow when carrying out maintenance work on an electric motor. Explain the steps in German.

Electric motor service plan

1 If there is dirt on the frame and in air passages, you should remove it. The motor could become hot when the dirt prevents the air flowing to cool it. ☐

2 If the air flow is weak and erratic, internal air passages might be clogged. The motor has to be removed for further inspection. ☐

3 If there is corrosion on the motor, it should be repainted. ☐

4 If the bearings are hot or noisy, they have to be lubricated. ☐

5 You should start the motor and check whether the brushes ride smoothly on the commutator. The brushes should not generate too much noise or too many sparks. ☐

6 The surfaces of the brushes must be polished, and the brushes themselves should be long enough to last until the next maintenance date. ☐

7 The commutator has to be clean and have a polished surface. If the surface of the commutator has grooves, the commutator has to be replaced at once. ☐

8 The bearing may also need lubricating. In this case, you have to make sure your lubrication equipment is clean before lubricating it. ☐

9 Ball bearings and roller bearings have to be greased with a grease gun until the grease comes out of the hole. ☐

10 When a bearing has to be washed, you do this with a solvent. ☐

11 When the bearing shows wear and tear, it has to be replaced. ☐

P **3** **SAFETY FIRST** ⚠
Find the most important safety rules for servicing an electric motor as described in exercise 2. Compare your lists in groups of four and create one list per group. Each group presents their list to the class.
→ **PHRASES:** Presentations

WORD BANK

ball bearing – Kugellager
commutator – Gleichrichter
electrical drive – elektrischer Antrieb
grease (v) – fetten
grease gun – Fettpresse
groove – Rille, Furche
lubricate (v) – schmieren
preventive maintenance – vorbeugende Wartung, vorbeugende Instandhaltung
roller bearing – Rollenlager
scheduled maintenance – planmäßige Wartung, planmäßige Instandhaltung
solvent – Lösungsmittel
wear and tear – Abnutzung, Verschleiß

R **4**
◉ A 2.11

Uli, a German trainee, has to service an electric motor. Rick, an exchange trainee from England, is helping him because all of the documentation is in English. Listen to the dialogue to find out which documents are the basis for the maintenance work.

R **5**
◉ A 2.11

Listen to the dialogue again and answer the questions.

1. Why are the documents in exercise 5 important when servicing the electric motor?
2. Which maintenance jobs has Uli already done?
3. Which jobs still need to be done?
4. Compare the list of jobs with the tasks described in the electric motor service plan on page 81. Which steps does Uli not do?

I **6**
👥

Your company, Friedrichwerke, has bought an electric motor from ELMET Motors in California. Unfortunately, it is not running properly. Prepare and act out a telephone call using the role cards for Speaker A and Speaker B in the Appendix.

→ **PHRASES:** Dealing with customers / Telephoning

7
⚠ Describe the maintenance work on an electric motor or another drive unit that you have done in your company. Present your results to the class.

P **8**

UNDERSTANDING TECHNICAL ENGLISH
The German term 'Instandhaltung' can be translated as 'maintenance' and 'service', and 'Instandsetzung' can be translated as 'maintenance' and 'repair', depending on the context. Translate the sentences correctly.

→ **PHRASES:** Presentations

1. Die Instandhaltung wird regelmäßig durchgeführt, um Störungen zu vermeiden.
2. Die Pumpe war ausgefallen und eine Instandsetzung war nötig.
3. Die Termine, an denen eine Instandhaltung durchgeführt wird, werden in einem Buch festgehalten.

9
🌐

Use the Internet to find out which problems can arise when ball bearings are not lubricated sufficiently. Collect your ideas in a table like the one below and present your findings to the class.

Example:

measured variable	measuring method	detectable damage
vibrations	acoustic test	fatigue

B | Maintenance of machines

M   **1**
KMK II

Sie sollen an einer Maschine Ihres Ausbildungsbetriebes eine Wartung vornehmen. Zur Überprüfung der Qualität des verwendeten Öls liegt ein Ablaufschema in englischer Sprache vor. Zur Vermeidung von Fehlern und auch als Arbeitserleichterung bei späteren Wartungsarbeiten bittet Sie Ihr Ausbildungsleiter, den Inhalt auf Deutsch zu übertragen. Stellen Sie dann der Klasse Ihre Lösung vor.

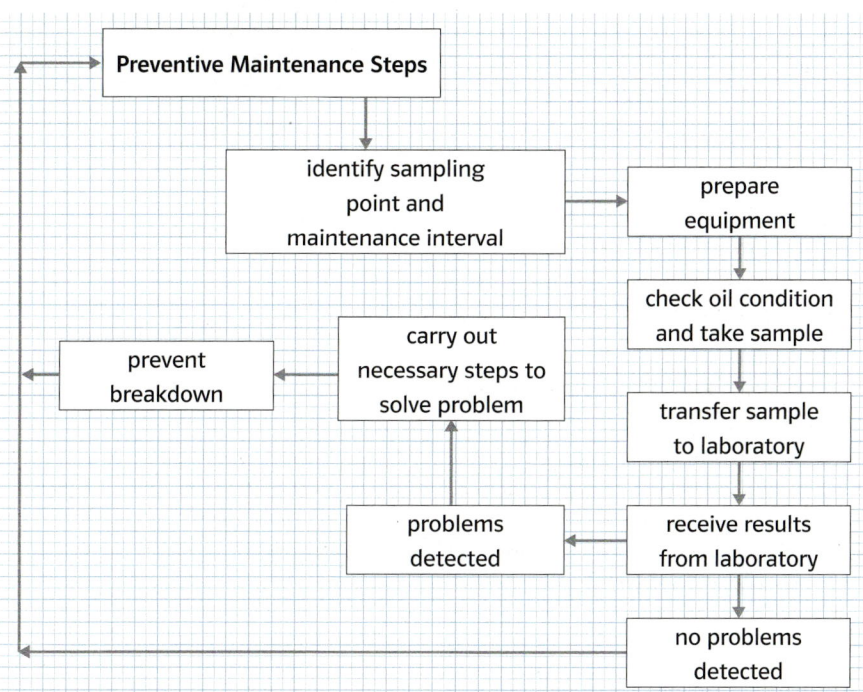

M   **2**
KMK II

 Ihr Ausbilder gibt Ihnen folgenden Text als Vorlage. Er bittet Sie, für die anderen Auszubildenden ein Poster zur Planung von Wartungsarbeiten auf Deutsch zu erstellen. Erstellen Sie dieses Poster in Partnerarbeit.

Before you start maintenance work

1. Make sure you have a work flow diagram of the maintenance work.
2. You must have the necessary skills to carry out the job.
3. All tasks must be described in detail and all necessary diagrams must be available.
4. A complete parts list as well as a list of the tools and equipment required must be enclosed in the documentation.
5. Have all necessary data sheets, acceptance records and risk assessment sheets ready.
6. Gather all of the parts, equipment and materials that you will need in one location.
7. Prepare a checklist for your maintenance activities to monitor the quality of your work. Report all observations on a separate sheet of paper.

P   **3**
KMK III

 Erstellen Sie mit Hilfe dieser Vorgabe in Partnerarbeit einen konkreten Plan auf Englisch für eine Wartungsarbeit, die Sie aus Ihrem Ausbildungsbetrieb bereits kennen.

→ **PHRASES:** Presentations

WORD BANK

fatigue – Ermüdung
measured variable – Meßgröße

WORD BANK ⊙

acceptance record – Abnahmeprotokoll
base plate – Grundplatte
commissioning – Inbetriebnahme
mounting – Befestigung
sag – Durchhang
spalling – Absplitterung
warping – Verziehen

⌕ V1 Company tour

lingua tv
we watch languages!

Before watching

1. Describe the photo.
2. Who do you think the men in the picture are?

While watching

3. Watch the film and find out the following:
   a. the number of countries SAND Machinery delivers to.
   b. the names of three departments that the men have visited.
   c. the number of people who work for the company.
   d. whether SAND Machinery has other sites and if so, where they are.
4. Watch the film again and answer the questions.
   a. What will Mr Kramer's main tasks be during the internship?
   b. What is made at the company's production site?

After watching

5. Explain the sentences from the clip in your own words.
   a. "I'm eager to get in and get my feet wet."
   b. "… around the globe, around the clock."

⌕ V2 Telephoning

lingua tv
we watch languages!

Before watching

1. Describe the photo.

While watching

2. What problem does Ralf have at the beginning of the call?
3. Watch the film again and answer the questions.
   a. Who is calling?
   b. Who does he want to speak to?
   c. What is the purpose of his call?
   d. Why can Ralf's boss not contact the caller until the 15th of the month?
4. Find out the following technical information about the vehicle in question:
   a. the engine size
   b. the top speed
   c. the distance that can be travelled on a single charge.

After watching

5. Use the information in parts 3 and 4 to write a short memo for Ralf's boss explaining who called and what the call was about, and giving other key information.
6. How does Ralf handle the phone call? Discuss what he did well and what he could improve.

🎬 V 3 Job interview

Before watching

1. Describe the photo.

While watching

2. Write down three of the questions that the interviewer asks.
3. Watch the film again and answer the questions.
   a. What is the applicant's name?
   b. What position is he applying for?
   c. What position did the applicant hold in his last job?
   d. According to the applicant, what is his greatest strength?
   e. What is the applicant's weakness?
   f. What questions does the applicant ask the interviewer?

After watching

4. Do you think the applicant will get the job? Give reasons for your answer.

🎬 V 4 Technical support

While watching

1. What does 'rebooting the system' mean?
2. Watch the video again and decide whether the following statements are true or false.

   a. The caller cannot connect to the Internet.
   b. He has been having problems for two days now.
   c. He has tried rebooting the system.
   d. Turning the modem on and off did not help the problem.
   e. The scanner is not connected to the caller's computer.
   f. The technical support employee is unable to solve the problem with the scanner.

After watching

3. Make a list of problems that employees may have with their computers.
4. Record the call by copying the headings onto a sheet of paper and filling in the information.

   Name of caller · Problem(s) · Solution(s) · Further action necessary: Yes/No

⚙V 5 Waste – the future's most valuable resource

Before watching

1. What things do you recycle every day, and how?
2. How many different waste bins does your city or community provide per household?

While watching

3. Watch the film and find out the following information:
   a. How many tons of rubbish does Germany produce each year?
   b. What nations are eager to pay for our rubbish?
   c. What metal is particularly desirable for recycling?

4. Watch the film again and answer the following questions:
   a. How many tons of copper were stolen in Germany?
   b. How much heat can one ton of residual waste produce?

After watching

5. Explain these phrases/sentences from the film in your own words.
   a. "modern urban warfare"
   b. "Our waste is getting a second lease on life."

⚙V 6 Pipe inspection

Before watching

1. What do pipelines transport?

While watching

2. Watch the film and find out the following information:
   a. What is the inspection device called?
   b. How long is it?
   c. How fast does the device travel?
   d. How many days does it take to inspect 300 km of pipeline?

3. Watch the film again and answer the following questions:
   a. Where are the data analyzed?
   b. How accurate is the data grid?
   c. What does the device use to identify defects?

After watching

4. What may cause defects in or damage to pipelines?

V7 High voltage work

Before watching

1. What do you think the men in the steel basket are preparing to do?

While watching

2. Watch the film and find out the following:
   a. what weather conditions are necessary for repairing overhead power lines.
   b. how many volts of electricity high-voltage lines carry.
   c. how the repairmen get to the damaged lines.
   d. what safety measures are taken.

3. Watch the film again and answer the following questions:
   a. How long does the job shown in the film take?
   b. Where is the electricity switched off and on?

After watching

4. Why is it important that the men work quickly?
5. Explain in your own words: "A power cut can quickly bring an entire city to its knees."

V8 Ras Laffan

While watching

1. Watch the film and find out the following:
   a. where Ras Laffan is located.
   b. what is processed there.
   c. how much is processed each year.
   d. how large the Ras Laffan industrial region is.

2. Watch the film again and answer the following:
   a. What problems do the construction workers face?
   b. How is the concrete cooled, and why?
   c. Why is the gas cooled?

After watching

3. Explain the phrase "liquid gold".

⊙✄ V9 Pipelines

Before watching

1. Name some things which are transported in pipelines.

While watching

2. Watch the film and find out the following:
   a. what alloy is popular for making long-distance pipelines.
   b. how thick are the steel plates that are formed into round pipes.
   c. the welding technique used in the factory shown.
   d. what the expander is for.

3. Watch the film again and answer the following:
   a. What conditions do offshore pipelines have to cope with?
   b. Why do they have an additional outer casing of concrete?

After watching

4. Explain why quality-control checks are important in the production of pipelines.

⊙✄ V10 Robots in the hospital

While watching

1. Watch the film and find out the following:
   a. What hospital is shown as an example? Which parts of the hospital do we see?
   b. How many robots do they have?
   c. What powers the robot couriers and how do they navigate?
   d. What is a 'lift-and-tunnel system'?

2. Watch the film again and answer these questions:
   a. What metal in the plates keeps the food warm?
   b. Do the robots distribute the food to the patients?
   c. How many containers are used to transport food?
   d. How does the hospital director feel about using robots to transport patients?

After watching

3. What else do you think the robots transport in the hospital?
4. Where else might transportation robots be used?

V11 Portable power stations

Before watching

1. Think of situations in which a portable power station like the one in the photo could be useful.

While watching

2. Watch the film and list the uses of electrical power 'out in the open' that the reporter mentions.

3. Watch the film again and answer the following:
   a. What supplies the power for the 12-volt portable power station?
   b. Why are batteries not such a good choice?
   c. Where was the portable power station invented?

After watching

4. Do you think the inventor will be able to sell his power station in Germany? Where might the need for it be greater?

V12 Car speed control

Before watching

1. What speed limit is acceptable
   a. on city streets?
   b. on the motorway?

While watching

2. Watch the film and find out the following:
   a. how many people die in road accidents in the UK every year.
   b. what the MIRA is working on.
   c. what the satellite positioning system does.

3. Watch the film again and answer the following:
   a. Is speed control popular with car manufacturers? Why or why not?
   b. Do speed cameras have any effect on driving habits?
   c. How is the speed-control system being tested?

After watching

4. Would you buy a car with a speed-control system? Give reasons for your answer.

KMK-Prüfungssätze

KMK Stufe I *(100 VP)*

1 Rezeption (Hörverstehen)   **20 VP**

⊙ A 6.1 Sie interessieren sich für eine Stelle im englischsprachigen Ausland, z. B. ein Praktikum oder eine längerfristige Anstellung nach der Gesellen- oder Facharbeiterprüfung. Die Virtual Employment Agency (VEA) vermittelt solche Praktika. Sie laden einen Podcast mit vier Stellenangeboten herunter. Erstellen Sie hierzu eine Tabelle mit folgenden Stichwörtern und hören Sie den Podcast zweimal an. Füllen Sie Ihre Tabelle auf Englisch aus.

Information number	1 (5 VP)	2 (5 VP)	3 (5 VP)	4 (5 VP)
trade / position offered				
length of practical				
company and location of practical				
requirements				
extra information: email address, telephone number if given				

2 Rezeption (Leseverstehen)   **20 VP**

Sie möchten Ihren Arbeitgeber überzeugen, Sie während Ihrer Ausbildung für ein Praktikum im Ausland freizustellen und haben dazu folgendes Informationsmaterial von der Internetseite der VEA heruntergeladen. Ihr Arbeitgeber bittet Sie, folgende Fragen zu diesem Text auf Deutsch zu beantworten.

1. Was erfahren wir über die Organisation der VEA? *(2 VP)*
2. Welche Vorteile eines Praktikums werden genannt? *(3 VP)*
3. Was konkret bietet die VEA an? *(3 VP)*
4. Was wird über eine Bezahlung/Kostenzuschuss für die Praktikanten gesagt? *(3 VP)*
5. Wie lange dauern die angebotenen Praktika? *(3 VP)*
6. Wer kann sich bei der VEA bewerben und welche Voraussetzungen sollten die Bewerber mitbringen? *(3 VP)*
7. Wie bewirbt man sich? Welche Unterlagen müssen geschickt werden? *(3 VP)*

London-based VEA offers job placements

Who we are

VEA is an organisation funded by the European Union and European companies. Our aim is to help to make European companies fit to
5 operate more effectively in a global world by giving their trainees a chance to work abroad, improve their English language skills and become acquainted with a new culture. The trainees who take part in the programme have a chance to see different work techniques and learn to adapt to new working conditions.

▶

10 *What we offer*

VEA helps trainees to find work placements in England, Scotland and Wales. We have lists of companies in all kinds of trades who offer work placements. All placements take place in an authentic work environment. We can help you to establish contacts with companies

15 and to plan your stay. We have a telephone hotline if problems should come up.

What payment is given

VEA does not pay trainees any money for the work placement, but we can pay a fixed amount towards your travelling expenses. However,

20 most of the companies that we have under contract offer small salaries that will enable you to cover daily expenses such as food and board.

How long do work placements last?

The duration of work placements depends on the companies. Placements usually last between eight and ten weeks, but most

25 companies are flexible if you want to arrange different periods. The shortest possible placement is three weeks.

Who can apply

All trainees can apply after their first or second year of training. The applicants should have a fair working knowledge of English. They

30 should be communicative, interested in our culture and willing to participate in social activities if these are offered by the company.

How to apply

Send an email and a CV as an attachment in English telling us why you would like to take part in our work placement programme. You

35 should also send written consent and a letter of recommendation from your company. And don't forget to mention the dates you would like to do the placement and the trade you would like to work in. Send your application by email to info@vea…biz subject matter "work placement."

(363 words)

---

3 Produktion   30 VP

Sie wollen sich per E-Mail bei der VEA um ein Praktikum bewerben (Adresse: info@vea…biz). Schreiben Sie, dass Ihre Firma es lieber hätte, wenn Sie zunächst einmal nur 3 Wochen auf ein Auslandspraktikum gingen. Geben Sie an, welchen Beruf Sie lernen und in welchem Jahr Ihrer Ausbildung Sie sich befinden. Nennen Sie einen Zeitraum von drei Wochen (mit genauem Datum), in dem Sie ein Praktikum machen möchten.

4 Mediation   30 VP

Auf der Internetseite befinden sich auch Erfahrungsberichte früherer Absolventen. Einer hat Ihnen besonders gefallen. Sie übertragen ihn ins Deutsche, um ihn ebenfalls Ihrem Arbeitgeber vorzulegen. Auf eine wörtliche Übersetzung legt er keinen Wert, lediglich auf eine inhaltlich korrekte Wiedergabe.

My name is Michael. I'm in my third year of training as a car mechanic. I've just come back from a three-month placement in South Wales. It was sponsored by the Leonardo Programme. My company in Germany ▶

encouraged me to apply for the placement. They even sponsored me

5 by paying my wages even though I wasn't working for them for three months.

I worked in a company based near Cardiff that makes parts for the automobile industry. First I spent a few days in each department of the company, and then I was fully involved in the production process.

10 I worked with a Welsh colleague in the CNC centre. Of course I had some experience with CNC from my own company. I must say, I learned a lot, especially how to work more efficiently and independently.

In the beginning the language was a bit of a problem, but after a couple of weeks we managed to communicate quite well, and I learned many

15 technical words and phrases.

This placement was a great opportunity for me, and my boss sees it as a real plus for our company and our business with British customers.

(193 words)

KMK Stufe II *(100 VP)*

1 Rezeption (Hörverstehen)   8 VP

⊙ A 6.2 **Ihre Firma stellt Hydraulikaggregate her. Sie werden gebeten, eine Nachricht auf dem Anrufbeantworter Ihrer Firma abzuhören und eine kurze Telefonnotiz auf Deutsch zu erstellen.**
Bevor Sie die Nachricht abhören, bereiten Sie auf einem Blatt eine Telefonnotiz mit folgenden Überschriften vor.

1. Name des Anrufers und der Firma *(2 VP)*
2. Sitz der Firma *(1 VP)*
3. Nachricht für … *(1 VP)*
4. Grund des Anrufes *(2 VP)*
5. Auftragsnummer *(1 VP)*
6. Rückrufnummer *(1 VP)*

2 Rezeption (Hörverstehen)   12 VP

⊙ A 6.3 **Für die Herstellung von Steuerungen und Motoren sind seltene Erden unverzichtbar. Ihr Ausbildungsleiter hat zu seltenen Erden einen englischen Podcast gefunden. Da der Ausbilder nicht so gut Englisch kann, bittet er Sie, sich den Podcast anzuhören und folgende Fragen auf Deutsch zu beantworten.**

1. Was wird über den Bedarf an seltenen Erden in der Einführung gesagt? *(1 VP)*
2. Welche Hinweise werden in der Einführung über die Rolle Chinas gegeben? *(2 VP)*
3. Ihr Ausbildungsleiter hat nicht genau verstanden, ob und wie seltene Erden wiederverwertet werden können. Notieren Sie die Aussage des Sprechers auf Deutsch. *(1 VP)*
4. Der Podcast nennt einige Bereiche, in denen seltene Erden unverzichtbar sind. Nennen Sie vier dieser Bereiche. *(2 VP)*
5. In welchem Bereich werden gleich mehrere Kilogramm an seltenen Erden pro Einheit gebraucht? *(1 VP)*

6. Wie selten sind seltene Erden nach Auskunft des Podcasts wirklich? *(1 VP)*
7. Es werden Produktionszahlen für China genannt: Wie hoch ist der Anteil der Chinesen an den geschätzten Reserven weltweit? *(1 VP)*
8. Welche anderen Länder werden genannt, in denen seltene Erden gefördert werden? *(2 VP)*
9. Welche Sorgen plagen das amerikanische Repräsentantenhaus? *(1 VP)*

3 **Rezeption (Leseverstehen)** **20 VP**

Im Umgang mit Druckluft müssen bestimmte Sicherheitsregeln beherzigt werden. Bei einem Druckluftwerkzeug, das Ihre Firma geliefert bekam, war folgendes Faltblatt beigefügt. Ihr Ausbilder stellt Ihnen dazu ein paar Fragen, die Sie anhand dieses Textes auf Deutsch auf einem gesonderten Blatt beantworten sollen.

1. Der Text zählt eine Reihe von Druckluftwerkzeugen auf. Nennen Sie acht davon in der Reihenfolge, in der der Text sie aufführt. *(4 VP)*
2. Welche Sicherheitsausrüstung muss laut Text benutzt werden? *(2 VP)*
3. Was muss zum Schutz Ihrer Mitarbeiter getan werden? *(2 VP)*
4. Wie sind laut Text Druckluftwerkzeuge zu behandeln? *(3 VP)*
5. Was wird über die Zusatzgeräte ausgesagt? *(1 VP)*
6. Welche allgemeinen Eigenschaften sollen die Schläuche haben (bitte in der Reihenfolge aufführen wie im Text)? *(2 VP)*
7. Welche speziellen Eigenschaften hinsichtlich des Druckes sind bei den Schläuchen einzuhalten? *(2 VP)*
8. Was müssen Sie laut Text tun, bevor Sie Werkzeuge an den Druckluftschlauch anschließen? *(1 VP)*
9. Welchen Anforderungen müssen die Schlauchverbindungen entsprechen? *(2 VP)*
10. Druckluft wird gerne auch zur Reinigung verwendet. Was wird über die Reinigung mit Druckluft in diesem Text ausgesagt? *(1 VP)*

What are pneumatic tools?
* Pneumatic tools are powered by compressed air. Common types of these air-powered hand tools that are used in industry include buffers, nailing and stapling guns, grinders, drills, jack hammers, chipping
5 hammers, riveting guns, sanders and wrenches.

How do you use pneumatic tools safely?
* Review the manufacturer's instruction before using a tool.
* Wear safety glasses or goggles, or a face shield and, where necessary, safety shoes or boots and hearing protection.
10 * Post warning signs where pneumatic tools are used. Set up screens or shields in areas where nearby workers may be exposed to flying fragments, chips, dust, and excessive noise.
* Ensure that the compressed air supplied to the tool is clean and dry. Dust, moisture, and corrosive fumes can damage a tool. An in-line
15 regulator filter and lubricator increases tool life.
* Keep tools clean and lubricated, and maintain them according to the manufacturer's instructions. ▶

- Use only the attachments that the manufacturer recommends for the tools you are using.
20 - Be careful to prevent hands, feet, or body from injury in case the machine slips or the tool breaks.
- Reduce physical fatigue by supporting heavy tools with a counter-balance wherever possible.

How should you handle air hoses?

25 - Use the proper hose and fittings of the correct diameter.
- Use hoses specifically designed to resist abrasion, cutting, crushing and failure from continuous flexing.
- Choose air-supply hoses that have a minimum working pressure rating of 1035 kPa (150 psig) or 150 % of the maximum pressure
30 produced in the system, whichever is higher.
- Check hoses regularly for cuts, bulges and abrasions. Tag and replace, if defective.
- Blow out the air line before connecting a tool. Hold hose firmly and blow away from yourself and others.
35 - Make sure that hose connections fit properly and are equipped with a mechanical means of securing the connection (e.g. chain, wire, or positive locking device).
- Install quick disconnects of a pressure-release type rather than a disengagement type. Attach the male end of the connector to the tool,
40 NOT the hose.
- Do not operate the tool at a pressure above the manufacturer's rating.
- Turn off the air pressure to hose when not in use or when changing power tools.
- Do not carry a pneumatic tool by its hose.
45 - Avoid creating trip hazards caused by hoses laid across walkways or curled underfoot.
- Do not use compressed air to blow debris or to clean dirt from clothes.

What should you avoid with compressed air?

- Cleaning with compressed air is dangerous.
50 - Do not use compressed air for cleaning unless no alternate method of cleaning is available. The nozzle pressure MUST remain below 207 kPa (30 psi). Personal protective equipment and effective chip guarding techniques must be used. (…)

(489 words)

---

4 Mediation   30 VP

Im Lernfeldunterricht Ihrer Berufsschule bekommen Sie folgenden (siehe nächste Seite) englischen Text vorgelegt. Lesen Sie ihn durch und übertragen Sie die wichtigsten Punkte in zusammenhängenden Sätzen ins Deutsche. Eine wörtliche Übersetzung ist nicht gewünscht.

Processes for joining metals

When metals are to be joined different processes can be applied such
as welding, soldering and brazing. There are two kinds of welding:
gas welding and electric-arc welding. By definition, welding is a
5 fusion process that joins materials of the same kind, usually metals or
thermoplastics. This is often done by melting the workpieces and adding
a filler to form a pool of molten material that cools to become a strong
joint; pressure is sometimes used together with high temperature, up to
3000°C, to produce the weld.
10 This is in contrast to soldering and brazing, which use a material with
a lower melting point between the workpieces to form a bond between
them without melting the workpieces.
The solder used in soldering has a melting point of up to 450°C. The
parts which are to be joined are heated, and the solder is pressed against
15 them. The solder melts and flows into the joint. After the material has
cooled down, the joint is finished.
Higher temperatures are needed in brazing: the solder has a melting
point of between 450°C and 900°C. Metals suitable for brazing are steel,
copper, silver and brass.
20 Electrical engineers apply soldering to join electronic parts onto a PCB
(printed circuit board), for example. Plumbers use this joining technique
to fit water or gas pipes, to join drain pipes or gutters, or to generate
roof sealings.

(233 words)

5 Produktion — 30 VP

Ihre Firma plant einen Messeauftritt auf der *Automotive Testing Expo* in Shanghai.
Zur Vorbereitung hatte sie zwei Monate vor dem Messetermin den Besuch eines
Mitarbeiters in Shanghai geplant, um mit chinesischen Zulieferern den Auftritt zu
besprechen. Leider wurde der Termin von chinesischer Seite kurzfristig um zwei
Wochen verschoben. Schreiben Sie eine E-Mail mit folgenden Punkten an das Royal
Victoria Hotel in Shanghai info@royalvictoria...com .

- Bedanken Sie sich für die Reservierung eines Einzelzimmers mit Dusche,
  Satellitenfernseher, schnurlosem Telefon und Internetanschluss für
  Nichtraucher sowie für die Reservierung eines Sitzungsraumes für kurze
  Geschäftsbesprechungen für den Zeitraum 01.–08.08.20…
- Teilen Sie mit, dass Sie die Reservierungen leider stornieren müssen, weil
  Ihre Geschäftsreise um zwei Wochen verschoben werden musste.
- Fragen Sie an, ob Sie Ihre Buchungen ebenfalls um zwei Wochen
  verschieben können, und zwar auf den 15.–22.08… .
- Bitten Sie um eine schriftliche Bestätigung der neuen Buchungen.
- Bitten Sie um die Empfehlung eines anderen Hotels für den Fall, dass das
  Royal Victoria Hotel zu dem gewünschten Termin keine Zimmer mehr
  frei hat.
- Denken Sie beim Verfassen Ihrer E-Mail auch an die äußere Form der
  E-Mail wie Betreff, Anrede, Schluss und Grußformel.

Role cards

Modul C Telephoning, B 3

Speaker A

Give your partner the following information:
1. The room is 54 m².
2. The wire needs to be 128.5 cm long.
3. The doors are 80 cm x 220 cm.
4. Each of the components weighs around 0.75 kg.

Modul 6 Sensors, B 3

→ **PHRASES:** Telephoning

Speaker B

You are Sean Miller. Do the following:
1. Ask about alternative sensors.
2. Give the features of the sensor that you agreed on with Karl Otten.
3. Agree to order the alternative sensor.
4. Give the address of the German company and spell the name of the street: AOP GmbH, Akazienweg 19, 52062 Aachen. Three sensors.
5. Delivery date must be no later than Friday, August 13.
6. Thank the person you called.

Modul 7 Hydraulics, A 4

→ **PHRASES:** Telephoning

Speaker A

Sie arbeiten beim Rettungsdienst Bristol in England und Sie erhalten einen Notruf. Nennen und erfragen Sie folgende Punkte:
1. Melden Sie sich vorschriftsgemäß.
2. Fragen Sie die Anruferin / den Anrufer, was genau passiert ist.
3. Teilen Sie der Anruferin/dem Anrufer mit, dass Sie sofort einen Krankenwagen schicken und erkundigen Sie sich danach, wo der Verletzte *(injured person)* zu finden ist.
4. Sagen Sie der Anruferin / dem Anrufer, dass sie / er das Öl mit Wasser abwaschen und alle öligen Kleidungsstücke entfernen soll.

Modul C Telephoning, B 3

Speaker B

Give your partner the following information:
1. The table is 2 m x 3 m.
2. The engine runs at 7500 rpm.
3. 220 V sockets are standard in Germany.
4. The customer would like the work surface to be 24 mm thick.

Modul 11 Maintenance, A 6

Speaker A: ELMET, California	Speaker B: Friedrichwerke, Frankfurt
Nehmen Sie den Anruf vorschriftsgemäß entgegen.	Melden Sie sich vorschriftsgemäß. Schildern Sie kurz Ihr Problem: Der Motor wird in letzter Zeit sehr heiß, wenn er eine Weile in Betrieb ist.
Fragen Sie, wie alt der Motor ist.	
Sagen Sie, dass dies dann noch ein Garantiefall wäre. Fragen Sie, ob die Luftdurchgänge bereits gereinigt wurden.	Sagen Sie, dass Sie den Motor erst vor zwei Monaten gekauft haben.
	Sagen Sie, dass Sie auch interne Luftdurchgänge überprüft haben, aber dass das Problem weiterhin besteht.
Fragen Sie, ob der Motor von Korrosion betroffen sein könnte.	
Erkundigen Sie sich, ob die Lager laut oder heiß sind.	Verneinen Sie die Frage. Sie haben den Motor schon geprüft.
Entgegnen Sie dem Kunden, dass er den Motor sorgfältig gewartet hat. Es muss sich um einen Produktionsfehler handeln. ELMET schickt schnellstmöglich das nötige Ersatzteil.	Bestätigen Sie dies. Fügen Sie jedoch hinzu, dass Sie sie bereits geschmiert haben.
	Bedanken Sie sich.
Entschuldigen Sie sich für die Unannehmlichkeiten *(inconvenience – Achtung: Dies wird nur im Singular verwendet.)*. Verabschieden Sie sich.	Verabschieden Sie sich ebenfalls.

Modul 7 Hydraulics, A 4

→ **PHRASES:** Telephoning

Speaker B

Sie machen ein Praktikum in der englischen Niederlassung Ihrer Firma. Bei der Reparatur eines Lecks an einem hydraulischen Schlauch ist Ihrem Kollegen ein Unfall passiert. Leider vergaß der Kollege, seine Schutzhandschuhe *(protective gloves)* anzuziehen und erlitt eine starke Verätzung *(burn)*. Rufen Sie den Rettungsdienst an.

1. Nennen Sie Ihren Namen und Ihre Firma.
2. Erklären Sie, was passiert ist und inwieweit Ihr Kollege verletzt ist.
3. Nennen Sie die Adresse Ihrer Firma: 15, Douglas Road Industrial Park, Bristol.
4. Sagen Sie, dass Sie dem Pförtner *(porter)* mitteilen, dass der Notdienst kommt.
5. Bedanken Sie sich für den Rat, den Sie vom Rettungsdienst erhalten.

Phrases

A | Meeting people

Formal greetings	Formelle Begrüßung
Good morning / afternoon / evening, Ms Robinson / Mr Jones.	Guten Morgen / Tag / Abend, Frau Robinson / Herr Jones.
Good morning / afternoon / evening, ladies and gentlemen.	Guten Morgen / Tag / Abend, meine Damen und Herren.
Informal greetings	**Informelle Begrüßung**
Good morning, Susan / James.	Guten Morgen, Susan / James.
Hi / Hello / Morning, Karl.	Tag / Morgen, Karl.
Hi everybody!	Tag zusammen!
Formal goodbyes	**Formelle Verabschiedung**
Goodbye! It's been nice / pleasant meeting you.	Auf Wiedersehen! Es war nett / angenehm, Sie kennen zu lernen!
Thank you for your help / your time. Let's keep in touch.	Danke für Ihre Hilfe / Ihre Zeit. Wir bleiben in Kontakt.
Informal goodbyes	**Informelle Verabschiedung**
Bye!	Tschüss / Ciao!
See you later!	Bis später!
See you around!	Wir sehen uns!
See you tomorrow / on Monday / next week!	Bis morgen / Montag / nächste Woche!
Formal introduction	**Formelle Vorstellung**
May I introduce myself?	Darf ich mich vorstellen?
Hello, my name is / I'm Lukas Hansen from ATW Shipping.	Hallo, mein Name ist / ich heiße Lukas Hansen von ATW Shipping.
Pleased to meet you. / Nice to meet you. / How do you do?	Angenehm. / Sehr erfreut.
It's a pleasure to finally meet you in person.	Es freut mich sehr, Sie endlich einmal persönlich kennen zu lernen.
Informal introduction	**Informelle Vorstellung**
Hi. I'm Peter, Peter James.	Hi. Ich bin Peter, Peter James.
Hello, my name is Sarah O'Neill.	Hallo, ich heiße Sarah O'Neill.
Hi Sarah. Nice to meet you.	Hi Sarah. Freut mich, dich kennen zu lernen.

Introducing others (formal)	Andere miteinander bekannt machen (formell)
Have you met our managing director?	Haben Sie schon unsere Geschäftsführerin / unseren Geschäftsführer kennen gelernt?
Ms Hall? May I introduce you to Christian Eriksen, our new intern? Christian, Georgina Hall from our sales department.	Frau Hall? Darf ich Sie Christian Eriksen, unserem neuen Praktikanten, vorstellen? Christian, das ist Georgina Hall von unserer Verkaufsabteilung.
Introducing others (informal)	**Andere miteinander bekannt machen (informell)**
Here's someone I'd like you to meet.	Ich möchte euch gerne jemanden vorstellen.
Christian, this is Joe. Joe, Christian.	Christian, das ist Joe. Joe, das ist Christian.
Let me introduce you to the team.	Darf ich dich dem Team vorstellen?
Use of first names	**Verwendung von Vornamen**
Please call me Martin.	Bitte nennen Sie mich ruhig Martin.
My name's Marianne.	Ich heiße Marianne.
My first name's Andrew, but everybody calls me Andy.	Mein Vorname ist Andrew, aber alle nennen mich Andy.
May I call you Anna?	Darf ich Anna zu Ihnen sagen?

B | Your company

Introducing the company	Die Firma vorstellen
Our company was founded in 1997.	Unsere Firma wurde 1997 gegründet.
In 2005 we were taken over by …	2005 wurden wir von … übernommen.
We are a leading manufacturer of engines.	Wir sind ein führender Hersteller von Motoren.
We are a medium-sized family firm.	Wir sind ein mittelständisches Familienunternehmen.
We are a manufacturer of industrial cleaning machines specializing in high-pressure cleaners.	Wir sind ein Hersteller von industriellen Reinigungsgeräten und sind auf Hochdruckreiniger spezialisiert.
I work for a major construction company.	Ich arbeite bei einem bedeutenden Bauunternehmen.
We are a subsidiary of …	Wir sind eine Tochtergesellschaft von …
We are a chain of electronics suppliers.	Wir sind eine Kette von Elektronik-Anbietern.
Describing the company's products / services	**Die Produkte / Dienstleistungen der Firma beschreiben**
We offer sustainable solutions.	Wir bieten nachhaltige Lösungen an.
Our products are environmentally friendly.	Unsere Produkte sind umweltfreundlich.
Our products are well-known in Europe.	Unsere Produkte sind europaweit bekannt.
Our components are both reliable and long-lasting.	Unsere Komponenten sind zuverlässig und haben eine lange Lebensdauer.
Our software is adapted to suit your requirements.	Unsere Software wird Ihren Bedürfnissen angepasst.
We manufacture high-tech shock absorbers.	Wir stellen High-Tech-Stoßdämpfer her.
Our products are designed using the latest CAD technology.	Unsere Produkte werden mit der neuesten CAD-Technologie entworfen.

Describing the job	Den Beruf beschreiben
I'm training to become a …	Ich mache eine Lehre / Ausbildung zur / zum …
I am a bricklayer / carpenter / technician / plumber / joiner.	Ich bin Maurer(in), Zimmermann / Zimmerin, Techniker(in), Klempner(in), Schreiner(in).
I work in the automotive industry.	Ich arbeite in der Automobilindustrie.
I work with automated machines.	Ich arbeite mit automatisierten Maschinen.
Describing the workplace	**Den Arbeitsplatz beschreiben**
I work on an assembly line / a machine.	Ich arbeite am Fließband / an einer Maschine.
I work in a large warehouse / factory.	Ich arbeite in einem großen Warenlager / einer großen Fabrik.
I work in a garage / workshop.	Ich arbeite in einer Autowerkstatt / Werkstatt.
I work on a building site.	Ich arbeite auf einer Baustelle.
Talking about tasks and responsibilities	**Über Aufgaben und Zuständigkeiten sprechen**
I am responsible for programming the machines.	Ich bin für die Programmierung der Maschinen zuständig.
I report to the foreman.	Ich bin dem Meister / Vorarbeiter unterstellt.
I work shifts.	Ich mache Schichtarbeit.
I often have to do overtime.	Ich muss oft Überstunden machen.
I repair electrical devices.	Ich repariere elektrische Geräte.

C | Telephoning

1. Answering the phone	Sich am Telefon melden
Introducing yourself	**Sich vorstellen**
Smart EDV GmbH, good morning. Hendrik Klopp speaking.	Smart EDV GmbH, guten Morgen. Hendrik Klopp am Apparat.
Offering help	**Hilfe anbieten**
How may I help you? / Can I help you?	(Wie) kann ich Ihnen helfen?
What can I do for you?	Was kann ich für Sie tun?
Asking for details	**Nach Details fragen**
Who's calling, please?	Wer ist am Apparat, bitte?
May I / Can I ask who's calling, please?	Darf ich fragen, wer anruft?
May I / can I take your name, please?	Könnten Sie mir bitte Ihren Namen nennen?
Could you spell that please?	Könnten Sie das bitte buchstabieren?

Connecting	Verbinden
One moment, please. I'm putting you through now.	Einen Moment bitte, ich verbinde Sie.
Shall I put you through to …?	Soll ich Sie mit … verbinden?
Hold the line, please. I'll put you through.	Bitte bleiben Sie am Apparat. Ich verbinde.

Your boss is not available	Der / die Vorgesetzte ist nicht zu sprechen
I'm afraid Mr Deschler is not in the office at the moment.	Es tut mir leid, Herr Deschler ist z. Zt. leider nicht in seinem Büro.
… He is on a building site.	… Er ist auf einer Baustelle.
… He has a visitor with him.	… Er hat Besuch.
… He is out at lunch.	… Er ist in der Mittagspause.

Offering to call back	Einen Rückruf anbieten
Shall I ask her to call you back?	Soll ich sie bitten, Sie zurückzurufen?
Can she call you back this afternoon?	Kann sie Sie heute Nachmittag zurückrufen?
Does he have your telephone number?	Hat er Ihre Telefonnummer?
Can I just confirm your number?	Kann ich Ihre Nummer nochmals überprüfen?
I'll just repeat that.	Ich wiederhole.

Taking a message	Eine Nachricht aufnehmen
Can I take a message?	Kann ich etwas ausrichten?
Can I give him a message?	Kann ich ihm etwas ausrichten?
Would you like to leave a message?	Möchten Sie eine Nachricht hinterlassen?
Can I just confirm that?	Kann ich das kurz überprüfen?
So that's twenty-four square metres, isn't it?	Das sind also vierundzwanzig Quadratmeter, oder?
I'll make sure he gets the message.	Ich werde mich darum kümmern, dass er die Nachricht bekommt.
I'll tell her as soon as she comes back.	Ich sage ihr Bescheid, sobald sie zurückkommt.

Problems	Probleme
Sorry, I didn't quite catch that. Could you repeat it more slowly, please?	Es tut mir leid, das habe ich nicht verstanden. Könnten Sie es bitte etwas langsamer wiederholen?
I'm afraid I didn't catch the telephone number. Could you repeat it, please?	Leider habe ich die Telefonnummer nicht mitbekommen. Würden Sie sie bitte wiederholen?
I'm sorry, but we are having a bad connection. Could you repeat that, please?	Es tut mir leid, aber die Verbindung ist schlecht. Könnten Sie das bitte nochmals wiederholen?

Ending the call	Das Telefongespräch beenden
You're welcome.	Bitteschön. / Gern geschehen.
Thanks for calling.	Vielen Dank für Ihren Anruf.
Goodbye.	Auf Wiederhören.

2. Making a call	Jemanden anrufen
Introducing yourself	**Sich vorstellen**
This is … from Fertighaus Henke.	Hier spricht … von Fertighaus Henke.
My name's … I'm calling from Smart EDV.	Mein Name ist … . Ich rufe von der Firma Smart EDV an.
Asking to speak to somebody	**Nach jemandem fragen**
Could I speak to Ms Sheringham, please?	Könnte ich bitte Frau Sheringham sprechen?
Could you put me through to Mr Ferguson?	Könnten Sie mich mit Herrn Ferguson verbinden?
Could you give me his / her extension number, please?	Könnten Sie mir bitte seine / ihre Durchwahl geben?
I'd like to speak to someone from the production planning department.	Ich möchte mit jemandem in der Fertigungsplanung sprechen.
Spelling your name	**Den Namen buchstabieren**
It's S-C-H-N-E-I-D-E-R. Schneider.	Das ist S-C-H-N-E-I-D-E-R. Schneider.
Giving your phone number	**Die Telefonnummer nennen**
It's 0049 for Germany, then 0391 458 547.	Das ist die 0049 für Deutschland, dann 0391 458 547.
It's 0391 458 547.	Das ist die 0391 458 547.
Leaving a message	**Eine Nachricht hinterlassen**
Yes, please. Could you tell him that …?	Ja bitte. Könnten Sie ihm ausrichten, dass …?
Thank you. I'll ring back later.	Danke sehr. Ich rufe später zurück.
I'm afraid I won't be in the workshop this afternoon. I'll give you my mobile number.	Leider bin ich heute Nachmittag nicht in der Werkstatt. Ich gebe Ihnen meine Handynummer.
Ending the call	**Das Telefongespräch beenden**
Thank you very much for your help.	Vielen Dank für Ihre Hilfe.
Goodbye.	Auf Wiederhören.

D | Written communication

Salutation	Anrede
Dear Sir or Madam	Sehr geehrte Damen und Herren
Dear Mr … / Dear Ms …	Lieber Herr … / Liebe Frau …
Dear Peter	Lieber Peter
Complimentary close	**Schlussformel**
Yours sincerely / Yours faithfully (rarely used)	Mit freundlichen Grüßen / Hochachtungsvoll (selten benutzt)
Best regards / Kind regards / Best wishes	Schöne Grüße / Herzliche Grüße

Enquiries	Anfragen
We have visited your website and …	Wir haben Ihre Webseite besucht und …
Your services have been recommended to us by …	Ihre Dienstleistungen wurden uns von … empfohlen.
We are a well-established manufacturer of …	Wir sind ein gut etablierter Hersteller von …
Our firm is a leading importer of …	Unsere Firma ist ein führender Importeur von …
Could you please let us have a brochure and a price list?	Wir bitten um einen Prospekt und eine Preisliste.
Please send us a quotation for …	Bitte machen Sie uns ein Angebot über …
Please quote your lowest prices for …	Bitte nennen Sie uns Ihre günstigsten Preise für …
We would be grateful for information on your terms of payment and delivery.	Wir bitten um nähere Angaben zu Ihren Liefer- und Zahlungsbedingungen.
A visit by your representative would be appreciated.	Wir wären dankbar für einen Besuch Ihres Vertreters.
We look forward to hearing from you.	Wir freuen uns darauf, bald von Ihnen zu hören.

Offers	Angebote
Many thanks for your enquiry of 30 May about our new range of …	Wir danken Ihnen vielmals für Ihre Anfrage vom 30. Mai wegen unseres neuen Sortiments von …
As requested, we are sending you enclosed our latest catalogue and price list.	Wie gewünscht fügen wir unseren neuesten Katalog und unsere Preisliste bei.
We can offer a 10 % quantity discount on orders of at least 500 units.	Für Aufträge über mindestens 500 Stück wird 10 % Mengenrabatt gewährt.
We take pleasure in submitting the following cost estimate:	Wir freuen uns, Ihnen folgenden Kostenvoranschlag zu unterbreiten:
Our usual terms of payment are: – cash with order – cash on delivery – 30 days net, 10 days 2 % – by irrevocable letter of credit	Unsere üblichen Zahlungsbedingungen lauten: – Barzahlung bei Auftragserteilung – Barzahlung bei Lieferung – 30 Tage netto, 10 Tage 2 % Skonto – durch unwiderrufliches und bestätigtes Akkreditiv
The delivery period is 6 weeks.	Die Lieferzeit beträgt 6 Wochen.
We look forward to welcoming you as our customers.	Wir freuen uns darauf, Sie als Kunden begrüßen zu dürfen.

Orders	Bestellungen
Please supply the following items on the terms stated below:	Bitte liefern Sie uns folgende Positionen zu den unten genannten Bedingungen:
As agreed, we will effect payment by bank transfer 30 days from date of invoice.	Wie vereinbart werden wir die Zahlung 30 Tage nach Rechnungsdatum per Banküberweisung vornehmen lassen.
Please note that the goods must reach us by 1 March at the latest.	Wir weisen darauf hin, dass die Ware bis spätestens 1. März hier eintreffen muss.
Please acknowledge this order promptly.	Bitte bestätigen Sie diesen Auftrag umgehend.
We look forward to receiving the goods in time and to doing further business with you.	Wir freuen uns, die Ware rechtzeitig entgegennehmen und weitere Geschäfte mit Ihnen machen zu können.

E | Applications

Mentioning the source of the advertisement	Die Quelle der Anzeige nennen
I would like to apply for the job / work placement which you advertised in the … of … / on the … website.	Ich möchte mich auf die in der … vom … / auf der … Website ausgeschriebenen Stelle / Praktikumsstelle bewerben.
I saw your advertisement for a … (job / work placement) in the … of … / on the … website and would like to apply for the position.	Ich habe Ihre Anzeige für eine Stelle / Praktikumsstelle in der … vom … / auf der … Website gesehen und möchte mich auf die Stelle bewerben.
I am writing in response to your advertisement of … in the … / on the … website for a … (job / work placement).	Ich melde mich auf Ihre Anzeige vom … in der … / auf der … Website für eine Stelle / Praktikumsstelle.
Introducing yourself	**Sich vorstellen**
I am particularly attracted to this position as …	Ich bin an dieser Stelle besonders interessiert, weil …
I am currently doing a one-year / two-year … apprenticeship at a vocational college in … (town), Germany.	Ich mache zurzeit eine ein-/zweijährige … Ausbildung an einer berufsbildenden Schule in …, Deutschland.
I am in the second year of an apprenticeship in …	Ich bin im zweiten Jahr einer Ausbildung als …
At present I am working as a … with … (company).	Zurzeit arbeite ich als … bei der Firma …
After completing my apprenticeship / At the end of the apprenticeship I will be a qualified (job title).	Nachdem ich meine Ausbildung beendet habe / Mit Abschluss meiner Ausbildung bin ich eine qualifizierte / ein qualifizierter (Berufsbezeichnung).
Talking about yourself and saying why you are a good applicant	**Über sich sprechen und begründen, warum man ein guter Bewerber / eine gute Bewerberin ist**
As you will see from my CV …	Wie aus meinem Lebenslauf zu ersehen ist, …
I have a good knowledge of …	Ich verfüge über gute Kenntnisse in …
I am motivated / reliable / hard-working / keen to learn / friendly / open / a good communicator.	Ich bin motiviert / zuverlässig / sehr fleißig / lernwillig / freundlich / aufgeschlossen / ein kommunikativer Mensch.
I have previous work experience as …	Ich verfüge bereits über Berufserfahrung als …
I have a wide range of interests including …	Ich bin vielseitig interessiert, u.a. an …
I am familiar with this kind of work, because …	Mit dieser Tätigkeit bin ich vertraut, da …
I would very much welcome the opportunity to work in …	Über die Möglichkeit, in … zu arbeiten, würde ich mich sehr freuen.
I believe that I would be a valuable / enthusiastic employee.	Ich bin überzeugt, dass ich ein(e) nützliche(r) / engagierte(r) Mitarbeiter(in) wäre.

Finishing the letter	Den Brief beenden
I hope that you will consider my application.	Ich hoffe, dass Sie meine Bewerbung in Betracht ziehen werden.
Thank you in advance for considering my application.	Ich danke Ihnen im Voraus, dass Sie meine Bewerbung in Betracht ziehen.
I look forward to hearing from you (soon).	Ich freue mich auf eine (baldige) Antwort.

F | Socialising

Ice breakers	Eisbrecher
How was your weekend? – Good, thanks. How about yours?	Wie war dein / Ihr Wochenende? – Gut, danke. Und bei dir / Ihnen?
Did you see the game last night? – Of course! It was unbelievable. What did you think about the red card / winning goal?	Hast du / Haben Sie das Spiel gestern abend gesehen? – Natürlich! Es war unglaublich. Was halten Sie von der roten Karte / vom Siegtor?
Quite cold / warm today, isn't it?	Ziemlich kalt / warm heute, oder?
I really like your watch. Where did you get it?	Ihre / deine Uhr gefällt mir wirklich gut. Woher haben Sie / hast du sie?
Did you read the story about … in the newspaper this morning?	Haben Sie heute Morgen den Bericht über … in der Zeitung gelesen?
Ah! I see you are also in need of a coffee / cup of tea.	Ah! Wie ich sehe brauchen Sie / brauchst du auch einen Kaffee / eine Tasse Tee.
Is this your first time in Germany?	Sind Sie / Bist du zum ersten Mal in Deutschland?
The food is pretty good here, isn't it? – You can say that again!	Das Essen hier ist ziemlich gut, oder? – Das können Sie / kannst du laut sagen.
Keeping the conversation going	**Das Gespräch in Gang halten**
Really? Is that right? You're joking!	Wirklich? Ist das wahr? Sie machen / du machst Scherze!
That's brilliant / hilarious / fascinating!	Das ist brilliant / sehr lustig / faszinierend!
And what happened then?	Und was passierte dann?
No, unfortunately I missed it. What happened?	Nein, leider habe ich es verpasst. Was ist passiert?
It's interesting you should say that, because …	Interessant, dass Sie das sagen, weil …
Talking about food, have you already tried the new Italian restaurant in the city centre?	Wo wir gerade über Essen sprechen: Haben Sie schon den neuen Italiener in der Innenstadt ausprobiert?
Changing the subject	**Das Thema wechseln**
I think it's best if we don't talk about politics.	Ich denke, es ist das Beste, wenn wir nicht über Politik sprechen.
If you don't mind, I'd rather not talk about that.	Wenn es Ihnen nichts ausmacht, würde ich lieber nicht darüber sprechen.
Yes … By the way, have you read …	Ja … Übrigens, haben Sie … gelesen?

Ending the conversation politely	Die Unterhaltung höflich beenden
Well, it's been good talking to you.	Nun, es war schön, mit Ihnen zu sprechen.
I suppose it's time to get back to work. See you around.	Ich denke, dass es Zeit ist, zur Arbeit zurückzukehren. Man sieht sich!
Excuse me, but I have just seen someone I need to speak to. It was nice talking to you.	Entschuldigen Sie, aber ich habe jemanden gesehen, mit dem ich sprechen muss. Es war nett, mit Ihnen zu reden.

Eating out	Essen gehen

Talking about preferences	Über Vorlieben sprechen
Do you eat meat / seafood / fish?	Essen Sie Fleisch / Meeresfrüchte / Fisch?
Do you like spicy food?	Mögen Sie scharfes Essen?
I'm a vegetarian / vegan.	Ich bin Vegetarier / Veganer.
I'm allergic to nuts.	Ich bin allergisch gegen Nüsse.
I'd prefer something light; I'm on a diet.	Ich würde etwas Leichtes bevorzugen – ich bin auf Diät.
I don't drink alcohol.	Ich trinke keinen Alkohol.

Talking about the menu	Über die Speisekarte sprechen
It's sweet / savoury / sour.	Es ist süß / herzhaft / sauer.
It's a starter / main dish / dessert.	Es ist ein(e) Vorspeise / Hauptgericht / Dessert.
What's in it?	Was ist da drin?
It's made of …	Es wird aus … gemacht.
It's boiled / fried / baked / roasted / filled with …	Es ist gekocht / gebraten/gebacken / geröstet / gefüllt mit …

Ordering	Bestellen
Are you ready to order?	Sind Sie bereit zum Bestellen?
As a starter, I'll take the … and then …	Als Vorspeise nehme ich …, und dann …
I'd like a side order of rice, please.	Ich hätte gerne (eine Portion) Reis als Beilage.
Shall we share a bottle of wine?	Sollen wir uns eine Flasche Wein teilen?
How do you like your steak? – Rare / medium / well-done, please.	Wie möchten Sie Ihr Steak? – Englisch / medium / durch, bitte.
What kind of wine / beer do you have?	Welche Weine / Biersorten haben Sie?

Talking about the food	Über das Essen sprechen
Enjoy your meal.	Guten Appetit!
How's your meal?	Wie ist Ihr Essen?
What's your … like?	Wie ist Ihr …?
The meat is very tender / a little tough.	Das Fleisch ist sehr zart / etwas zäh.
It's not as sweet as I expected.	Es ist nicht so süß, wie ich gedacht habe.
Excuse me, but my soup is cold.	Entschuldigen Sie, aber meine Suppe ist kalt.

Asking for the bill	Nach der Rechnung fragen
Excuse me, could we have the bill, please?	Entschuldigen Sie, könnten wir bitte die Rechnung haben?
Do you accept credit cards?	Akzeptieren Sie Kreditkarten?
This one's on me!	Das geht auf mich!
Shall we split the bill 50-50?	Sollen wir die Rechnung 50-50 teilen?

G | Presentations

Beginning the presentation	Die Präsentation beginnen
I should like to start by telling you about my company.	Zunächst möchte ich Ihnen etwas über meine Firma sagen.
My presentation will deal with …	Meine Präsentation behandelt …
I intend to keep my presentation as brief as possible.	Ich möchte meine Präsentation so kurz wie möglich halten.
I would welcome any questions at the end of my presentation.	Ich wäre gern bereit, etwaige Fragen am Ende meiner Präsentation zu beantworten.
The handout summarises the main points and gives an overview of the relevant figures and statistics.	Das Handout enthält die Hauptpunkte und gibt einen Überblick über die entsprechenden Zahlen und Statistiken.
Structuring the main part of your presentation	**Den Hauptteil der Präsentation strukturieren**
Now my second point is …	Ich komme nun zu Punkt 2 …
Thirdly, let me give you some basic statistics.	Drittens darf ich Ihnen ein paar grundlegende Statistiken zeigen.
I should now like to move on to the next topic.	Ich möchte nun gern zum nächsten Thema übergehen.
An excellent example of this is …	Ein hervorragendes Beispiel dafür ist …
I should like to give you an example to illustrate this point.	Ich möchte diesen Punkt mit einem Beispiel erläutern.
Concluding your presentation	**Die Präsentation beenden**
To sum up we can say that …	Zusammenfassend kann man sagen, dass …
I should like to finish by saying / thanking the organisers / pointing out …	Ich möchte schließen mit der Bemerkung / dem Dank an die Organisatoren / dem Hinweis …
Are there any questions?	Gibt es Fragen?
Thank you for your attention.	Vielen Dank für Ihre Aufmerksamkeit.

H | Dealing with customers

Making a complaint	Eine Beschwerde / Reklamation vorbringen
We are writing with reference to our order no. …	Wir nehmen Bezug auf unseren Auftrag Nr. …
On unpacking the cases our Incoming Goods Control discovered that 15 items are missing.	Beim Auspacken der Kisten stellte unsere Warenannahme fest, dass 15 Positionen fehlen.
We are afraid that several units are – seriously damaged / defective. – broken / badly scratched / stained.	Leider sind mehrere Teile – schwer beschädigt / schadhaft. – zerbrochen / stark zerkratzt / verschmutzt.
We are sorry to point out that the repair work has been poorly executed.	Wir müssen leider darauf hinweisen, dass die Reparatur schlecht ausgeführt wurde.
We believe the damage may be due to rough handling in transit.	Wir glauben, dass der Schaden auf unsachgemäße Behandlung beim Transport zurückzuführen ist.
This is very inconvenient for us because …	Dies kommt uns sehr ungelegen, da …
We would ask you to – replace the faulty goods at your expense. – grant us a price reduction of 10 %. – cut the price to € 550.	Wir möchten Sie bitten, – die mangelhafte Ware auf Ihre Kosten zu ersetzen. – uns einen Preisnachlass von 10 % zu gewähren. – den Preis auf € 550 zu senken.
We will keep the damaged goods until we hear from you.	Wir werden die beschädigten Waren behalten, bis wir von Ihnen hören.
Responding to a complaint	**Auf eine Beschwerde / Reklamation antworten**
Thank you for your email drawing a serious problem to our attention.	Danke für Ihre E-Mail, mit der Sie uns auf ein ernstes Problem aufmerksam gemacht haben.
We wish to apologise for this mistake.	Wir bitten für diesen Fehler um Entschuldigung.
We are extremely sorry for the poor service you have received.	Es tut uns außerordentlich leid, dass Sie einen unzureichenden Service erhalten haben.
We will investigate the matter thoroughly and inform you of the steps taken.	Wir werden die Angelegenheit gründlich untersuchen und Sie über die Schritte informieren, die wir unternommen haben.
Please return the faulty items at our expense.	Bitte senden Sie die mangelhaften Artikel auf unsere Kosten zurück.
We are prepared to reduce the price by 10 % if you decide to keep the goods.	Wir sind bereit, den Preis um 10 % zu senken, wenn Sie sich entschließen, die Ware zu behalten.
We hope that this proposal will find your approval.	Wir hoffen, dieser Vorschlag findet Ihre Zustimmung.

Audioscripts

⊙ A 2.1 Module 1 Tooling devices and robots, B 3, 4

Alan: Oh, this looks like a really modern machine here. What is it?

Detlev: You're right, this is the most modern machine in our workshop. We only got it last week. It's a CNC lathe. It looks fantastic, doesn't it?

Alan: Yes, it does. But what is so fantastic about it apart from its looks?

Detlev: I must admit, I really don't know too much about its functions. We can ask the instructor for more information.

Alan: Good idea!

Detlev: Hello Mr Lang. Can we ask you a few questions about the new lathe?

Mr Lang: Of course. What do you want to know?

Alan: What's a lathe for in the first place?

Mr Lang: Well, a lathe is used to machine metal workpieces. The workpiece is clamped in the chuck, that's the clamping device. The workpiece is then rotated while the cutting tools are applied by the saddle and cross-slide.

Alan: Oh, I understand. Then a lathe is different to a milling machine.

Mr Lang: Yes, it is. A milling machine is used to machine solid materials like high quality steel. There the tool rotates and the workpiece moves to the tool.

Detlev: Oh, now I understand.

Alan: But what are the different machine parts called?

Mr Lang: Well, here we have the chuck where the workpiece is clamped. Then we have the spindle which rotates the workpiece. Here's the PC-based control – you can see the PC panel here. That means we have a program which tells the machine what to do. And then there's the finished part catcher. It's like a box where all of the parts are collected.

Alan: Is the guard really necessary? We always wear safety glasses when we work on any machine.

Mr Lang: Well, you may wear glasses, Alan, but someone passing behind you may not. That's why the guard is important.

Detlev: What is so special about this machine?

Mr Lang: It machines precision parts such as automotive or bicycle parts, and also electronic and electrical parts.

Alan: Will we have a chance to work on it?

Mr Lang: Of course, you will in a few months' time after you have learned more about general tools and tooling devices.

⊙ A 1.1 Module A Meeting people, A 1, 2

Dialogue 1

Mr Neureuther: Neureuther, good morning.

Ms Hornbach: Good morning, Mr Neureuther.

Mr Neureuther: Good morning, Ms Hornbach.

Ms Hornbach: Mr Neureuther, the young man you were expecting from Denmark is here.

Mr Neureuther: Ah yes, please send him in. And Ms Hornbach, give Mr Dachs a call, will you please?

Ms Hornbach: I've already called him.

Christian: Hello, my name is Christian Eriksen. I come from Fanö in Denmark, and, uh, I'd like to work here as an intern for the next three months.

Mr Neureuther: Felix Neureuther. I'm the manager of the company.

Christian: Nice to meet you, Mr Neureuther.

Mr Neureuther: Nice to meet you too, Christian. I hope you had a pleasant trip.

Christian: Yes, it was fine, thank you. It's not far from Fanö to Kiel.

Mr Neureuther: Fine. Now, let me see, I guess you've handed all the necessary papers over to my secretary, Ms Hornbach?

Christian: Yes, I have.

Mr Neureuther: Oh good, Mr Dachs. I don't believe you've met Christian Eriksen. He'll be our new intern for the next three months. Christian, this is Mr Dachs, our personnel manager.

Mr Dachs: Nice to meet you Christian.

Christian: Nice to meet you too, Mr Dachs.

Mr Neureuther: Christian, Mr Dachs will take you to your team, so you can get to know them all. See you later, Christian.

Christian: See you later, Mr Neureuther.

Dialogue 2:

Mr Dachs: Morning, everybody.

All of them: Good morning, Mr Dachs.

Mr Dachs: I'd like you to meet our new colleague. He'll be working with us for the next three months. He's in his second year of training. Christian, would you like to introduce yourself?

Christian: Hello, my name is Christian Eriksen. I come from Fanö, that's an island off the coast of Denmark. The company I work for is a bit smaller than yours; there's just the boss, a skilled worker and two trainees.

Silke: Hi Christian, nice to meet you. My name is Silke, and I'm also in my second year of training.

Christian: Nice to meet you too, Silke. I'm glad you speak English, because my German is not so fluent. But I'm doing my best to improve.

Silke: No problem, we'll manage.

Josef: Hello Christian, I'm Josef, but everybody calls me Joe. I'm your foreman. My English is not perfect, but Silke can always help. I've been here for quite a long time. Isn't that right, Mr Dachs?

Mr Dachs: Yes, Joe has been with us for over 20 years now. I think for the first few weeks you'll work with him. Well, let's get back to work now. If you have any questions, you can ask Joe, but you can always come to my office, too.

Christian: Thank you, Mr Dachs.

⊙ A 2.2 Module 2 Electricity and electronics, A 5, 6

Joanna: Hi Daniel. Could you have a look at my circuit diagram before we go into class? I'm sure Mr Lang will check it very critically and I'd like to get a good mark for it.

Daniel: Of course, let me see …

Joanna: Hey, what's wrong with it? I know it's not perfect, but look at your face …

Daniel: Sorry, Joanna, but this doesn't work at all.

Joanna: Why not?

Daniel: Well, first of all you have to draw a circuit using straight lines. These lines are all curved.

Joanna: OK, OK. What else? Is the power source in the correct place?

Daniel: I'm afraid not. You start with the symbol for a power source on the left-hand side. Yours is on the right. The symbol for a power source isn't a square either, it's a rectangle.

Joanna: I see. Then the current flows along a path from the plus pole to the minus pole.

Daniel: Yes, so you should add the mathematical symbols for plus and minus to the power source in the diagram.

Joanna: And what comes next?

Daniel: Then we have to include three electronic components.

Joanna: Ah, yes, a lamp, a switch and a fuse.

Daniel: That's right. They have to be added to the path of the current.

Joanna: Which one comes first after the power source? I put the lamp first.

Daniel: Well, Mr Lang explained that a fuse comes after the power source because it is a protective device. You see, if there is too much current in the circuit, you get an over-current and then the fuse blows. The fuse basically protects the path and the lamp.

Joanna: I see. Where do I put the switch then? I remember Mr Lang telling us that the switch allows the current to flow or it stops the current flowing.

Daniel: Exactly. That's why I positioned the symbol for the switch to the right of the fuse, on the right-hand side of the diagram. Again, the two symbols have to be connected with a straight line, not a curved line.

Joanna: OK, I won't use curved lines any more. The lamp then comes after the switch on the path.

Daniel: I would draw the lamp symbol parallel to the symbol for the fuse. Then you draw a connecting line back to the source and you have a rectangular circuit diagram.

Joanna: Thanks for your help, Daniel. The whole circuit makes more sense to me now. And I'm sure Mr Lang will like this diagram much better than my first one.

Daniel: I'm sure he will. You're welcome.

⊙ A 1.2 Module B Your company, A 4

Herr Kirchner: OK, so we've covered human resources, accounting, sales and marketing, and purchasing. Now we come to the more technical side of the company, and – of course – the area where you will be spending your time. OK, do you have any questions before we continue?

Sean: Yes, just a general question really. How old is the company?

Herr Kirchner: Older than you, Sean, that's for sure! Krone Elektronik was founded by Dr Florian Krone in 1954, and is still a family-owned company to this day.

Sean: And is this the headquarters here in Bochum?

Herr Kirchner: Yes, it is. Krone has nine manufacturing plants and sales offices across Europe, but this is the largest. In fact, we also have two in the USA – in Chicago and Baltimore.

Sean: Are there any plants in Great Britain?

Herr Kirchner: No, there aren't but we are opening a new factory in South Korea next year.

Sean: And how many people work for Krone Elektronik?

Herr Kirchner: That's a good question, Sean. I don't know the exact number, but it is at least 10,000, if you include the USA. OK, let's go on with the tour, shall we? The building to your right is our research and development department. They are currently working on a new braking system for a major German car company.

Sean: And what goes on in the large building next to it?

Herr Kirchner: This is our main building, which has three functions. Firstly, it is where the production planners work – and this is where you will spend most of your time. Their job is to optimize the manufacturing process by keeping production times and costs down. Secondly, as you can see, here are also the production halls, where you will start your internship.

Sean: You mentioned three functions. So what else happens over there? It's a really big place.

Herr Kirchner: Yes, it's over 6,000 square metres. Those people you can see over there are responsible for quality control. They test all of the components and devices before they go to the customer.

Sean: How many components are made here in Bochum?

Herr Kirchner: Well, one of the main components we produce here are the cylinder heads, and we make thousands of them every year. And each and every one of them must be inspected by the guys in quality control.

Sean: I guess that's an important job. I'm really looking forward to getting to work.

Herr Kirchner: That's great. I will introduce you to the foreman this afternoon. OK, finally, behind this building we have the IT department. At the moment, they are very busy dealing with the problems caused by our new operating system.

Sean: Oh, that doesn't sound too good. What exactly is the problem?

Herr Kirchner: I'm not sure exactly, some kind of interface difficulties, I think. OK, let's go into the canteen and have some lunch, shall we? Then I can answer some more of your questions.

⊙ A 2.3 Module 3 Electronic devices, A 3

Markus: Hi Peter.

Peter: Hi Markus. Can I ask you about the safety regulations we discussed in Mr Lang's class?

Markus: Yes, of course. Didn't you understand everything he said?

Peter: I understood most of it but to be honest I'd feel better if we could go over my notes. Look, here I wrote *"freischalten"* for rule number 1. Does that have something to do with disconnecting the electronic circuit?

Markus: Yes, that's right. You have to disconnect and switch off an appliance you're going to repair or test.

Peter: OK, I see. So let's see rule number 2. I wrote down *"gegen Wiedereinschalten sichern"*. Can you explain what that means?

Markus: Well, I think you have to make sure that nobody turns on the appliance again while you are working.

Peter: That could happen if you were repairing equipment in another hall.

Markus: Yes. You have to make sure that everybody knows what you are doing and that nobody switches on the circuit breakers again.

Peter: In English we say "lock and tag". You lock the fuse and write a note called a tag that you put where everybody can see it.

Markus: I see, you did listen carefully. What about rule number 3? *"Spannungsfreiheit feststellen"*.

Peter: If I understood Mr Lang's explanation correctly, you have to check for live wires.

Markus: That's right. You use a multimeter, I think it's called.

Peter: But just imagine if the multimeter was defective and I didn't know that the wire was still live. Couldn't I get hurt then?

Markus: Certainly, that's why you always apply rule number 4.

Peter: I didn't get all of rule 4: "*erden* and something".

Markus: That's "*erden und kurzschließen*". That means "earth and short-circuit".

Peter: But didn't Mr Lang say that when you work with voltages of more than 1,000 V, you must apply rule number 4?

Markus: Yes, he did. A system is only safe when you've earthed and short-circuited it.

Peter: There's one last rule, number 5. It says "something, *unter Spannung stehende Geräte*" and I didn't get the rest.

Markus: That's "*benachbarte, unter Spannung stehende Geräte abdecken oder abschranken*".

Peter: "*Benachbart*". Does it have something to do with 'neighbours'?

Markus: Yes, it does. Here it means the neighbouring machines. You have to prevent any electric current from 'jumping' over to other machines. You must also make sure that you don't touch conductive wires. That's why you usually put a rubber mat over the other machines.

Peter: Or maybe you could put up some kind of a guard.

Markus: That's possible, too. How would you translate rule number 5 "*benachbarte, unter Spannung stehende Geräte*" into English?

Peter: You could say "cover up or fence off neighbouring machines". I'll just write that down. Now I've got all the rules in English and German. Thanks, Markus.

Markus: No problem. It helps me to learn the rules, too.

⊙ A 1.3 Module C Telephoning, B 5

Alex: Fertighaus Henke, Alex Bauder.

Caller: Yes, hello. Do you speak English?

Alex: Er, yes, a little. How can I help you?

Caller: Well, my name is Matthew Reid and your company is currently building my house. I'm a little confused. I thought this was Mr Deschler's telephone number. He is the construction manager, isn't he?

Alex: Yes, he is, but unfortunately he is off sick today, so all of his calls are being diverted to me. Can I help you with something?

Caller: Well, I was calling to give Mr Deschler some changes to our house.

Alex: OK, and what was your name again, please?

Caller: Reid, Matthew Reid.

Alex: Could you possibly spell that please?

Caller: Certainly. It's R-E-I-D.

Alex: R-I-E-D.

Caller: No, R-E for England, I for India, D.

Alex: Sorry, R-E-I-D. OK, Mr Reid, and what is the address of the house?

Caller: Well, so far it is only a foundation pit, but it is Ringstrasse 26 in Lernsdorf.

Alex: Ringstrasse 26, Lernsdorf. Ah, yes, I know the site. We are scheduled to begin on your cellar next week, I think. OK, if you give me the information, I will pass it on to Mr Deschler. Let me just find a piece of paper … OK, I'm ready.

Caller: First of all, in the kitchen we need to move the extractor fan twenty centimetres to the left, so that it is directly over the hob. And the hole needs to have a diameter of one hundred and eighty-four millimetres, and we also need …

Alex: Sorry Mr Reid, but I am afraid any changes to your kitchen need to be discussed with the kitchen fitters. Are there any changes to the plans for any other part of the house?

Caller: Er, just a moment. Let me look at my list. OK, we need to change the height of the toilets in the bathroom. At the moment they are planned to be forty-five centimetres and we would like them to be fifty. Plus, we need to add another two hundred and twenty volt socket to the right of the bathroom mirror for my electric razor.

Alex: OK, anything else?

Caller: Yes, my wife and I have decided that we will need a larger carport. I have spoken to a friend and he says we should make it eight metres by six metres by three metres. Can you find out how much extra this would cost, please?

Alex: Of course. Let me just confirm, eight metres long by six metres wide. And how high should it be?

Caller: Three metres high. Of course, this means that we will have a smaller garden, but I think a carport is very useful. You can also ask Mr Deschler how big our garden will be with the new carport. It is currently one hundred and thirty-five square metres.

Alex: OK, I will ask him to adjust the plan and get in touch with you as soon as he is back in the office.

Caller: That's great. Oh, just one more thing. My wife wants to put larger windows in the living room. At the moment, the windows in the plan are one hundred and forty-eight centimetres by one hundred and eleven. She would like them to be one hundred and eighty-six by two hundred and twenty-two.

Alex: One eight six by two two two. OK Mr Reid, I will pass this information on to Mr Deschler and ask him to give you a call. Does he have your telephone number?

Caller: Yes, I think so, but let me give you my work number, too. It is 0391 587660…. Thank you for your help Mr Bauder. Goodbye.

Alex: You're welcome Mr Reid. Goodbye.

⊙ A 2.4 Module 4 Automation systems, C 1, 2

Reporter: Good morning ladies and gentlemen. Today we are in Munich, broadcasting from the most important automation systems trade fair in Europe. And our guest is automation expert, Professor Alexander Winter. Professor Winter, good morning.

Professor Winter: Good morning and thank you for having me on your show.

Reporter: At 11 o' clock you will be giving a presentation here on automation systems. What will you be talking about?

Professor Winter: My topic will be automated production and, of course, automation technologies. These technologies are used in every manufacturing process from production, handling, assembly and storage to planning and design. The technologies are also used to control and monitor working processes. The keywords here are 'rationalisation of workflow', 'mechanisation' and 'automation of technical processes'.

Reporter: 'Rationalisation of workflow' sounds very complicated to me and I'm sure to many of our listeners, too.

Professor Winter: Well, let me explain. It is the first step towards automated production.

Reporter: I see.

Professor Winter: Rationalisation of workflow first of all means improving production processes in order to reach a maximum quality of the products. Of course, cutting costs at the same time is another important aspect.

Reporter: Could you explain how this can be done?

Professor Winter: In order to reach this goal, manpower is replaced by machines. Thus mechanisation means letting machines do what human workers did before. As a result, human input is reduced to checking and controlling the machines while they work.

Reporter: I see. Please continue.

Professor Winter: Automation of technical processes not only reduces physical labour, it also reduces the amount of work involved in planning and design. This part of production is being controlled more and more by specifically designed computer programs and electronic components.

Reporter: Very interesting, Professor Winter. But I see we are already approaching the end of our broadcasting time. Thank you for taking the time to talk to me.

Professor Winter: Thank you.

⊙ A 2.5 Module 5 Pneumatic control and components, A 5, 6

Chad: Hi Heiner, what's wrong? You're looking pretty desperate. Can I help?

Heiner: Oh, hi Chad. Yes, these parts are very confusing! Look at this for example. It looks like a 5/2 way solenoid valve, but I'm not sure.

Chad: OK, let me see. No, it's a 4/2 way valve. What do you need it for anyway?

Heiner: Well, the instructor told me to do some of the installations in the handbook. The exercise says to install a double-acting cylinder with a 5/2-way solenoid valve.

Chad: What's the problem?

Heiner: The problem is that I have absolutely no idea how this works, let alone what the different components do.

Chad: Well, I'll try to give you a brief overview of the components and actuators. Look here, these are all actuators, right?

Heiner: Yes, but how can I tell them apart?

Chad: That's easy. A single-acting cylinder has only got one port, a double-acting cylinder has got two. They are also called power components because you can see a motion output.

Heiner: Oh, I see. But when do I use which cylinder?

Chad: Well, single-acting cylinders only provide power on the push stroke, whereas double-acting cylinders provide power on both the push and the return stroke.

Heiner: And what do the two black plastic parts on the cylinder barrel do?

Chad: They're reed contacts. They're sensors which control the position of the piston.

Heiner: And what's the function of these two small screws?

Chad: They're cushioning screws and they allow you to adjust the end-position cushioning. The cushioning screws also help to prevent damage to the cylinder on impact.

Heiner: OK. And these components here are valves, aren't they?

Chad: Yes, they are. They're control elements and there are many different types of valves. You'll need this 5/2-way solenoid valve for your installation. The solenoid coils at the sides of the valve energize it. Look, you connect the working ports of the valve with the two ports of the double-acting cylinder.

Heiner: Then this must be the pressure port which is connected with the power supply.

Chad: Correct. And look, these are the two exhaust ports. They have silencers to reduce the noise. And this is the manual override so you can test the circuit without using the switches or moving the machine elements.

Heiner: OK, now I understand. Can we connect the solenoid valve with the connection unit?

Chad: Yes, just plug the two cables into the two solenoid coils. OK. And the other two ends go into the connection unit. Perfect!

Heiner: Are we using 230 volts?

Chad: No, that would be too dangerous! It's only 24 volts. But despite that, you should be careful with this type of installation.

Heiner: Can we try it out now?

Chad: Good idea! Why don't you start the simulation software on the PC?

Heiner: OK, let me see. Hey, it works! Thanks a lot! And now I know some of the basics of pneumatics. Next time we go to the pub, the first drink is on me.

Chad: Glad I could help. I never say no to a free drink.

Module E Applications, C 1

Andrea: Hi David, how are you doing?

David: Hi Andrea. I'm fine thanks. How are you?

Andrea: Yeah, I'm OK. Busy, but fine.

David: I heard that you were thinking about applying for a three-month internship in the Northampton branch. Is that true?

Andrea: Yes, that's right. I really want to spend some time in England. I guess it was the same with you and coming to Germany.

David: Exactly. I wanted to see how things worked over here. So, you want to spend some time with my old colleagues, eh? That's great.

Andrea: Well actually, I wanted to ask you for a bit of advice if that's OK with you?

David: Sure, what can I help you with?

Andrea: Well, I have to officially apply for the internship, which means a letter and a CV.

David: OK, would you like me to read your letter?

Andrea: Yes, that would be great. I am going to finish it this weekend, and then I will bring it to work on Monday. Thanks. But where I really need your advice is with the CV. I was wondering if you had any tips for me. I know there are some differences between German and English CVs.

David: Yes, there are, you're right. Hmm … tips … let me see. OK, the first thing to remember is that your CV should be no longer than two pages.

Andrea: Two pages, OK.

David: Also, make sure you use good-quality paper and never send your CV without a covering letter.

Andrea: OK …

David: And don't forget to highlight your strengths and achievements. And when you talk about your work experience, start with your most recent job.

Andrea: Do I need to include a picture?

David: In England, a CV does not have a picture, but you can have one if you like. What is important is that you include the name and contact details of two references. These could be a supervisor or maybe a teacher.

Andrea: OK, great. Anything else?

David: Yeah, make sure that everything you write in your CV is the truth. If you are asked to explain something during the interview and you can't, then it could be pretty embarrassing. Be confident and sell yourself, but don't lie. Er … once you have finished the CV, read through it and check the spelling and the grammar.

The best thing to do is to give it to a friend. And, when you send it, keep a copy for yourself to read before the interview.

Andrea: Thanks a lot for the advice, David. I'm really grateful.

David: Don't mention it, Andrea. Let me know if there is anything else I can do.

Andrea: Well … you did say somebody should read over it and check everything – and who'd be better than a native speaker …?

⊙ A 2.6 Module 6 Sensors, B 1, 2

Sean: Good morning ModTranSys, Sean Miller speaking.

Karl: Em, good morning Karl Otten at AOP in Aachen speaking.

Sean: Oh hello, Karl I remember you from that installation work last year.

Karl: That's right. We have a problem with the conveyor belt. The motor has started overheating slightly.

Sean: I see. Let me look at the model type. Yes, here it is. If the motor is only overheating a little, we could install a temperature sensor. The model I have in mind is highly sensitive to temperature and will switch the motor off automatically when it reaches a certain temperature.

Karl: That sounds OK.

Sean: I will just pull up the data sheet of the temperature sensor on the screen. Let me see … here I have a sensor for thermal protection.

Karl: We probably want a sensor that itself produces no extra heat.

Sean: Definitely, it should have a very low self-heating factor.

Karl: It should also be highly accurate and it has to be calibrated in degrees Celsius.

Sean: That's no problem. The model I'm looking at also has a digital output so you can check and compare signals.

Karl: That sounds good. Which applications is the sensor specified for?

Sean: It has a wide range of applications: it detects fires and it can be used in household appliances and for the thermal management of CPUs in computers.

Karl: OK, then it will have a high temperature range and it should meet our requirements.

Sean: I'm sure it will. What range are you thinking of?

Karl: We need a temperature sensor that switches off when the motor temperature exceeds 15 °C.

Sean: That's no problem. We installed three conveyor belt systems so you will need three sensors.

Karl: That's right.

Sean: I see here in your client file that the annual service is due around now. We could combine it with the installation of the sensors.

Karl: OK. How soon can you get here?

Sean: We can get the sensors to you by Friday so I'll book a flight for then, too. Would that suit you?

Karl: The sooner the better. Contact me when you have your flight details.

Sean: Of course. See you on Friday then, Karl.

Karl: Thank you. Goodbye.

Sean: Goodbye.

⊙ A 1.5 Module F Socialising, A 1

Fabian: Hi, I'm Fabian.

Jan: Hello Fabian, my name's Jan. I'm with the group from Warsaw, Poland.

Fabian: Welcome to our company. Is this your first visit to Germany?

Jan: Actually, I've been here before. But my German isn't very good.

Fabian: Don't worry, we can talk in English. I should really practice more anyway. How was your trip? Was it a long journey?

Jan: No, not really. We took the plane from Warsaw to Stuttgart. Then someone from your company met us at the airport.

Fabian: Jan, would you like something to drink: coffee, juice, lemonade?

Jan: Sure, a lemonade would be good.

Fabian: OK, let's go to our canteen and sit down for a while.

Fabian: Here we go; I hope it's cold enough.

Jan: Thanks. So, I guess that you are also a trainee. What year are you in?

Fabian: I'm in my third year. What about you?

Jan: I've just started. How many trainees are there in your company?

Fabian: Er … about ten, I think.

Jan: That's quite a lot. There are only three trainees in our company, all in metal engineering. I think your company is much bigger than ours.

Fabian: Yeah, we even have our own football team. We don't play in a league; it's just for fun.

Jan: That sounds great! You should visit us in Poland one day. Maybe we could arrange a match.

Fabian: That's a good idea. Are you a football fan?

Jan: Yeah. I don't play myself, but I like to watch.

Fabian: Which team do you like?

Jan: Manchester United.

Fabian: Really? They're my favourite team, too! Well, apart from VFB Stuttgart, of course.

Jan: Do you live in Stuttgart?

Fabian: No, I live in a small town nearby. I have to take the bus every morning. But when the weather's good, I can take my motorbike.

Jan: Cool! Unfortunately I don't have a motorbike. I get a lift from a colleague who works in the same department as me.

Fabian: What do you do in your free time?

Jan: I like going to clubs, and sometimes I go fishing with my friends. What about you? Playing football, I suppose.

Fabian: Yeah, football and riding my motorbike.

◎ A 2.7　Module 7　Hydraulics, A 4

Emergency services: Emergency services, hello. How can I help you?

Richard: Hello, Richard Anhorn from Hydra Experts speaking. There has been a serious accident in our company!

Emergency services: OK. What's the problem?

Richard: A colleague was repairing a leak in a hydraulic system and somehow, he got too close to the leak. The hot hydraulic fluid burnt the skin on his hand.

Emergency services: OK. I'll send an ambulance over right away. What's the address of your company?

Richard: It's 59 Harbour Road, Western Road Industrial Estate, Portsmouth. I'll send one of the apprentices to wait for you at the main gate.

Emergency services: All right. In the meantime, wash the oil off with lots of water. If any clothing is affected, you should remove it!

Richard: Yes, we'll do that. Thanks!

◎ A 1.6　Module G　Presentations, C 1

Good morning ladies and gentlemen. Today I would like to present our new range of wooden furniture, *Simply Wood*. The range, which is shown here on the first slide, includes chairs, a large table, a lounger, and benches. I would like to start by talking about the materials used in the furniture. All of the *Simply Wood* range is made from single softwood timber and has been hand-crafted by our highly-skilled carpenters and joiners. If you look at this picture, you can see that the benches and the seats are designed with a low back, deep seats and long arms to offer a great deal of comfort and convenience. Thanks to a special varnish, the furniture is 100 % weatherproof and will not suffer from discolouring. As you can see from this final slide, the furniture is also available in white, to give it a classic, timeless look. And do not worry, we have used a durable, white polyurethane coating that is suitable for every environment. On your handout you will see more details about each piece, including measurements. Thank you for your attention this morning. Are there any questions? Yes …

◎ A 2.8　Module 8　Assembly, A 1, 2

Marie and Andreas: Good morning, Mr Lang.

Mr Lang: Good morning. I've got a service job in Hall 3 and I need your help. One of the conveyor systems is making a funny noise so I'd like to have a look at it. Are you ready?

Marie and Andreas: OK, we're coming.

Mr Lang: What do you think could be wrong?

Marie: Well, Mr Lang, we had a similar problem in our firm last year shortly before one of the conveyor systems broke down.

Mr Lang: And what caused the problem?

Marie: The ball bearings were faulty. What do you think the reason is here?

Mr Lang: Em, faulty ball bearings sound like a probable option. We will have to see. Well here we are. OK, you two, what did I tell you about maintenance work last week?

Andreas: We need to dismantle the electric drive first.

Marie: Then we have to find the fault.

Mr Lang: And how do we dismantle the electric drive?

Andreas: We can use an electric drill to loosen the screws of the housing.

Marie: Once the housing is removed, we will probably have to unplug any wires that are in the way. And we have to see if there are any more screws or bolts that might have to be opened. Or we might have to weld off a welded seam.

Mr Lang: Good. What comes next?

Marie: Well, hopefully the fault won't be too difficult to find. Then we remove the faulty parts …

Andreas: … and we replace them. We will have to fit the new parts properly and tighten all of the screws and bolts again.

Marie: We will need the power drill as a screwdriver would be too weak to fasten these big bolts.

Mr Lang: OK. Anything else?

Andreas: We have to check that the new components are working before we replace the housing.

Mr Lang: Right. Thank goodness there aren't any rivets that we have to knock off.

Marie: What do we need rivets for anyway?

Mr Lang: Rivets are for permanent joints. You have to destroy them in order to undo them. That makes a lot more work.

Marie: I see.

Mr Lang: Well, let's get down to work.

⊙ A 1.7 ## Module H Dealing with customers, A 4

Answering machine: *Guten Tag. Sie sind mit Stefan Bauder verbunden. Leider bin ich im Moment nicht erreichbar. Bitte hinterlassen Sie eine Nachricht nach dem Ton. Danke!*

Brian: Hello Mr Bauder, this is Brian Jenkins calling from New Wave Marketing in Hamburg. I am calling about the new IT network that your technicians set up last week. Unfortunately, we have been experiencing some problems. Since your technicians were here, some employees have had difficulty connecting to the Internet, and others have no access to our network at all and cannot even log on to their computers! However, the worst thing is that some important files and documents seem to have been lost as a result of the migration to the new software. One of these files was a presentation for a very important client. This is a particular problem for us because we have a meeting with this client on Monday, and we need the presentation and do not have enough time to redo it. Could you please look into this problem for us urgently as time is running out? If we do not hear from you by the end of today, we will have to look elsewhere. I will be in meetings this afternoon, but you can contact me per e-mail under B dot Jenkins at NWM…de. Thank you.

⊙ A 2.9 ## Module 9 Measuring instruments, B 2, 3

Lisa: Hello you two.

Christoph: Hi, Lisa, we've just filled in a worksheet about oscilloscopes …

Ryan: … which was quite interesting, but now we have to do some measurements with an oscilloscope. Could you tell us again how an oscilloscope works?

Lisa: Yes, of course. Come over here and I'll show you. By the way, do you know what an oscilloscope is used for?

Ryan: It is an instrument that displays the behaviour of an electrical signal graphically. Right? It uses a time scale.

Lisa: That's right. The oscilloscope shows the behaviour of the voltage on the screen. But don't forget that measurements taken by an oscilloscope are less accurate than the ones you take with a voltmeter.

Christoph: I see. What about the time scale?

Lisa: It's the same thing. If you need the exact frequency, you have to use a frequency meter.

Christoph: Oh, good. I'll keep that in mind.

Lisa: Now the screen has a grid with two axes. The horizontal one is the x-axis and shows the time base. The vertical one is the y-axis and it shows you the voltage.

Ryan: And what are all those knobs for?

Lisa: That one is the input channel for the voltage signal and this knob lets you select the amplitude value.

Christoph: I see, the amplitude value means that the signal has to be made stronger before you can see it.

Lisa: Correct – you have to amplify the signal. This applies to the y-axis. But let's look at the x-axis, too.

Ryan: You set the time with those knobs somehow, don't you?

Lisa: You've got it. There's the selection knob to set how long the time or division for the signal is to get a basic temporal setting.

Christoph: I'm sorry – I didn't quite understand that. Could you give me an example?

Lisa: Of course. Look, if you have, for example, 10 ms/Div that means that the signal needs 0.1 seconds to travel the division or distance. 10 ms multiplied by 10 divisions equals 100 ms.

Ryan: And how do I see this on the screen?

Lisa: Look here. Do you see the dot? It's lit up electronically. The dot moves up and down, depending on the input signal for the vertical y-axis and the time base for the horizontal x-axis. If you don't give it an input signal, the dot just moves in a straight line from left to right across the screen.

Ryan: Well, Lisa, thanks for explaining it to us.

Lisa: No problem. Glad I could help.

⊙ A 2.10 Module 10 Mechatronics, B 2, 3

Moira: Let's sit down over there, Jonas. It's not so busy.

Jonas: OK. This lasagne looks good.

Moira: Well, enjoy!

Jonas: Thanks. You too.

Moira: That was an interesting lesson.

Jonas: Yes it was. Did you understand which elements belong to a PLC system?

Moira: Let me see what I wrote in my notes … There are operating elements such as the starter button. That starts the machine or the process. Then there are electric signals like limit switches.

Jonas: That's right. The limit switches detect the positions of handling devices. What is the function of final control elements such as control valves?

Moira: I think that they regulate the cylinders and actuators. That's how you regulate the flow of the process.

Jonas: What did you write down about a PLC? All I have is that "a PLC usually has a programming unit such as a touchscreen panel. The PLC is used to automate electrical and mechanical working processes".

Moira: Yes, that's right. It takes different kinds of input and output, and it organises and controls machines and industrial production lines. Have you written down the elements which are used in a PLC system?

Jonas: I think so. Let me see … OK, there's the control device on the machine. It receives a signal from one of the signal elements. A control program analyses and processes the incoming signal and addresses the final control elements.

Moira: OK, I get it. Then the actuators perform the movements in the process, which are defined and regulated by the control program.

Jonas: Exactly. The program is written by a programmer in the manufacturing department or by a mechatronics technician. The function of the program is to make sure that the steps in the manufacturing process are performed in the correct order.

Moira: I see. What did Mr Lang say about the EVA principle? I didn't get that at all.

Jonas: EVA is short for *"Eingabe – Verarbeitung – Ausgabe"*.

Moira: OK, I'll just write that down. What did you say again?

Jonas: *Eingabe – Verarbeitung – Ausgabe*. What's that in English?

Moira: *Eingabe* is 'input' and *Ausgabe* is 'output' and *Verarbeitung* is probably 'processing'.

Jonas: OK. 'Input, processing and output'. Signals come in, are sent to pre-determined addresses to perform tasks and they produce a particular result.

Moira: That sounds right. Is that the time? We must go to our afternoon lessons now.

Jonas: You're right. We don't want to be late.

⊙ A 2.11 Module 11 Maintenance, A 4, 5

Rick: Hello Uli. Sorry I'm late. How far have you got with the motor?

Uli: Oh, hello, Rick. I've only just started.

Rick: Do you have any idea of how to proceed? I mean, you haven't done this kind of thing before. How do you know that you won't forget any important checks?

Uli: Well, there's nothing more important for a good standard of maintenance than good documentation. The trainer gave me a number of documents but they're all in English. So here you are.

Rick: Let me see. OK, this is the acceptance record of the motor, which was done during its commissioning. And this is our maintenance plan. The acceptance record lists all faults that may occur in a system. So, if you check the system for those faults, many of them can be ruled out. And yes, this is a repair log, which is also very helpful, because it can tell you where the weak spots are in the system.

Uli: I see. But the maintenance plan is the most important document, isn't it?

Rick: That's right. It tells you which parts have to be checked, lubricated or cleaned after a certain period of time.

Uli: Well, I've already done the cleaning and lubrication, and I've checked the bearings. Could you do me a favour and tell me what the next step is?

Rick: Sure, here it says: Check the sag of the belt.

Uli: What's the 'sag of the belt'? What do I have to do?

Rick: The belt here must not hang more than 2.5 cm.

Uli: Oh, I see. The sag is 4 cm so I'll adjust it. …
OK, now it's 1.5 cm. Anything else I have to check?

Rick: Yes, the mounting of the motor. Check the bolts and the base plate for warping and spalling.

Uli: Warping and spalling? I don't know what that is.

Rick: Warping happens when the shape of the base plate is deformed. Spalling means that the coating of the base plate is damaged.

Uli: The base plate seems to be OK. As far as I can see, the bolts look fine, too. Is that everything?

Rick: Yes, I think it is. Well, why don't we go over to the canteen for a coffee?

Uli: Good idea. Let's go.

Grammar overview

Present Tense (Gegenwart)

Bildung: Present Tense (simple)		
Merke: Bei der 3. Person Einzahl *(he / she / it)* wird ein *s* an die Endung des Verbs angehängt.	I like / you like / he (she / it) likes we like / you like / they like	computer games.

Verwendung: Present Tense (simple)	
– bei allgemein bekannten Tatsachen und Aussagen – bei regelmäßigen Handlungen: Schlüsselwörter: *usually, normally, always, never, sometimes, often …* – bei Gewohnheiten – bei Fahrplänen, Öffnungszeiten etc. für die Zukunft	– Most cars run on petrol. – I usually start work at 7 o'clock. – He doesn't smoke. – My train leaves at 10 o'clock tomorrow morning.

Bildung: Present Tense (progressive)		
am / are / is + Infinitiv mit Endung *-ing*	I **am** / you **are** / he / she / it / **is** we **are** / you **are** / they **are**	work**ing** on a new project.

Verwendung: Present Tense (progressive)	
– bei Handlungen im Augenblick des Sprechens – bei vorübergehenden Handlungen – bei (fest) geplanten Handlungen in der Zukunft – bei gefühlsbetonten Aussagen mit *always* (negativ besetzt)	– I am reading a manual at the moment. – I'm staying at the Royal Excelsior Hotel. – I'm meeting Ms Winter next week. – He is always complaining about his boss.

Past Tense (Vergangenheit)

Bildung: Past Simple	
ed-Endung bei regelmäßigen Verben	I work**ed** in Munich last year.
2. Form bei unregelmäßigen Verben *(1. meet / 2. met / 3. met)*	He **met** Mr Miller yesterday.

Verwendung: Past Simple		
bei Vorgängen, die in der Vergangenheit abgeschlossen wurden; oft mit Zeitangabe. Signalwörter u. a.: *yesterday, in (1990), two weeks ago, last year, last month, last week.*	I finished my studies	in 2008. 3 years ago. last week.

Present Perfect (Vollendete Gegenwart)

Bildung: Present Perfect (simple)		
have oder *has* + *ed*-Endung (bei regelmäßigen Verben)	I / you / we / they **have** work**ed** He / she **has** work**ed**	as a trainee.
	It **has** work**ed** well for us.	
3. Form bei unregelmäßigen Verben *(1. see / 2. saw / 3. seen)*	I have **seen** the new car.	

Bildung: Present Perfect (progressive)		
have / has + *been* + Infinitiv mit *-ing*	I / you / we / they **have** He / she **has**	**been** living in Munich for 5 years.

Verwendung: Present Perfect (simple and progressive)	
– bei Handlungen in der Vergangenheit **ohne Zeitangabe**	– I have written three letters.
– bei noch andauernden Zeitbestimmungen	– We haven't had any complaints so far / today …
– bei Handlungen, die in der Vergangenheit begonnen haben, aber noch nicht abgeschlossen sind, wobei *for* bei Zeiträumen *(two hours / three weeks)* und *since* bei Zeitpunkten *(2001 / January)* benutzt wird	– I have been living in Stuttgart **for** 20 years. – I have been living in Stuttgart **since** 1982.
– Einige Verben werden in der Regel nicht in der Verlaufsform verwendet.	– I have **had** the car for five years. – I have **known** the company since 2010.

Future (Zukunft)

Bildung und Verwendung	
Shall / will drückt äußere Umstände aus.	Most of this year's teleworking jobs **will** be offered in autumn.
Will drückt die Bereitschaft oder Entschlossenheit aus, etwas zu tun, sowie Versprechungen.	I'**ll** do my best to get the job.
Will wird auch benutzt für eine spontane Entscheidung.	Wait a minute, I'**ll** help you!
Going to wird verwendet, um persönliche Planungen und Vorhaben auszudrücken.	I **am going to** apply for a job in teleworking. *(Ich habe vor…)*
Going to wird auch verwendet, wenn bereits Anzeichen dafür da sind, dass etwas eintreten wird.	Look at those clouds! It'**s going to** rain.
Present continuous wird verwendet um eine feste Vereinbarung (gewöhnlich mit Zeitangabe) mitzuteilen.	Jennifer is **meeting** her colleague this evening.
Present simple wird für die Zukuft verwendet in Verbindung mit Fahrplänen, Öffnungszeiten usw.	Jim's train **arrives** at 4.30 p.m. Our office **opens** at 9 o'clock tomorrow morning.

Comparison of adjectives (Steigerung des Adjektivs)

Bildung	
Einsilbige und zweisilbige Adjektive werden durch Anhängen von *-er* und *-est* (germanische Steigerung) gesteigert.	fast – faster – fastest
Aus *y* wird *i*.	easy – easier – easiest
Ein einzelner Endkonsonant wird nach einfachem betonten Vokal verdoppelt.	hot – hotter – hottest
Für die zweisilbigen gibt es keine eindeutigen Regeln. Gewöhnlich werden zweisilbige Adjektive, die auf *-y*, *-le*, *-er* oder *-ow* enden germanisch gesteigert, aber dies ist keine bindende Regel.	clever – cleverer – cleverest noble – nobler – noblest narrow – narrower – narrowest
Ebenfalls germanisch gesteigert werden zweisilbige Adjektive, wenn sie ihre Betonung auf der zweiten Silbe haben. Auch diese Regel ist nicht bindend. Daneben gibt es aber z. B. auch folgende Formen: *more / the most clever* oder *more / the most polite*.	polite – politer – politest sincere – sincerer – sincerest
Andere zweisilbige Adjektive werden in der Regel romanisch gesteigert.	nervous – more nervous – most nervous splendid – more splendid – most splendid
Alle drei- und mehrsilbigen Adjektive steigert man mit *more* und *the most* (romanische Steigerung).	expensive – more expensive – the most expensive beautiful – more beautiful – the most beautiful
Es gibt auch eine Reihe von unregelmäßigen Adjektiven.	good – better – the best bad – worse – the worst much / many – more – the most little – less – the least old – elder – the eldest (bei Familienangehörigen)

Verwendung	
Gleichheiten mit *as … as*	He is **as** skilful **as** I. (so geschickt / fachmännisch wie ich)
Komparative mit *than*	Mike is **less** helpful **than** Tim. (weniger … als)
Je … desto…	**The** more I work with this machine **the** better I like it.
Superlativ beim Vergleich von mehr als 2 Objekten	The new electric drill is **the most** expensive tool in the brochure.

Adverbs (Adverbien)

> Das Umstandswort (Adverb) dient zur näheren Beschreibung eines Eigenschaftswortes (Adjektives) oder eines Zeitwortes (Verbs).

Bildung

Von der Wortbildung her unterscheidet man zwei Arten von Adverbien:	
1. ursprüngliche und durch Zusammensetzung gebildete Adverbien	often, quite, here, soon always, already, yesterday
2. durch Ableitung gebildete Abverbien: Hier wird an das Adjektiv ein -ly angehängt.	clearly, usually, quickly, easily, badly
Manche Adjektive und Adverbien sind	
– gleichlautend oder	daily, weekly, monthly, yearly, early, fast
– unterschiedlich.	good – **well**
Die Steigerung des Adverbs ist der Steigerung des Adjektivs vergleichbar.	carefully – more carefully – most carefully fast – faster – the fastest
Unregelmäßige Formen der Steigerung	well – better – best badly – worse – worst
y wird zu **i**	happy + -ly = happily
stummes **e** fällt weg	true + -ly = truly
Verdoppelung des Endkonsonanten	beautiful + -ly = beautifully

Verwendung

Hier wird das Verb näher beschrieben.	The new machine **works well**.
Hier wird das Adjektiv *clear* näher beschrieben.	The small printer makes **remarkably clear** printouts.
Hier wird ein anderes Adverb *(quickly)* näher beschrieben.	Our new machine works **extremely quickly**.

Questions (Fragen)

Bildung: Alternative questions (Entscheidungsfragen)

Entscheidungsfragen, die mit ja oder nein beantwortet werden können, werden im Englischen immer mit einem Hilfsverb oder einer Form von *to do* eingeleitet.	**Do** you smoke? **Did** you see Mr Miller yesterday?
Erstes Hilfsverb steht vor dem Subjekt.	**Have** you met Mr Miller?

Verwendung: Alternative questions (Entscheidungsfragen)	
Does Sally speak French?	Yes, she **does**. / No, she **doesn't**.
Can these tools be used in milling as well as in turning?	Yes, they **can**. / No, they **can't**.
Is the lathe set properly for this job?	Yes, it **is**. / No, it **isn't**.
Did he meet the chief executive at the fair?	Yes, he **did**. / No, he **didn't**.
Will you finish this job by Friday?	Yes, I **will**. / No, I **won't**.

Bildung: Questions with interrogatives (Fragen mit Fragefürwörtern)	
Die Fragen werden mit dem Fragefürwort eingeleitet. Vor dem Subjekt steht die Form von to do (do / does; did), nach dem Subjekt steht das Vollverb im Infinitiv.	**How** do you **go** to work? **What** does she **do**?
Wird nach dem Subjekt oder einem Teil des Subjekts gefragt (who, what, which, whose), so wird die Form von 'to do' nicht verwendet.	**What** is his job?

Verwendung: Questions with interrogatives (Fragen mit Fragefürwörtern)	
Fragewort ist Subjekt.	Who operates this machine? Which tools do you need for this job?
Fragewort ist nicht Subjekt.	Who / Whom did he meet at the exhibition? Which tool have you chosen for this job?

Word order (Wortstellung)

Bildung	
Die Wortstellung folgt im englischen Aussagesatz der Regel S – P – O: Subject [They] – Predicate [have repaired] – Object [the broken tools]	They have repaired the broken tools.
Dies gilt auch im Nebensatz (im Deutschen steht ja im Nebensatz das Prädikat am Ende).	I was told that they had repaired the broken tools.
Zeitbestimmungen stehen in der Regel entweder am Anfang oder am Ende des Satzes.	Yesterday they repaired the broken tools. They repaired the broken tools a week ago.
Mehrere Umstandsbestimmungen folgen gewöhnlich folgender Reihenfolge: Manner – Place – Time (Art und Weise – Ort – Zeit)	The mechanic repaired the tools in the shop yesterday. The mechanic repaired the tools quite skilfully in the shop last night.
Adverbien der Häufigkeit (frequency) können auch vor dem Hauptverb stehen: always, ever, never, often, regularly, generally, rarely, seldom, occasionally.	The service people **always** come on time. The service people **never** come without calling ahead. The service people **usually** check the machine in May.
Diese Adverbien stehen aber nach dem Verb to be.	They are **generally** very reliable.
Bei Hilfsverben stehen die Adverbien der Häufigkeit zwischen dem Hilfsverb und dem Vollverb, bzw. nach dem Hilfsverb.	The machine has **sometimes** had problems. With old machines you can **never** tell.

Defining relative clauses (Notwendige Relativsätze)

> Ein Relativsatz ist notwendig, wenn die darin gegebene Information nötig ist, um deutlich zu machen, welche Person oder Sache gemeint ist.

Verwendung	
bei Personen *who* oder *that*	The man **who** / **that** is operating the CNC machine usually works at the training centre.
bei Sachen *which* oder *that*	The machine element **which** / **that** is moving the tool is the main spindle.
im Genitiv wird **whose** verwendet	Tom is an engineer **whose** skills are highly praised.
Das Relativpronomen als Satzobjekt kann weggelassen werden.	They called the technician (**who**) they saw standing at the milling machine. Sally read the operation plan (**which**) she had filled in this morning.

Non-defining relative clauses (Nicht notwendige Relativsätze)

> Ein Relativsatz ist nicht notwendig, wenn die darin gegebene Information nicht nötig ist, um deutlich zu machen, welche Person oder Sache gemeint ist.

Verwendung	
Ein Relativsatz ist nicht notwendig, wenn die darin enthaltene Information nicht nötig ist, um zu erkennen, welche Person oder Sache gemeint ist.	**Sally's friend**, who is a skilled worker, **is doing his final exams this summer.** **The machine**, which is DEG's latest model, **works perfectly.**
Relativpronomen als Satzobjekt	**The three German apprentices**, who Sally met at the training centre, **are in their last year of training.**

Reported speech (Indirekte Rede)

Die indirekte Rede wird benutzt, wenn berichtet wird oder wurde, was jemand sagt oder sagte, bzw. macht oder machte (**Aussage**), wenn jemandem gesagt wird oder wurde, was geschehen soll (**Aufforderung**), oder wenn gefragt wird oder wurde, was geschieht oder geschah (**Frage**).

Bildung / Verwendung	
Steht das Wort, welches die indirekte Rede einleitet, in der Gegenwart, so ändern sich die Zeitformen der direkten Rede nicht.	"We **are measuring** this machined component." → Sally explains that they are measuring the machined component.
Steht das Wort, welches die indirekte Rede einleitet, in der Vergangenheit, so ändern sich die Zeitformen der direkten Rede wie folgt.	
Simple past und *present perfect* werden zu *past perfect*.	Sally **explained that they were measuring** the machined component. "The trainee **forgot** to set the revolution speed." → The master **noticed that the trainee had forgotten** to check the revolution speed.
Will wird zu *would*.	"The drilling operation **will** have to be prepared by marking out and centring." → Oliver **remembered** that the drilling operation **would** have to be prepared by marking out and centring.
Pronomen werden angepasst.	"**I can't** find the measuring equipment." → **Sally told** me that she **couldn't find** the measuring equipment.
Orts- und Zeitbestimmungen werden angepasst.	"**We** are seeing the other students **tomorrow**." → Oliver **added** that **they** were seeing the other students **the next day**. "I programmed the CNC machine **two days ago**." → He said that he had programmed the CNC machine **two days earlier**.
Aufforderungen werden in der indirekten Rede im Infinitiv wiedergegeben.	"**Use** HSS twist drills to drill metal stock." → The instructor **advised** Sally **to use** HSS twist drills to drill metal stock.
Bei Fragen wird die Wortstellung wie im Aussagesatz verwendet, d.h. am Anfang steht das Fragewort, dann folgen Subjekt, Prädikat und Objekt.	"Why has Oliver used the impact drilling function?" → The master **wanted to know why Oliver had used** the impact drilling function. "When did you sharpen the drill?" → He asked **when he had sharpened** the drill.
Die Umschreibung mit 'to do' wird nur bei Verneinungen angewendet.	"Why **don't** you call the salesman?" → She **asked** Sally why she **didn't call** the salesman.

Passive voice (Passiv)

Bildung	
Form von *to be* + *ed*-Endung (wie bei *simple past*) bei regelmäßigen Verben Form von *to be* + 3. Form bei unregelmäßigen Verben (*1. take / 2. took / 3. taken*. Siehe Liste der unregelmäßigen Verben.)	The machine **is equipped** with an emergency stop. He **is taken** to hospital.

Aktiv:	We *Subjekt*	recharge *Prädikat*	the batteries. *Objekt*
Passiv:	*Subjekt* The batteries	*Prädikat* are recharged	*Objekt (by-agent)* (by us).

Formen	
Present Tense (Simple)	The goods are transported every day.
Present Tense (Progressive)	The goods are being transported at the moment.
Past Tense (Simple)	The goods were transported yesterday.
Past Tense (Progressive)	The goods were being transported when the truck crashed.
Future 1 (will)	The goods will be transported next Monday, I promise.
Future 1 (going to)	The goods are going to be transported next month.
Present Perfect	The goods have already been transported.
Past Perfect	The goods had been transported before the order arrived.

Verwendung	
Das Passiv wird hauptsächlich verwendet, wenn der Ausführende (*by-agent*) unwichtig oder unbekannt ist oder nicht genannt werden soll. Deshalb wird der *by-agent* nur bei besonderer Betonung genannt.	The batteries **are recharged** (**by us**) when they are empty. A few years ago the first cars **were equipped** with airbags (**by the manufacturers**).
Die Passivkonstruktion wird besonders bei technischen Beschreibungen, Anweisungen in Handbüchern usw. verwendet. Bei der Umwandlung von Aktiv in Passiv wird das Objekt des Aktivsatzes zum Subjekt des Passivsatzes.	Aktiv: We recharge **the batteries**. Passiv: **The batteries** are recharged (by us).
Im Gegensatz zum Deutschen können bestimmte Verben im Englischen im Passiv verwendet werden. Die Übersetzung ins Deutsche erfolgt durch eine Konstruktion mit 'man'.	The fuel cell is considered to be a very promising invention. *(Man hält die Brennstoffzelle für eine sehr zukunftsweisende Erfindung.)*
Die Verlaufsform ist im Passiv nur im *Present Tense* und *Past Tense* gebräuchlich.	He **is being** taken to hospital. *(Er wird gerade ins Krankenhaus gebracht.)* He **was being** taken to hospital. *(Er wurde gerade ins Krankenhaus gebracht.)*

Gerund (Gerundium)

Wie im Deutschen kann man auch im Englischen aus einem Verb ein Substantiv machen. Beispiel: Durch häufiges **Messen** können Fehler vermieden werden.

Bildung	
Anhängen von *-ing* an den Infinitiv (Grundform) des Verbs	check + ing = checking drill + ing = drilling
Verdoppelung eines Endkonsonanten (Mitlaut) nach einem Vokal (Selbstlaut)	put – putting travel – travelling control – controlling refuel – refuelling
Stummes *e* fällt weg: aber: *agree – agreeing; see – seeing*	file – filing measure – measuring

Verwendung	
Ein *gerund* kann Subjekt (Satzgegenstand) sein. Ebenso kann es die Funktion eines Objekts (Satzergänzung) haben.	**Filing** is rarely done by hand. He began **cleaning** the machine.
Nach Präpositionen (Verhältniswörtern) oder präpositionalen Ausdrücken steht ebenfalls das *gerund*.	He was afraid of **setting** the lever to a higher speed. They objected **to trying** the new software **without having** made a backup of the hard drive. The manager apologised **for being** late. They prevented the visitors **from entering** the production area without a hard hat. He was tired **of hearing** the same complaint.
Nach bestimmten Verben (Zeitwörtern) steht das *gerund*.	Try to **avoid overheating** the machine. The trainer **recommended turning** the machine off. We cannot **risk losing** this customer. Phillip **suggested using** a different production method.
Weitere Verben, die ein *gerund* nach sich haben.	enjoy, like, dislike, remember, stop He enjoys working in Italy.

Prepositions (Verhältniswörter)

Präpositionen geben das Verhältnis von Personen oder Dingen zueinander an (z.B. räumlich oder zeitlich).

Räumliche Präpositionen			
above	oberhalb	**into**	in … hinein
across	durch, quer durch	**off**	von … herunter, von … weg
at	neben, bei	**on, upon**	auf
opposite	gegenüber		

Räumliche Präpositionen

behind	hinter	out, out of	aus, heraus
below	unter, unterhalb	through	durch
beneath	unter, unterhalb	to	zu, nach, in Richtung auf
beside	neben	towards	auf … zu (Richtung)
between	zwischen	under	unter
in	in	within	innerhalb

Zeitliche Präpositionen

at	an, in	from	von
before	vor	in	am, im (Jahre)
between	zwischen	on	an, am
by	bis, bis spätestens	since	seit (Zeitpunkt)
during	während	until, till	bis
for	seit (Zeitraum)		

Modale Präpositionen und Präpositionen des Grundes

according to	entsprechend, gemäß	despite, in spite of	trotz
because of	wegen	with	mit
besides	außer	without	ohne

Verwendung

Laut Gebrauchsanweisung sollte **das Auswechseln** der Werkzeuge kein Problem darstellen.	**According to** the manual, there should be no problem **with** changing the tools.
… **hinten** im Raum	The machine is **at** the back of the room.
… **unten** auf jeder Seite	You'll find the number of the module **at** the bottom of every page.
… **am** Eingang	They were waiting **at** the entrance when it happened.
… ist **gegenüber / auf der anderen Seite**	The printer is **across** the hall.
… rannte quer **über** die Straße	The dog ran **across** the road.
… **zwischen** zwei Aktenmappen (räumlich)	He found the letter **between** two folders.
… **zwischen** 9 und 10 Uhr (zeitlich)	Why don't we meet **between** nine and ten?
… nur **während**	Smoking is allowed **during** the lunch break only!
… **von** … **bis**	He worked in Cardiff **from** December **until** January.
… **auf** der Straße	You should not park your car **in** the street.
… **bis** (spätestens)	You must be back **by** six o'clock at the latest.

Modal auxiliaries (Modale Hilfsverben)

> Die modalen Hilfsverben werden im Englischen oft auch *defective* (d.h. unvollstän-
> dige) *auxiliaries* genannt, denn sie können in der Regel nur das Präsens bilden. Für
> die übrigen Zeiten müssen Ersatzformen verwendet werden.

Bildung		
Hilfsverb	**Ersatzform**	**deutsche Bedeutung**
can	to be able to	können, fähig sein, in der Lage sein
can	to be allowed to	dürfen, die Erlaubnis haben
may	to be allowed to	dürfen, die Erlaubnis haben
must	to have to	müssen
mustn't	not to be allowed to	nicht dürfen
needn't	not to have to	nicht brauchen, nicht müssen

Verwendung	
Present Tense: You **must** read the installation instructions very carefully.	**Simple past:** Yesterday he **had to** read the installation instructions twice because they were badly translated.
After the installation is completed you **needn't reboot** your system.	I **didn't have to** reboot my system when I installed the screensaver the other day.
Present Tense: He **can** handle software problems quite well.	**Present perfect:** Up to now he **has been able** to handle software problems quite well.
Present Tense: You **must not smoke** in the office.	**Future:** You **will not be allowed** to smoke in the office.

Participles (Partizipien)

Bildung	
Present Participle Infinitiv + *-ing*	Wind turbines are a **promising** option.
Past Participle 3. Stammform: *damaged* (*ed*-Endung wie bei *simple past*); (3. Form bei unregelmäßigen Verben: *1. know / 2. knew / 3. known*. Siehe Liste der unregelmäßigen Verben.)	After the storm we had to replace three **damaged** solar panels.

Verwendung	
als Adjektiv	It is a **known** fact that solar power can be used as an alternative energy.
Partizipialkonstruktionen dienen zur **Verkürzung** von: 1. adverbialen Nebensätzen mit Konjunktion *(when, although, as, while,...)* 2. adverbialen Nebensätzen ohne Konjunktion 3. Relativsätzen	When **planning** to build a home, you should consider using solar energy to heat your water. **Unlocking** the warehouse door, he smelled gas. Wind farms **built** along the coast are most efficient.
Partizipialkonstruktionen zur **Verknüpfung** von zwei Hauptsätzen.	The guide led us through the factory. He warned us to stay away from the machines. The guide led us through the factory **warning** us to stay away from the machines.

If-clauses (Bedingungssätze)

Man unterscheidet drei Arten von Bedingungen:
1. erfüllbare Bedingungen
2. Bedingungen, deren Erfüllung unwahrscheinlich ist
3. Bedingungen, die überhaupt nicht mehr erfüllt werden können.
Zusätzlich zu den drei Typen gibt es noch einen weiteren Typ, der Regeln und Naturgesetze ausdrückt.

Bildung und Verwendung	
Type I (probable condition)	If you **lubricate** this machine regularly, it **will run** smoothly for a long time. *(Wenn man die Maschine regelmäßig ölt, läuft sie lange Zeit problemlos.)*
Type II (improbable condition)	If you **lubricated** this machine regularly, **it would** run smoothly for a long time. *(Wenn man diese Maschine regelmäßig ölen würde, würde sie für lange Zeit problemlos laufen.)*
Type III (impossible condition)	If you **had lubricated** this machine regularly, it **would have run** smoothly for a long time. *(Wenn man die Maschine regelmäßig geölt hätte, wäre sie lange Zeit problemlos gelaufen (jetzt läuft sie aber offensichtlich nicht mehr).*
Rules and laws of nature Hier handelt es sich im eigentlichen Sinne nicht mehr um eine Bedingung, sondern um ein Naturgesetz. Deshalb steht im Hauptsatz auch kein Futur, sondern ebenfalls das Präsens.	If you **heat** ice, it **melts**. *(Wenn man Eis erhitzt, schmilzt es.)*
Besonderheit bei Formen von *to be*	If I **were** you, I wouldn't use a combination spanner here.

Chronological word list

🌐 **Videotraining: Englische Aussprache**

Perfekte englische Aussprache leicht gemacht:
Mit dem Lernprogramm zur englischen Lautschrift
können Sie alle Laute einüben. Wählen Sie einfach
in der Navigation rechts den entsprechenden Reiter
(*Vowels* oder *Consonants*) aus und klicken Sie dann
auf das gewünschte phonetische Symbol. Sprechen
Sie die Wörter laut nach.

Unter www.klett.de geben Sie bitte den Code unter
der Abbildung rechts ein.

🌐 n633sn

Abkürzungen und Zeichen

etw. = etwas	sth. = something
Pl. = Plural	BE = britisches Englisch
jmdn., jmdm. = jemanden, jemandem	AE = amerikanisches Englisch
sb. = somebody	◉ = Vokabeln zu den Hörtexten

Module 1 Tooling devices

to apply to [əˈplaɪ tə] anwenden
manufacturing [ˌmænjəˈfæktʃərɪŋ]
　Fertigung, Produktion
to automate [ˈɔːtəmeɪt] automatisieren
to include [ɪnˈkluːd] einschließen
therefore [ˈðeəfɔː] deshalb, darum
equipment [ɪˈkwɪpmənt] Ausrüstung,
　Ausrüstungsgegenstände
workshop [ˈwɜːkʃɒp] Werkstatt
wire stripper [ˈwaɪə ˌstrɪpə] Abisolierzange
multimeter [ˈmʌltɪˌmiːtə] Multimeter,
　Vielfachmessgerät
long nose pliers [ˌlɒŋnəʊz ˈplaɪəz] Spitzzange
spanner [ˈspænə] Schraubenschlüssel
screwdriver [ˈskruːˌdraɪvə] Schraubendreher
to measure [ˈmeʒə] messen
to drill [drɪl] bohren
to mill [mɪl] fräsen
to strip [strɪp] abisolieren
to grip [grɪp] greifen

to drive in (a nail) [ˌdraɪvˈɪn] (einen Nagel)
　einschlagen
to bend [bend] biegen
to screw [skruː] schrauben

A | General tools

internship [ˈɪntɜːnʃɪp] Praktikum
trainer [ˈtreɪnə] Ausbilder(in)
test leads [ˈtest ˌliːds] Prüfspitzen

B | Working with tooling devices

apart from [əˈpɑːt frəm] abgesehen von
power drill [ˈpaʊə ˌdrɪl] Bohrmaschine
feeder [ˈfiːdə] Beschickungsapparat, Füllapparat
welding equipment [ˈweldɪŋ ˌɪˈkwɪpmənt]
　Schweißausrüstung
gripper [ˈgrɪpə] Greifer
crimping device [ˈkrɪmpɪŋ dɪˌvaɪs]
　Crimpzange, Quetschzange
PC panel [ˌpiːsiː ˈpænl] Bildschirm mit Tastatur

column drill ['kɒləm ˌdrɪl] Ständerbohrmaschine

grinding machine ['graɪndɪŋ məˌʃiːn] Schleifmaschine

to solder ['səʊldə] löten

fuse [fjuːz] Sicherung

workpiece ['wɜːkpiːs] Werkstück

circuit board ['sɜːkɪt ˌbɔːd] Leiterplatte

lathe [leɪð] Drehbank

to fasten ['fɑːsn] befestigen

to operate ['ɒpreɪt] betreiben

to machine [məˈʃiːn] mit einer Maschine bearbeiten

looks [lʊks] Aussehen

to admit [ədˈmɪt] zugeben, eingestehen

to clamp [klæmp] einspannen, befestigen

to rotate [rəʊˈteɪt] rotieren, sich drehen

cutting tool ['kʌtɪŋ ˌtuːl] Schneidewerkzeug

milling machine ['mɪlɪŋ məˌʃiːn] Fräsmaschine

catcher ['kætʃə] Auffangschale

to collect [kəˈlekt] sammeln

to design [dɪˈzaɪn] entwerfen, bauen

headstock ['hedstɒk] Spindelstock, Antriebskasten

spindle ['spɪndl] Spindel

chuck [tʃʌk] Spannfutter, Bohrfutter

base [beɪs] Standfuß, Grundbefestigung

to install [ɪnˈstɔːl] installieren

precision [prɪˈsɪʒn] Präzision

C | Robots

commonly ['kɒmənli] üblicherweise

joint [dʒɔɪnt] Gliedmaß, Verbindungsteil

to equip [ɪˈkwɪp] ausstatten, ausrüsten

spray painter ['spreɪ ˌpeɪntə] Farbsprühdüse

to perform [pəˈfɔːm] ausführen

various ['veəriəs] verschieden

researcher [rɪˈsɜːtʃə] Forscher(in)

continually [kənˈtɪnjuəli] permanent, fortwährend

to search for ['sɜːtʃ fə] suchen nach

to develop [dɪˈveləp] entwickeln

care assistant for the elderly ['keər ˌəˌsɪstənt fə ðiˈeldəli] Altenpfleger(in)

old people's home ['əʊld ˈpiːplz ˌhəʊm] Altenheim

to predict [prɪˈdɪkt] vorhersagen

to replace [rɪˈpleɪs] ersetzen

nuclear accident [ˌnjuːkliər ˈæksɪdənt] Atomunfall

hazardous ['hæzədəs] gefährlich

versatile ['vɜːsətaɪl] vielseitig

competitive [kəmˈpetɪtɪv] konkurrenzfähig

workmate ['wɜːkmeɪt] Arbeitskollege, Arbeitskollegin

advantage [ədˈvɑːntɪdʒ] Vorteil

disadvantage [ˌdɪsədˈvɑːntɪdʒ] Nachteil

D | Safety at work

safety ['seɪfti] Sicherheit

statement ['steɪtmənt] Aussage

baggy ['bægi] weit

trousers ['traʊzəz] Hose

overall ['əʊvrɔːl] Arbeitskittel, -mantel

goggles ['gɒglz] Sicherheitsbrille

to switch off [ˌswɪtʃˈɒf] ausschalten

Module A Meeting people

confident ['kɒnfɪdənt] sicher, selbstbewusst

appropriate [əˈprəʊpriət] angemessen, passend

A | Saying "hello" and "goodbye" and giving your name

existing [ɪgˈzɪstɪŋ] bestehend

trade fair ['treɪd ˌfeə] Messe

job fair ['dʒɒb ˌfeə] Jobmesse

B | Intercultural awareness

politeness [pəˈlaɪtnəs] Höflichkeit

pleasantry ['plezntri] höfliche Floskel

profitability [ˌprɒfɪtəˈbɪləti] Rentabilität

to chat [tʃæt] sich unterhalten

health [helθ] Gesundheit

pleasant ['pleznt] angenehm

to waste time [ˌweɪst ˈtaɪm] Zeit verschwenden

impression [ɪmˈpreʃn] Eindruck

conference ['kɒnfrəns] Tagung

minutes ['mɪnɪts] Protokoll

polite [pəˈlaɪt] höflich

usual ['juːʒl] gewöhnlich, üblich, normal

upset [ʌpˈset] verärgert

stranger ['streɪndʒə] Unbekannte(r)

on the other hand [ɒn ðiˈʌðə ˌhænd] andererseits

in charge of [ɪn ˈtʃɑːdʒ əv] verantwortlich für

cash register ['kæʃ ˌredʒɪstə] Kasse

given name [ˌgɪvn ˈneɪm] Vorname

family name [ˌfæmli ˈneɪm] Nachname

to intend [ɪnˈtend] beabsichtigen

Module 2 Electricity and electronics

sub-field [ˈsʌbˌfiːld] Unterfeld
voltage [ˈvəʊltɪdʒ] Spannung
device [dɪˈvaɪs] Gerät, Vorrichtung
substation [ˈsʌbˌsteɪʃn] Umspannwerk
sliding door [ˌslaɪdɪŋ ˈdɔː] Schiebetür
portable [ˈpɔːtəbl] tragbar
closed circuit TV (CCTV) [ˌkləʊzd ˌsɜːkɪt ˌtiːˈviː, ˌsiːsiːtiːˈviː] Videoüberwachung
switch [swɪtʃ] Switch, Schalter

A | A complete circuit

circuit [ˈsɜːkɪt] Stromkreis
path [pɑːθ] Pfad
to flow [fləʊ] fließen
component [kəmˈpəʊnənt] Bauelement
power source [ˈpaʊə ˌsɔːs] Stromquelle
load [ləʊd] Ladung
milling machine [ˈmɪlɪŋ məˌʃiːn] Fräsmaschine
workshop [ˈwɜːkʃɒp] Werkstatt
transistor [trænˈzɪstə] Transistor
resistor [rɪˈzɪstə] Widerstand (als elektrisches Bauteil)
alternating current (AC) [ˌɔːltəneɪtɪŋ ˈkʌrnt, ˌeɪˈsiː] Wechselstrom
direct current (DC) [dɪˌrekt ˈkʌrnt, ˌdiːˈsiː] Gleichstrom
combination [ˌkɒmbɪˈneɪʃn] Zusammenschluss, Verbindung
lamp [læmp] Lampe, Glühbirne
resistor [rɪˈzɪstə] Widerstand
to link [lɪŋk] verbinden
current [ˈkʌrnt] Strom
electrician [ˌelɪkˈtrɪʃn] Elektriker(in)
interrupted [ˌɪntəˈrʌptɪd] unterbrochen
unintentionally [ˌʌnɪnˈtenʃnli] unbeabsichtigt
faulty [ˈfɔːlti] defekt
lead [liːd] Zuleitung, Zuführung
to interrupt [ˌɪntəˈrʌpt] unterbrechen
short-circuit [ʃɔːtˈsɜːkɪt] Kurzschluss
over-current [ˈəʊvəˌkʌrnt] Überstrom
circuit diagram [ˈsɜːkɪt ˌdaɪəgræm] Schaltplan, Schaltbild
fuse [fjuːz] Sicherung

⊙ **critically** [ˈkrɪtɪkli] kritisch, sorgfältig
mark [mɑːk] Note

to draw [drɔː] zeichnen
curved [kɜːvd] gebogen
to add [æd] hinzufügen
to include [ɪnˈkluːd] einschließen
protective [prəˈtektɪv] Schutz-
to blow [bləʊ] durchbrennen
to protect [prəˈtekt] (be-)schützen
to position [pəˈzɪʃn] positionieren
to connect [kəˈnekt] verbinden
parallel [ˈpærəlel] parallel
rectangle [ˈrektæŋgl] Rechteck
square [skweə] Quadrat
to make more sense [ˌmeɪk mɔː ˈsens] mehr Sinn machen

B | Working with electronic components

sophisticated [səˈfɪstɪkeɪtɪd] anspruchsvoll, kompliziert
electrical connector [ɪˌlektrɪkl kəˈnektə] elektrischer Anschluss
soldering iron [ˈsəʊldrɪŋˌaɪən] Lötkolben
capacitor [kəˈpæsɪtə] Kondensator
sensor [ˈsensə] Sensor
diode [ˈdaɪəʊd] Diode
conductor [kənˈdʌktə] elektrischer Leiter, Draht
semiconductor [ˌsemɪkənˈdʌktə] Halbleiter

C | Electric current

to divide into [dɪˈvaɪd ˌɪntuː] einteilen in
accumulator [əˈkjuːmjəleɪtə] Akku
to receive [rɪˈsiːv] erhalten
mains supply [ˌmeɪnz səˈplaɪ] Netzteil
solar cell [ˌsəʊlə ˈsel] Solarzelle
movement [ˈmuːvmənt] Bewegung
to monitor [ˈmɒnɪtə] aufzeichnen, darstellen
sinusoidal [ˌsaɪnəˈsɔɪdl] sinusförmig
wave [weɪv] Welle
electricity supply [ˌelæɪkˈtrɪsəti səˌplaɪ] Stromversorgung
popularity [ˌpɒpjəˈlærəti] Beliebtheit
photovoltaic system [ˌfəʊtəʊvɒlˌteɪɪk ˈsɪstəm] Photovoltaik
inverted rectifier [ɪnˌvɜːtɪd ˈrektɪfaɪə] Wechselrichter
to feed in [ˌfiːdˈɪn] einspeisen
national grid [ˌnæʃnl ˈgrɪd] Stromversorgungsnetz
appliance [əˈplaɪəns] Gerät

Module B Your company

regardless of [rɪ'gɑːdləs ˌəv] ungeachtet, unabhängig von
furniture ['fɜːnɪtʃə] Möbel
likely ['laɪkli] wahrscheinlich
supplier [sə'plaɪə] Lieferant
skill [skɪl] Fähigkeit, Fertigkeit
to express [ɪk'spres] zum Ausdruck bringen
grease [griːs] Fett
ratchet ['rætʃɪt] Knarre
tool [tuːl] Werkzeug

A | The company and its departments

department [dɪ'pɑːtmənt] Abteilung
to distribute [dɪ'strɪbjuːt] vertreiben, verteilen
damaged ['dæmɪdʒd] beschädigt
employee [ɪm'plɔɪiː] Beschäftigte(r), Angestellte(r)
accounts [ə'kaʊnts] Buchhaltung
raw materials [ˌrɔː mə'tɪəriəlz] Rohstoffe
human resources [ˌhjuːmən 'riːzɔːsɪz] Personal-abteilung
to recruit [rɪ'kruːt] rekrutieren, anstellen
purchasing (department) ['pɜːtʃəsɪŋ dɪˌpɑːtmənt)] Einkauf(-sabteilung)
to maintain [meɪn'teɪn] warten, in Stand halten
R&D (Research and Development) [rɪˌsɜːtʃ ən dɪ'veləpmənt] Forschungs- und Entwicklungsabteilung
to develop [dɪ'veləp] entwickeln
in charge of [ɪn 'tʃɑːdʒ ˌəv] zuständig für

⊙ **to cover** ['kʌvə] abdecken, bedecken
headquarters [ˌhed'kwɔːtəz] Hauptsitz
to found [faʊnd] gründen
family-owned [ˌfæmli'əʊnd] in Familienbesitz
manufacturing plant [ˌmænjə'fæktʃərɪŋ ˌplɑːnt] Produktionsbetrieb
currently ['kʌrəntli] derzeit, zurzeit, momentan
braking system ['breɪkɪŋ ˌsɪstəm] Bremsanlage
internship (AE) ['ɪntɜːnʃɪp] Praktikum
device [dɪ'vaɪs] Gerät
cylinder head ['sɪlɪndə ˌhed] Zylinderkopf
to inspect [ɪn'spekt] prüfen
operating system ['ɒpreɪtɪŋ ˌsɪstəm] Betriebssystem
interface ['ɪntəfeɪs] Schnittstelle, Interface

B | Tasks and responsibilities

task [tɑːsk] Aufgabe
responsibility [rɪˌspɒnsə'bɪləti] Verantwortung
to manufacture [ˌmænjə'fæktʃə] herstellen
to occur [ə'kɜː] vorkommen
apprenticeship [ə'prentɪʃɪp] Ausbildung, Lehre
branch [brɑːnʃ] Niederlassung
precision [prɪ'sɪʒn] Genauigkeit
essential [ɪ'senʃl] wesentlich, unbedingt erforderlich
to drill [drɪl] bohren
to shape [ʃeɪp] formen, fräsen
to polish ['pɒlɪʃ] abschleifen, polieren
to intervene [ˌɪntə'viːn] einschreiten
to vibrate [vaɪ'breɪt] vibrieren
workpiece ['wɜːkpiːs] Werkstück
to monitor ['mɒnɪtə] überwachen, kontrollieren, beobachten
to measure ['meʒə] messen
dimension [daɪ'menʃn] Maß, Abmessung
lubricated ['luːbrɪkeɪtɪd] geölt
lubricating oil ['luːbrɪkeɪtɪŋ ˌɔɪl] Schmieröl
generally ['dʒenrəli] normalerweise, im Allgemeinen
shift [ʃɪft] Schicht
to prefer [prɪ'fɜː] bevorzugen
rarely ['reəli] selten
accuracy ['ækjərəsi] Genauigkeit
to include [ɪn'kluːd] einbeziehen, einschließen
to swap [swɒp] tauschen

C | Organisational structure

to employ [ɪm'plɔɪ] beschäftigen
to support [sə'pɔːt] unterstützen
to split [splɪt] aufteilen
core area [ˌkɔː 'eəriə] Kernbereich
to report to [rɪ'pɔːt tuː] unterstehen
to belong to [bɪ'lɒŋ tuː] gehören zu
experienced [ɪk'spɪəriənst] erfahren
capable ['keɪpəbl] fähig
closely ['kləʊsli] eng

Module 3 Electronic devices

device [dɪ'vaɪs] Vorrichtung, Gerät
complex ['kɒmpleks] aufwändig, kompliziert
transistor [træn'zɪstə] Transistor
rectifier ['rektɪfaɪə] Gleichrichter
varistor ['veərɪstə] Varistor
zener diode ['ziːnə ˌdaɪəʊd] Zener-Diode

capacitor [kə'pæsɪtə] Kondensator
op-amp ['ɒp͵æmp] Operationsverstärker
to amplify ['æmplɪfaɪ] verstärken
current ['kʌrnt] Strom
to switch [swɪtʃ] schalten
voltage ['vəʊltɪdʒ] Spannung
electric charge [ɪ͵lektrɪk 'tʃɑːdʒ] elektrische Ladung
circuit board ['sɜːkɪt ͵bɔːd] Leiterplatte
circuit diagram ['sɜːkɪt ͵daɪəgræm] Schaltplan
to convert [kən'vɜːt] verwandeln, umwandeln
to conduct [kən'dʌkt] leiten
input terminal ['ɪnpʊt ͵tɜːmɪnl] Eingangspol,
Netzwerkeingang

A | A frequency converter

frequency converter ['friːkwənsi kən͵vɜːtə]
Frequenzumrichter
frequency changer ['friːkwənsi ͵tʃeɪndʒə]
Frequenzumrichter
application [͵æplɪ'keɪʃn] Anwendung
pump [pʌmp] Pumpe
fan [fæn] Ventilator
national grid [͵næʃnl 'grɪd] Stromversorgungsnetz
to transmit [trænz'mɪt] übermitteln
to apply [ə'plaɪ] anwenden, einsetzen
torque [tɔːk] Drehmoment
to provide [prə'vaɪd] versorgen
power station ['paʊə ͵steɪʃn] Kraftwerk
production line [prə'dʌkʃn ͵laɪn] Fertigungsstraße
to guarantee [͵gærn'tiː] garantieren
accuracy ['ækjərəsi] Genauigkeit

honest ['ɒnɪst] ehrlich
to disconnect [͵dɪskə'nekt] ausschalten, abklemmen
circuit ['sɜːkɪt] Schaltkreis
circuit breaker ['sɜːkɪt ͵breɪkə] Sicherung, Leitungsschutzschalter
to lock [lɒk] abschließen
to tag [tæg] beschildern, mit einem Zettelanhänger
versehen
tag [tæg] Zettel, Anhänger
live wire [͵laɪv 'waɪə] stromführender Draht
multimeter ['mʌlti͵miːtə] Multimeter, Mehrfachmessgerät
defective [dɪ'fektɪv] defekt
to earth [ɜːθ] erden
to short-circuit [ʃɔːt'sɜːkɪt] kurzschließen
to prevent [prɪ'vent] verhindern
rubber mat [͵rʌbə 'mæt] Gummimatte

guard [gɑːd] Schutzschild, Schutzgitter
to cover up [͵kʌvər͵'ʌp] abdecken
to fence off [͵fens͵'ɒf] abschranken, abgrenzen

B | Semiconductors

conductive [kən'dʌktɪv] Strom führend
conductor [kən'dʌktə] Leiter, stromführendes Kabel
to adjust [ə'dʒʌst] anpassen, einstellen
manufacture [͵mænjə'fæktʃə] Herstellung
to decrease [dɪ'kriːs] abnehmen, sinken
to increase [ɪn'kriːs] zunehmen
insulator ['ɪnsjəleɪtə] Isolator, Isolierung
property ['prɒpəti] Eigenschaft
range [reɪndʒ] Bereich
light-emitting diode (LED) [͵laɪtɪmɪtɪŋ 'daɪəʊd,
͵eliˈdiː] LED, Leuchtdiode
to flow [fləʊ] fließen
thermistor [θɜː'mɪstə] Thermistor, Heißleiter,
NTC-Widerstand
dopant ['dəʊpnt] Dotand, Dotierstoff,
Dotierungssubstanz
extrinsic semiconductor [ek'strɪnsɪk ͵semɪkən'dʌktə]
Extrinsic-Halbleiter, Störstellenhalbleiter
intrinsic semiconductor [ɪn͵trɪnsɪk ͵semɪkən'dʌktə]
Eigenhalbleiter, i-Halbleiter, Intrinsic-Halbleiter

C | Ohm's Law

Ohm's Law ['əʊmz ͵lɔː] Ohmsches Gesetz
physicist ['fɪzɪsɪst] Physiker(in)
to discover [dɪ'skʌvə] entdecken
to react [ri'ækt] reagieren
to label ['leɪbl] benennen
proportional to [prə'pɔːʃnl tə] verhältnisgleich
dependent (on) [dɪ'pendnt ͵ɒn] abhängig (von)
cross-section ['krɒssekʃn] Querschnitt
conventional [kən'venʃnl] herkömmlich, traditionell
interchangeable [͵ɪntə'tʃeɪndʒəbl] austauschbar
scientist ['saɪəntɪst] Wissenschaftler(in)
to measure ['meʒə] messen
Greek [griːk] Griechisch

Module C Telephoning

line [laɪn] *(hier:)* Branche
to fix [fɪks] reparieren
leak [liːk] undichte Stelle

to install [ɪnˈstɔːl] installieren, montieren, anschließen

complaint [kəmˈpleɪnt] Beschwerde, Reklamation

order [ˈɔːdə] Bestellung, Auftrag

necessary [ˈnesəsri] nötig, notwendig

delay [dɪˈleɪ] Verspätung, Verzögerung

breakdown [ˈbreɪkdaʊn] Panne, Störung

solution [səˈluːʃn] Lösung

confused [kənˈfjuːzd] verwirrt

crash [kræʃ] Absturz

A | Making and receiving a phone call

meeting [ˈmiːtɪŋ] Sitzung, Besprechung

country code [ˈkʌntri ˌkəʊd] Ländervorwahl

area code [ˈeəriə ˌkəʊd] Vorwahl

extension number [ɪkˈstenʃn ˌnʌmbə] Durchwahl

suitable [ˈsuːtəbl] geeignet, passend

polite [pəˈlaɪt] höflich

although [ɔːlˈðəʊ] obwohl

to remain [rɪˈmeɪn] bleiben

request [rɪˈkwest] Bitte

grateful [ˈɡreɪtfl] dankbar

whereas [weəˈræz] während

impolite [ˌɪmpəˈlaɪt] unhöflich

B | Giving information over the phone

valuable [ˈvæljuəbl] *(hier:)* wichtig

figures [ˈfɪɡəz] Nummern, Daten

clearly [ˈklɪəli] deutlich, klar

---

confused [kənˈfjuːzd] verwirrt

to divert [daɪˈvɜːt] weiterleiten

extractor fan [ɪkˈstræktəfæn] Dunstabzug

hob [hɒb] Kochfeld

diameter [daɪˈæmɪtə] Durchmesser

socket [ˈsɒkɪt] Steckdose

Module 4 Automation systems

automation system [ˌɔːtəˈmeɪʃn ˌsɪstəm] Automatisierungssystem

to apply [əˈplaɪ] anwenden

manufacturing [ˌmænjəˈfæktʃərɪŋ] Fertigung

computer-controlled [kəmˌpjuːtə kənˈtrəʊld] computergesteuert

operator [ˈɒpreɪtə] Bediener(in)

to replace [rɪˈpleɪs] ersetzen

to a great extent [tu ə ˌɡreɪt ˌɪkˈstent] in großem Ausmaß, großteils

reliable [rɪˈlaɪəbl] zuverlässig, verlässlich

hygienic [haɪˈdʒiːnɪk] hygienisch

to increase [ɪnˈkriːs] zunehmen

delivery time [dɪˈlɪvri ˌtaɪm] Lieferzeit

significantly [sɪɡˈnɪfɪkəntli] deutlich

warehouse [ˈweəhaʊs] Lager

assembly line [əˈsembli ˌlaɪn] Fertigungsstraße

plant [plɑːnt] Fabrikanlage

machine tool [məˈʃiːn ˌtuːl] Werkzeugmaschine

to operate [ˈɒpreɪt] bedienen

A | Automated working processes

to feed [fiːd] zuführen, bestücken

to monitor [ˈmɒnɪtə] überwachen

panel [ˈpænl] Bedienplatte, Bedienfeld, Eingabefeld

control unit [kənˈtrəʊl ˌjuːnɪt] Steuerung

conveyor belt [kənˈveɪə ˌbelt] Förder-, Montageband

to recognise [ˈrekəɡnaɪz] erkennen

device [dɪˈvaɪs] Gerät, Vorrichtung

to load [ləʊd] laden, aufladen

PLC (programmable logic controller) [prəˌɡræməbl ˈlɒdʒɪk kənˌtrəʊlə] SPS (speicherprogrammierbare Steuerung)

actual [ˈæktʃuəl] tatsächlich

actuator [ˈæktʃueɪtə] Aktor

transmitter [trænzˈmɪtə] Sender

piston [ˈpɪstn] Kolben

switch [swɪtʃ] Switch, Schalter

bi-directional [ˌbaɪdɪˈrekʃnl] in zwei Richtungen

fieldbus system [ˈfiːldbʌs ˌsɪstəm] Feldbussystem

redundancy [rɪˈdʌndənsi] Redundanz

personnel [ˌpɜːsnˈel] Personal

fault [fɔːlt] Fehler

distributor [dɪˈstrɪbjətə] Anbieter

cable [ˈkeɪbl] Kabel

transmission [trænzˈmɪʃn] Übertragung

to transmit [trænzˈmɪt] übertragen

interface [ˈɪntəfeɪs] Schnittstelle, Interface

switch cabinet [ˈswɪtʃ ˌkæbɪnət] Verteilerkasten

wiring [ˈwaɪərɪŋ] elektrische Verdrahtung

to diagnose itself [ˈdaɪəɡnəʊz ɪtˌself] selbstständig Fehler erkennen

to maintain [meɪnˈteɪn] warten, in Stand halten

service person [ˈsɜːvɪs ˌpɜːsn] Wartungspersonal

among [əˈmʌŋ] unter

to allow [əˈlaʊ] ermöglichen

transfer [ˈtrænsfɜː] Übertragung, Übermittlung

to exchange [ɪks'tʃeɪndʒ] austauschen, auswechseln
to alter ['ɔːltə] verändern
replacement [rɪ'pleɪsmənt] Ersatz
to handle ['hændl] handhaben, abwickeln, bearbeiten

B | Planning an automated system

effective [ɪ'fektɪv] wirksam
sequence ['siːkwəns] Abfolge
to examine [ɪg'zæmɪn] untersuchen
sequence description ['siːkwəns dɪˌskrɪpʃn] Ablaufbeschreibung
positional sketch [pəˌzɪʃnl 'sketʃ] Technologie-schema
circuit diagram ['sɜːkɪt ˌdaɪəgræm] Schaltplan
displacement-step diagram [dɪˌspleɪsmənt 'step ˌdaɪəgræm] Wegschrittdiagramm
motion sequence [ˌməʊʃn 'siːkwəns] Bewegungs-abfolge
control element [kən'trəʊlˌelɪmənt] Steuergerät
signal flow ['sɪgnl ˌfləʊ] Signalfluss
outlet port ['aʊtlet ˌpɔːt] Entlüftungsanschluss
exhaust [ɪg'zɔːst] Abluftanschluss
retracted-end position [rɪˌtræktɪdˌ'end pəˌzɪʃn] hintere Endstellung
inlet port ['ɪnlet ˌpɔːt] Druckanschluss
supply port [sə'plaɪ ˌpɔːt] Druckluftanschluss
forward-end position [ˌfɔːwədˌ'end pəˌzɪʃn] vordere Endstellung

C | Automated processes

to broadcast ['brɔːdkɑːst] senden
trade fair ['treɪd ˌfeə] Messe
assembly [ə'sembli] Montage
storage ['stɔːrɪdʒ] Lagerung
mechanisation [ˌmekənaɪ'zeɪʃn] Mechanisierung
workflow ['wɜːkfləʊ] Arbeitsablauf
manpower ['mænˌpaʊə] Arbeitskraft
labour ['leɪbə] Arbeit
to summarize ['sʌmraɪz] zusammenfassen
To sum up ... [tə ˌsʌmˌ'ʌp] Zusammenfassend, Ich fasse zusammen ...
to perform [pə'fɔːm] ausführen, durchführen

feed system ['fiːd ˌsɪstəm] Zuführungssystem
pick and place application [ˌpɪkˌən 'pleɪsˌæplɪˌkeɪʃn] Pick-and-Place-Anwendung

machine vision system [məˌʃiːn 'vɪʒn ˌsɪstəm] Bildverarbeitungssystem
standstill ['stændstɪl] Stillstand

Module D Written communication

essential [ɪ'senʃl] sehr wichtig
workshop ['wɜːkʃɒp] Werkstatt
efficiently [ɪ'fɪʃntli] effizient
necessary ['nesəsri] nötig, notwendig
enquiry [ɪn'kwaɪəri] Anfrage
promptly ['prɒmtli] sofort
offer ['ɒfə] Angebot
order ['ɔːdə] Bestellung
to replace [rɪ'pleɪs] ersetzen
lesser ['lesə] geringer
advantage [əd'vɑːntɪdʒ] Vorteil
disadvantage [ˌdɪsəd'vɑːntɪdʒ] Nachteil
confidential [ˌkɒnfɪ'denʃl] vertraulich
time-consuming ['taɪmkənˌsjuːmɪŋ] zeitraubend
reliable [rɪ'laɪəbl] zuverlässig
misunderstanding [ˌmɪsʌndə'stændɪŋ] Missverständnis

A | Enquiries

enquiry [ɪn'kwaɪəri] Anfrage
car mechanic ['kɑː mɪˌkænɪk] Automechaniker(in)
appropriate [ə'prəʊpriət] angemessen, passend
salutation [ˌsæljə'teɪʃn] (Brief:) Anrede
supplier [sə'plaɪə] Lieferant, Zulieferer
subject line ['sʌbdʒɪkt ˌlaɪn] (Brief:) Betreffzeile
bonnet (BE) ['bɒnɪt] Motorhaube
family-run [ˌfæmli'rʌn] in Familienbesitz, familiengeführt
to expand [ɪk'spænd] erweitern, vergrößern
catalogue ['kætəlɒg] Katalog
discount ['dɪskaʊnt] Rabatt, Preisnachlass
terms of payment [ˌtɜːmzˌəv 'peɪmənt] Zahlungsbedingungen
delivery times [dɪ'lɪvri ˌtaɪmz] Lieferzeiten
sample ['sæmpl] Muster
closing phrase ['kləʊzɪŋ ˌfreɪz] Schlussworte
complimentary close [ˌkɒmplɪmentri 'kləʊz] Grußformel (am Briefende)
to recommend [ˌrekə'mend] empfehlen
cost estimate ['kɒstˌestɪmət] Kostenvoranschlag
to configure [kən'fɪgə] konfigurieren

to appreciate [ə'priːʃieɪt] etw. (wert-)schätzen
to supply from stock [sə.plaɪ frəm 'stɒk] ab Lager
    liefern

B | Offers

bank transfer ['bæŋk ,trænsfɜ:] Banküberweisung
working day [,wɜːkɪŋ 'deɪ] Werktag
attachment [ə'tætʃmənt] Anhang
stock [stɒk] Bestand, Vorrat
to require [rɪ'kwaɪə] benötigen
ratchet ['rætʃɪt] Knarre, Ratsche
socket ['sɒkɪt] Stecknuss
(adjustable) wrench [ə,dʒʌstəbl 'renʃ] (verstellbarer)
    Schraubenschlüssel
screwdriver ['skruːdraɪvə] Schraubendreher
to dispatch [dɪ'spætʃ] versenden, verschicken
DIY (Do-it-yourself) [,diːaɪ'waɪ] Heimwerken

C | Orders

sum [sʌm] Betrag
consignment [kən'saɪnmənt] Lieferung, Sendung
torque wrench ['tɔːk ,renʃ] Drehmomentschlüssel

Module 5 Pneumatic control
    and components

to compete [kəm'piːt] konkurrieren, mithalten
manufacturer [,mænjə'fæktʃərə] Hersteller,
    Produzent
to improve [ɪm'pruːv] besser werden,
    sich verbessern
goal [gəʊl] Ziel
to achieve [ə'tʃiːv] erreichen, erzielen
manpower ['mænpaʊə] Arbeitskräfte
metal cutting shears ['metl.kʌtɪŋ ʃɪəz] Blechschere
tyre fitting machine ['taɪə.fɪtɪŋ məʃiːn]
    Reifenmontiermaschine
nail gun ['neɪl ,gʌn] Nagelpistole
briefly ['briːflɪ] kurz und knapp
brake chamber ['breɪk ,tʃeɪmbə] Bremszylinder
compressed air [kəm,prest ,'eə] Druckluft

A | Pneumatics and
    pneumatic components

to require [rɪ'kwaɪə] benötigen
to transmit [trænz'mɪt] übertragen
hose ['həʊz] Schlauch

valve [vælv] Ventil
pilot valve ['paɪlət ,vælv] Steuerventil
relay ['riːleɪ] Relais
actuator ['æktʃueɪtə] Aktuator
double-acting cylinder [,dʌbl.æktɪŋ 'sɪlɪndə]
    doppelt wirkender Zylinder
piston cylinder ['pɪstn ,sɪlɪndə] Kolbenzylinder
inlet port ['ɪnlet ,pɔːt] Druckanschluss
outlet port ['aʊtlet ,pɔːt] Entlüftungsanschluss
cylinder barrel ['sɪlɪndə ,bærl] Zylinderrohr
piston rod ['pɪstn ,rɒd] Kolbenstange
cushioning screw ['kʊʃənɪŋ ,skruː] Dämpfungs-
    schraube
scraper ring ['skreɪpə ,rɪŋ] Abstreifring
bearing cap ['beərɪŋ ,kæp] Lagerdeckel
bearing bush ['beərɪŋ ,bʊʃ] Lagerbuchse
to prevent [prɪ'vent] verhindern
pressure port ['preʃə ,pɔːt] Druckanschluss
to seal [siːl] abdichten, versiegeln
to guide [gaɪd] führen, leiten
to perform [pə'fɔːm] ausführen
stroke [strəʊk] Hub
to house [haʊz] eingebaut sein
control valve [kən'trəʊl ,vælv] Steuerventil
manual override [,mænjuəl 'əʊveraɪd]
    manueller Eingriff
5/2 way solenoid valve [faɪv'tuː ,weɪ 'səʊlənɔɪd ,vælv]
    5/2 Wege Elektromagnetventil
to indicate ['ɪndɪkeɪt] angeben, nennen
to actuate ['æktʃueɪt] betätigen
circuit ['sɜːkɪt] Schaltkreis

⊙   **desperate** ['despərət] verzweifelt
    confusing [kən'fjuːzɪŋ] verwirrend
    let alone [,letə'ləʊn] ganz zu schweigen von
    whereas [weər'æz] während, wohingegen
    reed contact ['riːd ,kɒntækt] Reedkontakt
    piston ['pɪstn] Kolben
    end-position cushioning [,endpə,zɪʃn 'kʊʃənɪŋ]
        Endlagendämpfung
    impact ['ɪmpækt] Anschlag
    silencer ['saɪlənsə] Schalldämpfer
    to plug [plʌg] stecken

B | Pneumatic solutions

to feed [fiːd] zustellen
production line [prə'dʌkʃn ,laɪn] Fertigungsstraße
adhesive [əd'hiːsɪv] Klebstoff

in quick succession [ɪn ˌkwɪk sək'seʃn] in schneller Abfolge

to mount [maʊnt] montieren, anbringen

slide [slaɪd] Gleitschiene

conveyor belt [kən'veɪə ˌbelt] Förder-, Montageband

significant [sɪg'nɪfɪkənt] beachtlich

drive system ['draɪv ˌsɪstəm] Antriebssystem

two-magazine [ˌtu:mægə'zi:n] mit zwei Magazinen

motion sequence ['məʊʃn ˌsi:kwəns] Bewegungsabfolge

alternately [ɒl'tɜ:nətli] abwechslungsweise

Module E Applications

to sign [saɪn] unterschreiben

application [ˌæplɪ'keɪʃn] Bewerbung

opportunity [ˌɒpə'tju:nəti] Möglichkeit

to decide [dɪ'saɪd] sich entscheiden

branch [brɑ:nʃ] Niederlassung

advert ['ædvɜ:t] Anzeige

letter of application [ˌletər̩əv̩ˌæplɪ'keɪʃn] Bewerbungsschreiben

CV (curriculum vitae) [ˌsi:'vi:, kəˌrɪkjələm 'vi:taɪ] Lebenslauf

job interview ['dʒɒbˌɪntəvju:] Vorstellungsgespräch

employment contract [ɪm'plɔɪmənt ˌkɒntrækt] Arbeitsvertrag

to invite [ɪn'vaɪt] einladen

skill [skɪl] Fähigkeit

industry ['ɪndəstri] *(hier:)* Branche

hard-working [ˌhɑ:d'wɜ:kɪŋ] fleißig

A | Job advertisements

recently ['ri:sntli] kürzlich

willing to learn [ˌwɪlɪŋ tə 'lɜ:n] lernbereit, lernwillig

responsible [rɪ'spɒnsəbl] verantwortlich

punctual ['pʌŋktʃuəl] pünktlich

pleasant ['pleznt] angenehm, sympathisch

working atmosphere [ˌwɜ:kɪŋˌætməsfɪə] Arbeitsklima

valid ['vælɪd] gültig

troubleshooting ['trʌblˌʃu:tɪŋ] Fehlersuche

to maintain [meɪn'teɪn] bewahren

leading ['li:dɪŋ] führend

supplier [sə'plaɪə] Lieferant, Zulieferer

vacancy ['veɪknsi] freie Stelle

fault [fɒlt] Fehler

assembly [ə'sembli] Montage

summary ['sʌmri] Zusammenfassung

B | Letter of application

internship (AE) ['ɪntɜ:rnʃɪp] Praktikum

theoretical [θɪə'retɪkl] theoretisch

to gain [geɪn] *(hier:)* sammeln

reliable [rɪ'laɪəbl] zuverlässig

to consider [kən'sɪdə] betrachten

to require [rɪ'kwaɪə] benötigen

C | The CV

advice [əd'vaɪs] Rat

tip [tɪp] Tipp, Hinweis

to highlight ['haɪlaɪt] betonen

strength [streŋθ] Stärke

achievement [ə'tʃi:vmənt] Leistung

supervisor ['su:pəvaɪzə] Leiter(in), Kontrolleur(in)

truth [tru:θ] Wahrheit

embarrassing [ɪm'bærəsɪŋ] peinlich

to spell [spel] buchstabieren

grateful ['greɪtfl] dankbar

Module 6 Sensors

device [dɪ'vaɪs] Vorrichtung, Gerät

to convert [kən'vɜ:t] verwandeln, umwandeln

to record [rɪ'kɔ:d] aufzeichnen

presence ['prezns] Präsenz

toxic ['tɒksɪk] giftig

to detect [dɪ'tekt] erkennen

in turn [ɪn 'tɜ:n] wiederum

to overheat [ˌəʊvə'hi:t] überhitzen

application [ˌæplɪ'keɪʃn] Anwendung

pressure ['preʃə] Druck

input ['ɪnpʊt] Eingabe

control loop [kən'trəʊl ˌlu:p] Regelkreis

to regulate ['regjəleɪt] regulieren

conveyor belt [kən'veɪə ˌbelt] Förder-, Montageband

validation [ˌvælɪ'deɪʃn] Fahrscheinentwertung

smoke detector ['sməʊk dɪˌtektə] Rauchmelder

proximity sensor [prɒk'sɪməti ˌsensə] Näherungssensor

A | The working principles of sensors

working principle [ˌwɜ:kɪŋ 'prɪnsəpl] Arbeitsweise

feeler ['fi:lə] Fühler

to monitor ['mɒnɪtə] überwachen

to control [kən'trəʊl] steuern

surroundings [sə'raʊndɪŋz] Umgebung

component [kəm'pəʊnənt] Bauteil

capacitive proximity sensor [kə,pæsətɪv prɒk'sɪməti ,sensə] kapazitiver Näherungssensor

to amplify ['æmplɪfaɪ] verstärken

capacitor [kə'pæsɪtə] Kondensator

electric charge [ɪ,lektrɪk 'tʃɑːdʒ] elektrische Ladung

coil [kɔɪl] Spule

in addition [ɪn ə'dɪʃn] außerdem

to calibrate ['kælɪbreɪt] abgleichen

oscillator ['ɒsɪleɪtə] Oszillator

inductive proximity sensor [ɪn,dʌktɪv prɒk'sɪməti ,sensə] induktiver Näherungssensor

reference signal ['refrns ,sɪgnl] Referenzsignal

analogue voltage signal [,ænəlɒg 'vəʊltɪdʒ ,sɪgnl] analoges Spannungssignal

current signal ['kʌrnt ,sɪgnl] Stromsignal

optical ['ɒptɪkl] optisch

to embed [ɪm'bed] einbetten

to process ['prəʊsəs] verarbeiten

backlighting ['bæk,laɪtɪŋ] Hintergrundbeleuchtung

to register ['redʒɪstə] anzeigen

inaudible [ɪn'ɔːdɪbl] nicht hörbar

to connect [kə'nekt] verbinden

control unit [kən'trəʊl ,juːnɪt] Steuerungseinheit

as follows [əz 'fɒləʊz] wie folgt

B | Choosing a suitable sensor

sensitive ['sensətɪv] empfindlich

to pull up [,pʊl 'ʌp] aufrufen

data sheet ['deɪtə ,ʃiːt] Datenblatt

thermal protection [,θɜːml prə'tekʃn] Wärmeschutz

self-heating [,self'hiːtɪŋ] Eigenerwärmung

output ['aʊtpʊt] Ausgabe

appliance [ə'plaɪəns] Gerät

thermal management [,θɜːml 'mænɪdʒmənt] Wärmemanagement

range [reɪndʒ] Bereich, Bandbreite

requirement [rɪ'kwaɪəmənt] Anforderung

to exceed [ɪk'siːd] übersteigen, übertreffen

annual service [,ænjuəl 'sɜːvɪs] alljährliche Wartung

due [djuː] fällig

to suit [suːt] passen

to agree on [ə'griː ,ɒn] sich auf etwas einigen

feature ['fiːtʃə] Eigenschaft, Merkmal

resistance [rɪ'zɪstns] elektrischer Widerstand

to prevent [prɪ'vent] verhindern, vermeiden

remote installation [rɪ,məʊt ,ɪnstə'leɪʃn] Remote-installation

environmental [ɪn,vaɪrn'mentl] Umwelt-

within [wɪ'ðɪn] innerhalb

resolution [,rezə'luːʃn] Auflösung

sophisticated [sə'fɪstɪkeɪtɪd] technisch ausgereift

heating system ['hiːtɪŋ ,sɪstəm] Heizungssystem

to compare [kəm'peə] vergleichen

precision [prɪ'sɪʒn] Genauigkeit

housing ['haʊzɪŋ] Gehäuse

to spell [spel] buchstabieren

delivery [dɪ'lɪvri] Lieferung

to apologise [ə'pɒlədʒaɪz] sich entschuldigen

confirmation [,kɒnfə'meɪʃn] Bestätigung

C | Intelligent sensors

combination [,kɒmbɪ'neɪʃn] Verbindung

switch [swɪtʃ] Switch, Schalter

to evaluate [ɪ'væljueɪt] auswerten

bus system ['bʌs ,sɪstəm] Bussystem

standardized ['stændədaɪzd] genormt

teach-in-mode [,tiːtʃ,ɪn ,məʊd] Teach-in-Modus, Teach-in-Funktion

configuration [kən,fɪgə'reɪʃn] Einstellung

interchangeable [,ɪntə'tʃeɪndʒəbl] austauschbar

to distribute [dɪ'strɪbjuːt] vertreiben

leakage ['liːkɪdʒ] Leck, Durchsickern

short-circuit [ʃɔːt'sɜːkɪt] Kurzschluss

default [dɪ'fɔːlt] Standardwert, Standardeinstellung

gradual contamination [,grædʒuəl kən,tæmɪ'neɪʃn] allmähliche Verschmutzung

to reduce [rɪ'djuːs] reduzieren, vermindern

necessity [nə'sesəti] Notwendigkeit

standstill ['stænstɪl] Stillstand

to adopt [ə'dɒpt] übernehmen

parameter [pə'ræmɪtə] Parameter, Einstellung

to ensure [ɪn'ʃɔː] sicherstellen, gewährleisten

flow [fləʊ] Fluß, Ablauf

to refine [rɪ'faɪn] verbessern, verfeinern

participating [pɑː'tɪsɪpeɪtɪŋ] teilnehmend

via [vaɪə] über

to equip [ɪ'kwɪp] ausstatten, ausrüsten

bus coupler ['bʌs ,kʌplə] Buskoppler

properly ['prɒpli] ordnungsgemäß

Module F Socialising

relationship [rɪ'leɪʃnʃɪp] Beziehung

A | Small talk

subsidiary [səb'sɪdɪəri] Tochtergesellschaft
trainee [ˌtreɪ'niː] Auszubildende(r)
appropriate [ə'prəʊprɪət] angemessen, passend

B | Small talk in business

to dismiss [dɪ'smɪs] nicht beachten
common ground [ˌkɒmən 'graʊnd] gemeinsame Basis
trivial ['trɪvɪəl] unwichtig
uneasiness [ʌn'iːzɪnəs] Unbehagen
tension ['tenʃn] Spannung
to avoid [ə'vɔɪd] vermeiden
awkward ['ɔːkwəd] peinlich, unangenehm

C | Eating out

well-done [ˌwel'dʌn] (Steak) gut durchgebraten
pork [pɔːk] Schweinefleisch
side order ['saɪdˌɔːdə] Beilage
bill [bɪl] Rechnung
game [geɪm] (hier:) Wild
dessert [dɪ'zɜːt] Nachtisch, Nachspeise
fork [fɔːk] Gabel
main dish [ˌmeɪn 'dɪʃ] Hauptgericht
beef [biːf] Rindfleisch
poultry ['pəʊltri] Geflügel
starter ['stɑːtə] Vorspeise
tip [tɪp] Trinkgeld

Module 7 Hydraulics

construction site [kən'strʌkʃn ˌsaɪt] Baustelle
to power [paʊə] antreiben
liquid ['lɪkwɪd] Flüssigkeit
fluid ['fluːɪd] Flüssigkeit
damage ['dæmɪdʒ] Beschädigung, Schaden
failure ['feɪljə] Versagen
elevator ['eləveɪtə] Aufzug, Fahrstuhl
excavator ['ekskəveɪtə] Bagger
car lift ['kɑːˌlɪft] Hebebühne
dump truck ['dʌmpˌtrʌk] Muldenkipper
forklift truck [ˌfɔːklɪft 'trʌk] Gabelstapler

A | Installing a hydraulic hose

hose ['həʊz] Schlauch
to consist of [kən'sɪstˌəv] bestehen aus

drive unit ['draɪv juːnɪt] Antriebseinheit
fitting ['fɪtɪŋ] Verschraubung
leak [liːk] Leck
to relieve [rɪ'liːv] abbauen
drain pan ['dreɪnˌpæn] Ablaufwanne
counterclockwise [ˌkaʊntə'klɒkwaɪz] gegen den Uhrzeigersinn
to align [ə'laɪn] fluchten, ausrichten
load [ləʊd] Last
transducer [trænz'djuːsə] Meßwertgeber
servo controller ['sɜːvəʊ kənˌtrəʊlə] Stellantrieb
flow-control valve ['fləʊkəntrəʊlˌvælv] Stromventil
piston pump ['pɪstnˌpʌmp] Kolbenpumpe
control valve [kən'trəʊlˌvælv] Steuerventil
flow position ['fləʊ pəˌzɪʃn] Durchflussstellung
forward stroke [ˌfɔːwəd 'strəʊk] Vorwärtshub

B | Troubleshooting and hydraulic systems

troubleshooting ['trʌblˌʃuːtɪŋ] Fehlersuche
fault [fɒlt, fɔːlt] Fehler
to solve [sɒlv] lösen
contaminant [kən'tæmɪnənt] Fremdkörper
to pour [pɔː] gießen
crackle test ['kræklˌtest] Knistertest
plate [pleɪt] Platte
workbench ['wɜːkbenʃ] Werkbank
to detect [dɪ'tekt] feststellen, wahrnehmen
ferrous ['ferəs] eisenhaltig, Eisen-
sample ['sɑːmpl] (Stich-)probe
ultrasonic tester [ʌltrəsɒnɪk 'testə] Ultraschall-prüfgerät
cavitation [ˌkævɪ'teɪʃn] Hohlraumbildung
aeration [eə'reɪʃn] Sauerstoffanreicherung
inlet port ['ɪnletˌpɔːt] Einlassöffnung
foam [fəʊm] Schaum
air entrainment [ˌeərˌɪn'treɪnmənt] Luftmitführung
to release [rɪ'liːs] abgeben
operating pressure ['ɒpreɪtɪŋ preʃə] Betriebsdruck
predictive maintenance [prɪˌdɪktɪv 'meɪntnəns] vorausschauende Instandhaltung
degree [dɪ'griː] Maß
reliability [rɪˌlaɪə'bɪləti] Zuverlässigkeit

Module G Presentations

required [rɪ'kwaɪəd] erforderlich, verlangt, erwünscht
service ['sɜːvɪs] Dienstleistung

positional sketch [pəˌzɪʃnl ˈsketʃ] Technologie-
    schema
to develop [dɪˈveləp] entwickeln
to improve [ɪmˈpruːv] besser werden,
    sich verbessern
meeting [ˈmiːtɪŋ] Sitzung, Besprechung
graph [grɑːf] Diagramm
chart [tʃɑːt] Schaubild, Diagramm
preparation [ˌpreprˈeɪʃn] Vorbereitung
to explain [ɪkˈspleɪn] erklären
sales pitch [ˈseɪlz ˌpɪtʃ] Verkaufspräsentation
reason [ˈriːzn] Grund

A | Preparing a presentation

audience [ˈɔːdiəns] Zuhörer (Pl.), Publikum
body language [ˈbɒdi ˌlæŋgwɪdʒ] Körpersprache
handout [ˈhændaʊt] Informationsblatt
to prepare [prɪˈpeə] vorbereiten
visual aids [ˌvɪʒuəlˈeɪdz] Anschauungsmaterial,
    visuelle Hilfen
to describe [dɪˈskraɪb] beschreiben
summary [ˈsʌmri] Zusammenfassung
overview [ˈəʊvəvjuː] Überblick
to reinforce [ˌriːɪnˈfɔːs] verstärken, betonen
guidelines [ˈgaɪdlaɪnz] Leitlinien

B | Describing materials and products

sturdy [ˈstɜːdi] robust
shiny [ˈʃaɪni] glänzend
robust [rəˈbʌst] stabil
state-of-the-art [ˌsteɪt əv ðiˌˈɑːt] auf dem neuesten
    Stand (der Technik)
user-friendly [juːzəˈfrendli] benutzerfreundlich
reliable [rɪˈlaɪəbl] zuverlässig
hand-crafted [ˌhænˈkrɑːftɪd] handgefertigt

C | Delivering a presentation

carpenter [ˈkɑːpɪntə] Tischler(in), Zimmerer,
    Zimmerin
furniture [ˈfɜːnɪtʃə] Möbel
trade show [ˈtreɪd ʃəʊ] Messe

⊙ **lounger** [ˈlaʊndʒə] Liegesessel
softwood [ˈsɒftˌwʊd] Weichholz
timber [ˈtɪmbə] Holz, Bauholz
joiner [ˈdʒɔɪnə] Tischler(in), Schreiner(in)
convenience [kənˌviːniəns] Zweckmäßigkeit,
    Bequemlichkeit

varnish [ˈvɑːnɪʃ] Lack
durable [ˈdjʊərəbl] haltbar
polyurethane coating [ˌpɒlɪjʊərəθeɪn ˈkəʊtɪŋ]
    Polyurethanbeschichtung

Module 8 Assembly

assembly [əˈsembli] Montage
to join [dʒɔɪn] verbinden
joint [dʒɔɪnt] Verbindung
permanent [ˈpɜːmnənt] dauerhaft
non-permanent [ˌnɒnˈpɜːmnənt] nicht dauerhaft
screw [skruː] Schraube
nail [neɪl] Nagel
fastener [ˈfɑːsnə] Befestigung
to loosen [ˈluːsn] lösen
to unscrew [ʌnˈskruː] aufschrauben
to take apart [ˌteɪk əˈpɑːt] auseinandernehmen
maintenance [ˈmeɪntnəns] Wartung
to replace [rɪˈpleɪs] ersetzen
to wear out [ˌweərˈaʊt] abnutzen
to weld [weld] schweißen
to braze [ˈbreɪz] hartlöten
to solder [ˈsəʊldə] löten
to rivet [ˈrɪvɪt] nieten, vernieten
seam [siːm] Naht
to destroy [dɪˈstrɔɪ] zerstören
to dismantle [dɪˈsmæntl] abbauen, abmontieren
container [kənˈteɪnə] Behälter
sheet [ʃiːt] Platte
bolt [bəʊlt] Bolzen
column drill [ˈkɒləm ˌdrɪl] Ständerbohrmaschine
wire [waɪə] Kabel
terminal [ˈtɜːmɪnl] Anschluss
butterfly screw [ˈbʌtəflaɪ ˌskruː] Flügelschraube

A | Assembling processes

to include [ɪnˈkluːd] einschließen, beinhalten
to tighten [ˈtaɪtn] festziehen
screwdriver [ˈskruːˌdraɪvə] Schraubenzieher
power drill [ˈpaʊə ˌdrɪl] Schlagbohrmaschine
conveyor system [kənˈveɪə ˌsɪstəm] Förderband
ball bearing [ˌbɔːl ˈbeərɪŋ] Kugellager
faulty [ˈfɔːlti] defekt
probable [ˈprɒbəbl] wahrscheinlich
electric drive [ɪˌlektrɪk ˈdraɪv] Antrieb, Motor
housing [ˈhaʊzɪŋ] Gehäuse

apprenticeship [ə'prentɪʃɪp] Berufsausbildung, Lehre

to remove [rɪ'muːv] entfernen

to unplug [ʌn'plʌg] abziehen

to desolder [diː'səʊldə] ablöten

Thank goodness! [θæŋk 'gʊdnəs] Gott sei Dank!

rivet ['rɪvɪt] Gewindeniet

to knock off [ˌnɒk 'ɒf] abschlagen, zerschlagen

to undo [ʌn'duː] auflösen, aufschrauben

stud bolt ['stʌd ˌbəʊlt] Gewindestift

nut [nʌt] Mutter

washer ['wɒʃə] Unterlegscheibe

B | Soldering and brazing

to braze [breɪz] hartlöten

plumbing ['plʌmɪŋ] Sanitär-

electrical engineer [ɪˌlektrɪkl ˌendʒɪ'nɪə] Elektrotechniker(in)

board [bɔːd] Platine, Leiterplatte

plumber ['plʌmə] Klempner(in), Installateur(in)

melting point ['meltɪŋ ˌpɔɪnt] Schmelzpunkt

solder ['səʊldə] Lot, Lötmetall

soldering station ['səʊldrɪŋ ˌsteɪʃn] Lötstation

soldering iron tip ['səʊldrɪŋ ˌaɪən ˌtɪp] Lötkolbenspitze

soldering piston tip ['səʊldrɪŋ ˌpɪstn ˌtɪp] Lötkolbenspitze

iron holder ['aɪən ˌhəʊldə] Lötkolbenhalter

solder paste ['səʊldə ˌpeɪst] Lötfett

solder tin ['səʊldə ˌtɪn] Lötzinn

solder wire ['səʊldə ˌwaɪə] Lötdraht

brazing torch ['breɪzɪŋ ˌtɔːtʃ] Lötlampe

mixer ['mɪksə] Mischregler

oxygen ['ɒksɪdʒən] Sauerstoff

acetylene [ə'setɪliːn] Azetylen

brass [brɑːs] Messing

hose [həʊz] Schlauch

regulator ['regjəleɪtə] Regler

processor-soldering station [ˌprəʊsesə 'səʊldrɪŋ ˌsteɪʃn] Prozessor-Lötstation

to prolong [prə'lɒŋ] verlängern

key [kiː] Taste

operating mode ['ɒpreɪtɪŋ ˌməʊd] Betriebsmodus

preset ['priːset] vorgegeben

feature ['fiːtʃə] (Leistungs-)Merkmal

C | Assembly lines

assembly line [ə'sembli ˌlaɪn] Fertigungsstraße, Montageband

stage [steɪdʒ] Station, Abschnitt

to carry out [ˌkæri 'aʊt] ausführen

manually ['mænjuəli] von Hand

skilled [skɪld] ausgebildet

sub-assembly ['sʌbəˌsembli] Vor-, Teilmontage

inspection [ɪn'spekʃn] Inspektion, Kontrolle

to feed [fiːd] zuführen, bestücken

secondary operation [ˌsekndri ˌɒpr'eɪʃn] Sekundärbetriebsart, Nebenbetriebsart

grease [griːs] Fett

Module H Dealing with customers

to deal with ['diːl wɪð] umgehen mit, sich befassen mit

customer ['kʌstəmə] Kunde, Kundin

success [sək'ses] Erfolg

appointment [ə'pɔɪntmənt] Termin

enquiry [ɪn'kwaɪəri] Anfrage

complaint [kəm'pleɪnt] Beschwerde

essential [ɪ'senʃl] sehr wichtig

builder ['bɪldə] Bauunternehmer(in)

building site ['bɪldɪŋ ˌsaɪt] Baustelle

to explain [ɪk'spleɪn] erklären

A | Complaints

solution [sə'luːʃn] Lösung

delay [dɪ'leɪ] Verzögerung, Verspätung

price reduction ['praɪs rɪˌdʌkʃn] Preisnachlass

faulty ['fɒlti] fehlerhaft, defekt, mangelhaft

damaged ['dæmɪdʒd] beschädigt

unsatisfactory [ʌnˌsætɪs'fæktri] unbefriedigend, ungenügend, unzureichend

to replace [rɪ'pleɪs] ersetzen

air freight ['eə ˌfreɪt] Luftfracht

surplus ['sɜːpləs] überschüssig

credit note ['kredɪt ˌnəʊt] Gutschrift

specific [spə'sɪfɪk] bestimmt, spezifisch

access ['ækses] Zugang

to log on [ˌlɒg 'ɒn] sich anmelden, sich einwählen

migration [maɪ'greɪʃn] *(hier:)* Umstellung

to redo [ˌriː'duː] noch einmal machen

to look into sth. [ˌlʊk 'ɪntə] einer Sache nachgehen

technician [tek'nɪʃn] Techniker(in)

plumbing and heating [ˌplʌmɪŋ ənd 'hiːtɪŋ] Heizung und Sanitär

B | Customer service

upset [ʌpˈset] verärgert

to avoid [əˈvɔɪd] vermeiden

argument [ˈɑːgjəmənt] Streit, Auseinandersetzung

to calm sb. [kɑːm] jmdn. beruhigen

to reassure [ˌriːəˈʃʊə] beruhigen

patient [ˈpeɪʃnt] geduldig

to solve [sɒlv] lösen

frame of mind [ˌfreɪm‿əv ˈmaɪnd] geistige
Verfassung

furious [ˈfjʊəriəs] wütend

to affect [əˈfekt] Einfluss nehmen auf

mood [muːd] Laune

to blame sb./sth. for sth. [bleɪm] jmdm./etw. die
Schuld an etw. geben, jmdn. verantwortlich
machen

excuse [ɪkˈskjuːs] Ausrede

Module 9 Measuring
instruments

measuring instrument [ˈmeʒrɪŋ‿ˌɪnstrəmənt]
Messgerät

whether [ˈweðə] ob

live wire [ˌlaɪv ˈwaɪə] stromführendes Kabel

voltage [ˈvəʊltɪdʒ] Spannung

insulated [ˈɪnsjəleɪtɪd] isoliert

mains tester [ˈmeɪnz ˌtestə] Phasenprüfer

voltmeter [ˈvəʊltˌmiːtə] Spannungsmessgerät

oscilloscope [əˈsɪləskəʊp] Oszilloskop

to deal with [ˈdiːl wɪð] sich beschäftigen mit

direct current [ˌdaɪrekt ˈkʌrənt] Gleichstrom

alternating current [ˌɒltəneɪtɪŋ ˈkʌrənt]
Wechselstrom

micrometer [maɪˈkrɒmɪtə] Bügelmessschraube

vernier calliper [ˌvɜːniə ˈkælɪpə] Messschieber

value [ˈvæljuː] Wert

scale [skeɪl] Skala

weight [weɪt] Gewicht

height [haɪt] Höhe

length [leŋθ] Länge

width [wɪdθ] Breite, Tiefe

depth [depθ] Tiefe

A | Using a vernier calliper
and a micrometer

metric vernier scale [ˈmetrɪk ˌvɜːniə ˌskeɪl]
metrischer Nonius

external measuring jaw [ɪkˌstɜːnl ˈmeʒrɪŋ ˌdʒɔː]
Messschneide

slide [slaɪd] Schieber

depth gauge rod [ˈdepθ ˌgeɪdʒ ˌrɒd] Tiefenmass

inch main scale [ˈɪntʃ ˌmeɪn ˌskeɪl] Zoll-Skala

internal measuring jaw [ɪnˌtɜːnl ˈmeʒrɪŋ ˌdʒɔː]
Messspitze

clamp screw [ˈklæmp ˌskruː] Klemmschraube

fixed jaw [ˌfɪkst ˈdʒɔː] fester Messschenkel

metric main scale [ˈmetrɪk ˌmeɪn ˌskeɪl]
metrische Skala

movable jaw [ˌmuːvəbl ˈdʒɔː] beweglicher
Messschenkel

rule [ruːl] Lineal

inch vernier scale [ˈɪntʃ ˌvɜːniə ˌskeɪl] Zoll-Nonius

frame [freɪm] Bügel

carbide tip [ˌkɑːbaɪd ˈtɪp] Hartmetallplättchen

spindle [ˈspɪndl] Spindel

sleeve [sliːv] Skalenhülse

thimble [ˈθɪmbl] Skalentrommel

ratchet [ˈrætʃɪt] Ratsche-Kupplung

wire [waɪə] Draht

shaft [ʃɑːft] Welle

diameter [daɪˈæmətə] Durchmesser

slot [slɒt] Kerbe, Nut

to consist of [kənˈsɪst‿əv] bestehen aus

arc [ɑːk] Bügel, Bogen

reading [ˈriːdɪŋ] Ablesung, Messwert

fraction [ˈfrækʃn] Bruchteil

screw [skruː] Schraube

measurement [ˈmeʒəmənt] Messung, Abmessung

nowadays [ˈnaʊədeɪz] heutzutage

to clamp [klæmp] einklemmen, festklemmen

anvil [ˈænvɪl] Amboss

range [reɪndʒ] Messbereich

to rotate [rəʊˈteɪt] rotieren

external [ɪkˈstɜːnl] extern-

rotation [rəʊˈteɪʃn] Rotation, Drehung

internal [ɪnˈtɜːnl] intern-

B | Working with an oscilloscope

adjustable [əˈdʒʌstəbl] einstellbar

speed [spiːd] Geschwindigkeit

applied [əˈplaɪd] angewendet(e)

from bottom to top [frəm ˌbɒtəm tə ˈtɒp]
von unten nach oben

to observe [əbˈzɜːv] beobachten, erkennen

periodic [ˌpɪəriˈɒdɪk] periodisch, regelmäßig,
wiederkehrend

frequency ['fri:kwənsi] Frequenz, Häufigkeit

amplitude ['æmplɪtju:d] Amplitude, Ausschlag

shape [ʃeɪp] Form

to perform [pəˈfɔːm] ausführen

by the way [ˌbaɪ ðə ˈweɪ] übrigens

behaviour [bɪˈheɪvjə] Verhalten

graphically ['græfɪkli] graphisch

to draw [drɔː] zeichnen

frequency meter ['fri:kwənsi ˌmiːtə] Frequenz-
messer

to keep sth. in mind [ˌkiːp ɪn ˈmaɪnd] an etwas
denken

grid [grɪd] Gitter

axis ['æksɪs] Achse

knob [nɒb] Knopf, Drehknopf

input ['ɪnpʊt] Eingabe-

channel ['tʃænl] Kanal

to amplify ['æmplɪfaɪ] verstärken

to apply to [əˈplaɪ tə] betreffen, gelten für

selection [səˈlekʃn] Auswahl-

division [dɪˈvɪʒn] Bereich

to travel ['trævl] durchlaufen

multiplied by ['mʌltɪplaɪd baɪ] mal

equal ['iːkwl] gleich

dot [dɒt] Signal

to depend on [dɪˈpend ɒn] abhängen von

Module 10 Mechatronics

manufacturing process [ˌmænjəˈfæktʃərɪŋ ˌprəʊses]
Herstellungsverfahren

food processing ['fuːd ˌprəʊsesɪŋ] Nahrungsmittel-
herstellung

fun park ['fʌn ˌpɑːk] Erlebnispark

entertainment [ˌentəˈteɪnmənt] Unterhaltung

sector ['sektə] Bereich, Sektor

control system [kənˈtrəʊl ˌsɪstəm] Regelungssystem

to control [kənˈtrəʊl] steuern, überwachen

to monitor ['mɒnɪtə] beobachten, überwachen

actuator ['æktʃueɪtə] Aktor

to operate ['ɒpreɪt] betreiben

current ['kʌrənt] elektrischer Strom

to weld [weld] schweißen

to detect [dɪˈtekt] feststellen, wahrnehmen

to read [riːd] lesen, ablesen

A | Examples of mechatronic systems

smart [smɑːt] intelligent

to optimize ['ɒptɪmaɪz] optimieren, verbessern

to apply [əˈplaɪ] anwenden

to develop [dɪˈveləp] entwickeln

to require [rɪˈkwaɪə] benötigen

ABS (anti-lock braking system) [ˌeɪbiːˈes, ˌæntɪlɒk
ˈbreɪkɪŋ ˌsɪstəm] Antiblockiersystem

automatic drive [ˌɔːtəmætɪk ˈdraɪv] Automatik

device [dɪˈvaɪs] Gerät

feature ['fiːtʃə] Ausstattung

numerically controlled [njuːˈmerɪkli kənˈtrəʊld]
numerisch gesteuert

handling ['hændlɪŋ] Handhabungs-

peripheral [pəˈrɪfrl] Peripheriegerät

electronic stability control [ˌelektrɒnɪk stəˈbɪləti
kənˌtrəʊl] ESP, Fahrdynamikregelung

prime example [ˌpraɪm ɪgˈzɑːmpl] Paradebeispiel

steering unit ['stɪərɪŋ ˌjuːnɪt] Steuerung

application [ˌæplɪˈkeɪʃn] Anwendung

brake [breɪk] Bremse

to skid [skɪd] ins Schleudern kommen

to discover [dɪˈskʌvə] entdecken

frequently ['friːkwntli] häufig

to assemble [əˈsembl] montieren, zusammenbauen

to combine with [kəmˈbaɪn wɪð] miteinander
verbinden

calculator ['kælkjəleɪtə] Taschenrechner

predecessor ['priːdɪsesə] Vorgänger

apart from [əˈpɑːt frəm] abgesehen von

B | Mechatronic components

to contain [kənˈteɪn] enthalten, beinhalten

beam splitter ['biːm ˌsplɪtə] Strahlteiler

focusing lens ['fəʊkəsɪŋ ˌlenz] Fokussierlinse

image processing ['ɪmɪdʒ ˌprəʊsesɪŋ]
Bildverarbeitung

contamination [kənˌtæmɪˈneɪʃn] Verschmutzung

windscreen ['wɪnskriːn] Windschutzscheibe

PLC control system [ˌpiːelsiː kənˈtrəʊl ˌsɪstəm]
SPS-Steuerung

final control element [ˌfaɪnl kənˈtrəʊl ˌeləmənt]
Stellglied

operating element ['ɒpreɪtɪŋ ˌeləmənt]
Bedienelement

presence ['prezns] Vorhandensein

limit switch ['lɪmɪt ˌswɪtʃ] Grenztaster

handling device ['hændlɪŋ dɪˌvaɪs] Handhabungsgerät

starter button ['stɑːtə ˌbʌtn] Startknopf

valve [vælv] Ventil

cylinder ['sɪlɪndə] Zylinder

panel ['pænl] Eingabefeld, Bedienleiste

input ['ɪnpʊt] Eingabe

output ['aʊtpʊt] Ausgabe

control device [kən'trəʊl dɪˌvaɪs] Steuerungselement

signal element ['sɪɡnl̩ˌeləmənt] Signalgeber

to perform [pə'fɔːm] ausführen

mechatronics technician [ˌmekə'trɒnɪks tek̩nɪʃn]
Mechatroniker(in)

pre-determined [ˌpriːdɪ'tɜːmɪnd] vorherbestimmt,
vorgegeben

accurately ['ækjərətli] genau

to keep a record [ˌkiːp ə 'rekɔːd] dokumentieren

control task [kən'trəʊl ˌtɑːsk] Steuerungsaufgabe

reliable [rɪ'laɪəbl] zuverlässig

wiring ['waɪərɪŋ] Verdrahtung

space-saving [ˌspeɪs'seɪvɪŋ] Platz sparend, kompakt

efficient [ɪ'fɪʃnt] leistungsfähig, wirksam

economical [ˌiːkə'nɒmɪkl] kostengünstig,
wirtschaftlich

C | A mechatronics project

fleet [fliːt] Flotte

forklift truck [ˌfɔːklɪft 'trʌk] Gabelstapler

to cruise [kruːz] herumfahren

shop floor [ˌʃɒp 'flɔː] Fabrikhalle, Werkstatt

carelessness ['keələsnəs] Unachtsamkeit

axle ['æksl] Achse

inexperience [ˌɪnɪk'spɪəriəns] Unerfahrenheit

overloading [ˌəʊvə'ləʊdɪŋ] Überlastung

to tip forwards [ˌtɪp 'fɔːwədz] vornüber kippen

load limit ['ləʊd ˌlɪmɪt] verbleibende Achslast

back wheel [ˌbæk 'wiːl] Hinterrad

grip [ɡrɪp] Bodenhaftung

to reach [riːtʃ] erreichen

to indicate ['ɪndɪkeɪt] anzeigen

to steer [stɪə] steuern

to light up [ˌlaɪt̩'ʌp] aufleuchten

to prevent [prɪ'vent] verhindern

damage ['dæmɪdʒ] Beschädigung, Schaden

goods [ɡʊdz] Waren

weight [weɪt] Gewicht

assembly [ə'sembli] Montage

reasonable ['riːznəbl] angemessen

to affect [ə'fekt] beeinträchtigen

to approve [ə'pruːv] genehmigen

load sensor ['ləʊd ˌsensə] Beladungszähler,
Kraftaufnehmer

horn [hɔːn] Hupe

to mount [maʊnt] montieren

cab [kæb] Fahrerkabine

Module 11 Maintenance

maintenance ['meɪntnəns] Wartung

to require [rɪ'kwaɪə] benötigen

to carry out [ˌkæriˌ'aʊt] ausführen

scheduled maintenance [ˌʃedjuːld 'meɪntnəns]
planmäßige Wartung, planmäßige Instandhaltung

preventive maintenance [prɪˌventɪv meɪntnəns]
vorbeugende Wartung, vorbeugende Instandhaltung

downtime ['daʊntaɪm] Ausfallzeit

to arise [ə'raɪz] entstehen, auftreten

to lubricate ['luːbrɪkeɪt] schmieren

bearing ['beərɪŋ] Lager

gearbox ['ɡɪəbɒks] Getriebe

cutting fluid ['kʌtɪŋ ˌfluːɪd] Kühlschmierstoff

interval ['ɪntəvl] Abstand

A | Maintaining an electric motor

electrical drive [ɪˌlektrɪkl 'draɪv] elektrischer Antrieb

breakdown ['breɪkdaʊn] Panne, Störung

frame [freɪm] Rahmen

air passage ['eə ˌpæsɪdʒ] Luftkanal

to remove [rɪ'muːv] entfernen

erratic [ɪ'rætɪk] unstet

to clog [klɒɡ] blockieren, verstopfen

brush [brʌʃ] Bürste

to ride [raɪd] laufen

commutator ['kɒmjʊteɪtə] Gleichrichter

spark [spɑːk] Funken

surface ['sɜːfɪs] Oberfläche

groove [ɡruːv] Rille, Furche

to replace [rɪ'pleɪs] ersetzen

ball bearing [ˌbɔːl 'beərɪŋ] Kugellager

roller bearing [ˌrəʊlə 'beərɪŋ] Rollenlager

to grease [griːs] fetten

grease gun ['griːs ˌɡʌn] Fettpresse

solvent ['sɒlvnt] Lösungsmittel

wear and tear [ˌweərˌən 'teə] Abnutzung, Verschleiß

to proceed [prə'siːd] vorgehen

acceptance record [ək'septəns ˌrekɔːd] Abnahmeprotokoll

commissioning [kə'mɪʃnɪŋ] Inbetriebnahme

to rule out [ˌruːlˈaʊt] ausschließen

sag [sæg] Durchhang

mounting [ˈmaʊntɪŋ] Befestigung

base plate [ˈbeɪs ˌpleɪt] Grundplatte

warping [ˈwɔːpɪŋ] Verziehen

spalling [ˈspɔːlɪŋ] Absplitterung

measured variable [ˌmeʒəd ˈveərɪəbl] Meßgröße

detectable [dɪˈtektəbl] meßbar

fatigue [fəˈtiːg] Ermüdung

B | Maintenance of machines

work flow diagram [ˈwɜːkfləʊ ˌdaɪəgræm] Arbeitsablaufdiagramm

to enclose [ɪnˈkləʊz] beifügen

data sheet [ˈdeɪtə ʃiːt] Datenblatt

risk assessment [ˈrɪsk əˌsesmənt] Risikobewertung

to gather [ˈgæðə] sammeln, zusammentragen

Alphabetical word list

diameter Durchmesser   74

diode Diode   18

direct current (DC) Gleichstrom   17, 72

disadvantage Nachteil   36

to disconnect ausschalten, abklemmen   25

discount Rabatt, Preisnachlass   37

to discover entdecken   77

to dismantle abbauen, abmontieren   64

to dismiss nicht beachten   54

to dispatch versenden, verschicken   38

displacement-step diagram Weg-schrittdiagramm   34

to distribute vertreiben   51

distributor Anbieter   33

to divide into einteilen in   19

division Bereich   75

DIY (Do-it-yourself) Heimwerken   38

dopant Dotand, Dotierstoff, Dotierungssubstanz   26

dot Signal   75

double-acting cylinder doppelt wirkender Zylinder   41

downtime Ausfallzeit   80

drain pan Ablaufwanne   57

to draw zeichnen   17

to drill bohren   8

to drive in (a nail) (einen Nagel) einschlagen   8

drive system Antriebssystem   43

drive unit Antriebseinheit   57

due fällig   50

dump truck Muldenkipper   56

durable haltbar   63

E

to earth erden   25

economical kostengünstig, wirtschaftlich   78

effective wirksam   34

efficient leistungsfähig, wirksam   78

efficiently effizient   36

electrical connector elektrischer Anschluss   18

electrical drive elektrischer Antrieb   81

electrical engineer Elektrotechniker(in)   66

electric charge elektrische Ladung   24

electric drive Antrieb, Motor   65

electrician Elektriker(in)   17

electricity supply Stromversorgung   19

electronic stability control ESP, Fahrdynamikregelung   77

elevator Aufzug, Fahrstuhl   56

embarrassing peinlich   47

to embed einbetten   49

employment contract Arbeits-vertrag   44

to enclose beifügen   83

end-position cushioning Endlagen-dämpfung   42

enquiry Anfrage   68

to ensure sicherstellen, gewährleisten   51

entertainment Unterhaltung   76

environmental Umwelt-   50

equal gleich   75

to equip ausstatten, ausrüsten   51

equipment Ausrüstung, Ausrüstungs-gegenstände   8

erratic unstet   81

essential sehr wichtig   68

to evaluate auswerten   51

to examine untersuchen   34

excavator Bagger   56

to exceed übersteigen, übertreffen   50

to exchange austauschen, auswechseln   33

excuse Ausrede   71

exhaust Abluftanschluss   34

existing bestehend   13

to expand erweitern, vergrößern   37

to explain erklären   68

extension number Durchwahl   29

external extern-   74

external measuring jaw Messschneide   73

extrinsic semiconductor Extrinsic-Halbleiter, Störstellenhalbleiter   26

F

failure Versagen   56

family name Nachname   15

family-run in Familienbesitz, familiengeführt   37

fan Ventilator   25

to fasten befestigen   10

fastener Befestigung   64

fatigue Ermüdung   82

fault Fehler   33, 45, 59

faulty fehlerhaft, defekt, mangelhaft   17, 65, 69

feature Ausstattung, (Leistungs-) Merkmal   67, 77

to feed zuführen, bestücken   33

feeder Beschickungsapparat, Füllapparat   9

to feed in einspeisen   19

feed system Zuführungssystem   35

feeler Fühler   49

to fence off abschranken, abgrenzen   25

ferrous eisenhaltig, Eisen-   59

fieldbus system Feldbussystem   33

figures Nummern, Daten   31

final control element Stellglied   78

fitting Verschraubung   57

to fix reparieren   28

fixed jaw fester Messschenkel   73

fleet Flotte   79

flow Fluß, Ablauf   51

to flow fließen   17

flow-control valve Stromventil   58

flow position Durchflussstellung   58

fluid Flüssigkeit   56

foam Schaum   59

focusing lens Fokussierlinse   78

food processing Nahrungsmittel-herstellung   76

fork Gabel   55

forklift truck Gabelstapler   56

forward-end position vordere Endstellung   34

forward stroke Vorwärtshub   58

fraction Bruchteil   74

frame Rahmen   81

frame of mind geistige Verfassung   71

frequency Frequenz, Häufigkeit   75

piston pump Kolbenpumpe 58

piston rod Kolbenstange 41

plant Fabrikanlage 32

plate Platte 59

PLC (programmable logic controller) SPS (speicherprogrammierbare Steuerung) 33

PLC control system SPS-Steuerung 78

pleasant angenehm 15

pleasantry höfliche Floskel 15

to plug stecken 42

plumber Klempner(in), Installateur(in) 66

plumbing Sanitär- 66

plumbing and heating Heizung und Sanitär 70

polite höflich 15

politeness Höflichkeit 15

polyurethane coating Polyurethan-beschichtung 63

popularity Beliebtheit 19

pork Schweinefleisch 55

portable tragbar 16

to position positionieren 17

positional sketch Technologieschema 60

poultry Geflügel 55

to pour gießen 59

to power antreiben 56

power drill Schlagbohrmaschine 65

power source Stromquelle 17

power station Kraftwerk 25

precision Genauigkeit 50

predecessor Vorgänger 77

pre-determined vorherbestimmt, vorgegeben 78

to predict vorhersagen 11

predictive maintenance voraus-schauende Instandhaltung 59

preparation Vorbereitung 60

to prepare vorbereiten 61

presence Präsenz 48

preset vorgegeben 67

pressure Druck 48

pressure port Druckanschluss 41

to prevent verhindern 41

preventive maintenance vorbeugende Wartung, vorbeugende Instandhaltung 80

price reduction Preisnachlass 69

prime example Paradebeispiel 77

probable wahrscheinlich 65

to proceed vorgehen 82

to process verarbeiten 49

processor-soldering station Prozessor-Lötstation 67

production line Fertigungsstraße 25

profitability Rentabilität 15

to prolong verlängern 67

promptly sofort 36

properly ordnungsgemäß 51

property Eigenschaft 26

proportional to verhältnisgleich 27

to protect (be-)schützen 17

protective Schutz- 17

to provide versorgen 25

proximity sensor Näherungssensor 48

to pull up aufrufen 50

pump Pumpe 25

punctual pünktlich 45

R

range Messbereich 74

ratchet Ratsche-Kupplung 74

to reach erreichen 79

to react reagieren 27

to read lesen, ablesen 76

reading Ablesung, Messwert 74

reason Grund 60

reasonable angemessen 79

to reassure beruhigen 71

to receive erhalten 19

recently kürzlich 45

to recognise erkennen 33

to recommend empfehlen 37

to record aufzeichnen 48

rectangle Rechteck 17

rectifier Gleichrichter 24

to redo noch einmal machen 69

to reduce reduzieren, vermindern 51

redundancy Redundanz 33

reed contact Reedkontakt 42

reference signal Referenzsignal 49

to refine verbessern, verfeinern 51

to register anzeigen 49

to regulate regulieren 48

regulator Regler 66

to reinforce verstärken, betonen 61

relationship Beziehung 52

relay Relais 41

to release abgeben 59

reliability Zuverlässigkeit 59

reliable zuverlässig 36

to relieve abbauen 57

to remain bleiben 30

remote installation Remoteinstallation 50

to remove entfernen 81

to replace ersetzen 64

replacement Ersatz 33

request Bitte 30

to require benötigen 80

required erforderlich, verlangt, erwünscht 60

requirement Anforderung 50

researcher Forscher(in) 11

resistance elektrischer Widerstand 50

resistor Widerstand 17

resolution Auflösung 50

responsible verantwortlich 45

retracted-end position hintere Endstellung 34

to ride laufen 81

risk assessment Risikobewertung 83

rivet Gewindeniet 65

to rivet nieten, vernieten 64

robust stabil 62

roller bearing Rollenlager 81

to rotate rotieren 74

rotation Rotation, Drehung 74

rubber mat Gummimatte 25

rule Lineal 73

to rule out ausschließen 82

S

safety Sicherheit 11

sag Durchhang 82

sales pitch Verkaufspräsentation 60

salutation (Brief:) Anrede 37

sample Muster, (Stich-)probe 37, 59

scale Skala 72

scheduled maintenance planmäßige Wartung, planmäßige Instandhaltung 80

scientist Wissenschaftler(in) 27

scraper ring Abstreifring 41

screw Schraube 64
to screw schrauben 8
screwdriver Schraubendreher 8
to seal abdichten, versiegeln 41
seam Naht 64
to search for suchen nach 11
secondary operation Sekundärbetriebsart, Nebenbetriebsart 67
sector Bereich, Sektor 76
selection Auswahl- 75
self-heating Eigenerwärmung 50
semiconductor Halbleiter 18
sensitive empfindlich 50
sensor Sensor 18
sequence Abfolge 34
sequence description Ablaufbeschreibung 34
service Dienstleistung 60
service person Wartungspersonal 33
servo controller Stellantrieb 58
shaft Welle 74
shape Form 75
sheet Platte 64
shiny glänzend 62
shop floor Fabrikhalle, Werkstatt 79
short-circuit Kurzschluss 17
to short-circuit kurzschließen 25
side order Beilage 55
to sign unterschreiben 44
signal element Signalgeber 78
signal flow Signalfluss 34
significant beachtlich 43
significantly deutlich 32
silencer Schalldämpfer 42
sinusoidal sinusförmig 19
to skid ins Schleudern kommen 77
skill Fähigkeit 44
skilled ausgebildet 67
sleeve Skalenhülse 74
slide Schieber 73
sliding door Schiebetür 16
slot Kerbe, Nut 74
smart intelligent 77
smoke detector Rauchmelder 48
socket Stecknuss 38
softwood Weichholz 63
solar cell Solarzelle 19
solder Lot, Lötmetall 66
to solder löten 10, 64
soldering iron Lötkolben 18

soldering iron tip Lötkolbenspitze 66
soldering piston tip Lötkolbenspitze 66
soldering station Lötstation 66
solder paste Lötfett 66
solder tin Lötzinn 66
solder wire Lötdraht 66
5/2 way solenoid valve 5/2 Wege
Elektromagnetventil 42
solution Lösung 28
to solve lösen 71
solvent Lösungsmittel 81
sophisticated technisch ausgereift 50
space-saving Platz sparend,
kompakt 78
spalling Absplitterung 82
spanner Schraubenschlüssel 8
spark Funken 81
specific bestimmt, spezifisch 69
speed Geschwindigkeit 75
to spell buchstabieren 50
spindle Spindel 74
spray painter Farbsprühdüse 11
square Quadrat 17
stage Station, Abschnitt 67
standardized genormt 51
standstill Stillstand 35, 51
starter Vorspeise 55
starter button Startknopf 78
statement Aussage 11
state-of-the-art auf dem neuesten
Stand (der Technik) 62
to steer steuern 79
steering unit Steuerung 77
stock Bestand, Vorrat 38
storage Lagerung 35
stranger Unbekannte(r) 15
strength Stärke 47
to strip abisolieren 8
stroke Hub 41
stud bolt Gewindestift 65
sturdy robust 62
sub-assembly Vor-, Teilmontage 67
sub-field Unterfeld 16
subject line (Brief:) Betreffzeile 37
subsidiary Tochtergesellschaft 53
substation Umspannwerk 16
success Erfolg 68
to suit passen 50
suitable geeignet, passend 30

sum Betrag 39
to summarize zusammenfassen 35
summary Zusammenfassung 61
To sum up ... Zusammenfassend,
Ich fasse zusammen ... 35
supervisor Leiter(in), Kontrolleur(in) 47
supplier Lieferant, Zulieferer 45
to supply from stock ab Lager
liefern 37
supply port Druckluftanschluss 34
surface Oberfläche 81
surplus überschüssig 69
surroundings Umgebung 49
switch Switch, Schalter 16
to switch schalten 24
switch cabinet Verteilerkasten,
Schaltschrank 33
to switch off ausschalten 11

T

tag Zettel, Anhänger 25
to tag beschildern, mit einem
Zettelanhänger versehen 25
to take apart auseinandernehmen 64
teach-in-mode Teach-in-Modus,
Teach-in-Funktion 51
technician Techniker(in) 69
tension Spannung 54
terminal Anschluss 64
terms of payment Zahlungsbedingungen 37
test leads Prüfspitzen 9
Thank goodness! Gott sei Dank! 65
theoretical theoretisch 46
therefore deshalb, darum 8
thermal management Wärme-
management 50
thermal protection Wärmeschutz 50
thermistor Thermistor,
Heißleiter, NTC-Widerstand 26
thimble Skalentrommel 74
to tighten festziehen 65
timber Holz, Bauholz 63
time-consuming zeitraubend 36
tip Trinkgeld 55
to tip forwards vornüber kippen 79
torque Drehmoment 25
torque wrench Drehmomentschlüssel 39

United Kingdom

USA

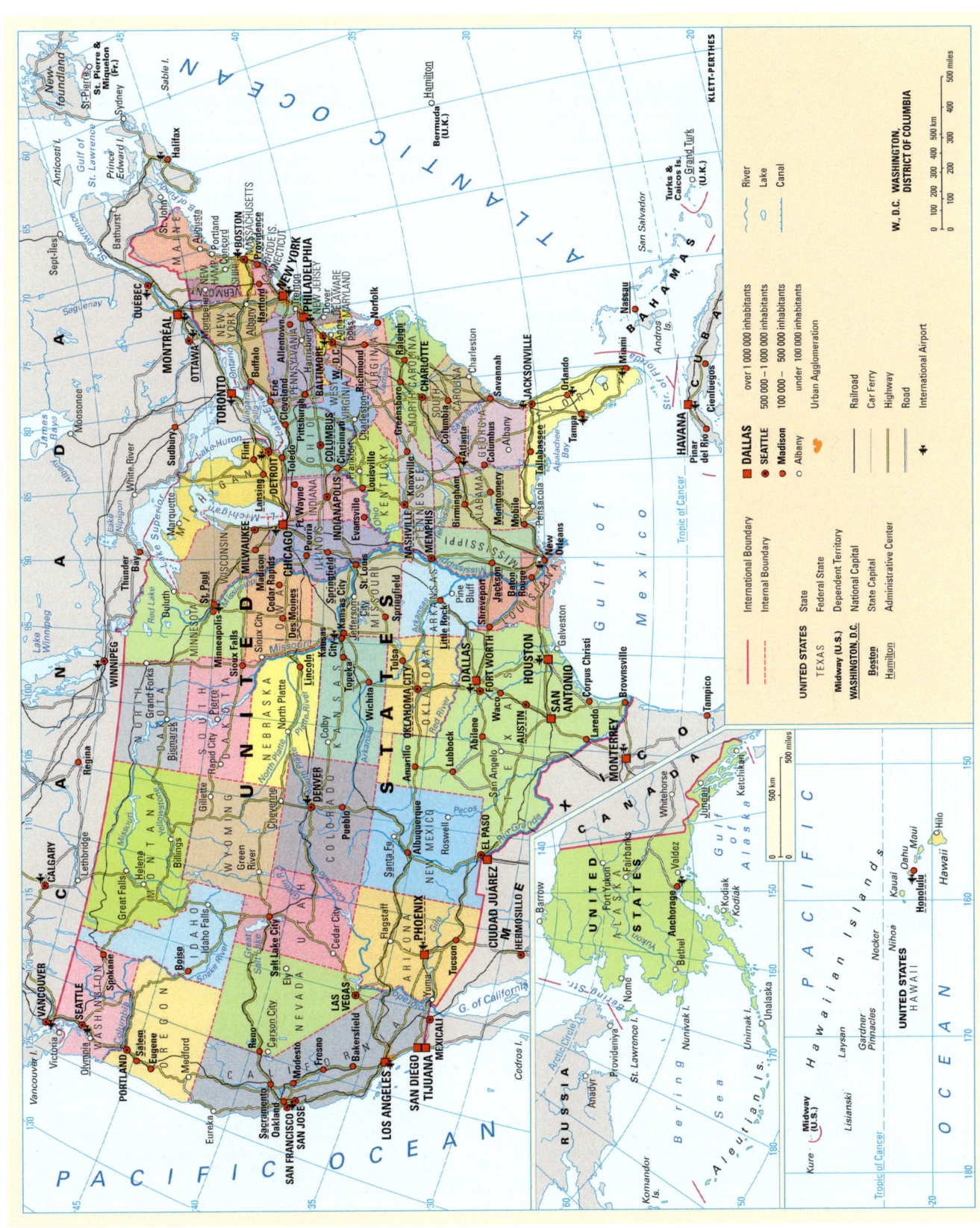

Bildquellenverzeichnis

4 shutterstock (Lightfactor), New York, NY; **4** shutterstock (Rainer Plendl), New York, NY; **5** dreamstime.com (Kellydt), Brentwood, TN; **5** shutterstock (ag-photos), New York, NY; **5** shutterstock (Nomad_Soul), New York, NY; **6** LinguaTV GmbH, Berlin; **6** Video(s) supplied by BBC Motion Gallery, London; **6** ZDF, Mainz; **6** ZDF Enterprises GmbH, Mainz; **8** shutterstock (Tish1), New York, NY; **8** shutterstock (Nomad_Soul), New York, NY; **8** shutterstock (Nikola Bilic), New York, NY; **8** shutterstock (wellphoto), New York, NY; **9** Fotolia.com (HandmadePictures), New York; **9** shutterstock (Brian Mueller), New York, NY; **9** shutterstock (Maksim Dubinsky), New York, NY; **9** Thinkstock (iStockphoto), München; **9** shutterstock (kudrashka-a), New York, NY; **9** Fotolia.com (Diana Kosaric), New York; **10** Robert Bosch GmbH, Stuttgart; **11** shutterstock (Theodore Littleton), New York, NY; **12** iStockphoto (daniel rodriguez), Calgary, Alberta; **12** Thinkstock (Stockbyte), München; **12** iStockphoto (David Jones), Calgary, Alberta; **12** iStockphoto (Helder Almeida), Calgary, Alberta; **14** iStockphoto (Dean Mitchell), Calgary, Alberta; **15** iStockphoto (4x6), Calgary, Alberta; **16** shutterstock (mycola), New York, NY; **16** shutterstock (Brian A Jackson), New York, NY; **16** shutterstock (Rd), New York, NY; **16** shutterstock (Steve Mann), New York, NY; **18** iStockphoto (Herbert Kratky), Calgary, Alberta; **18** iStockphoto (Gethin Lane), Calgary, Alberta; **18** iStockphoto (YouraPechkin), Calgary, Alberta; **18** iStockphoto (.iga .etrti.), Calgary, Alberta; **20** shutterstock (Dmitry Kalinovsky), New York, NY; **20** Thinkstock (BananaStock), München; **20** iStockphoto (sturti), Calgary, Alberta; **20** Thinkstock (iStockphoto), München; **22** shutterstock (Dmitry Kalinovsky), New York, NY; **23** iStockphoto (mediaphotos), Calgary, Alberta; **24** shutterstock (Lightfactor), New York, NY; **25** CC-BY-SA-3.0 (C J Cowie, CC BY-SA 3.0), siehe *3; **28** iStockphoto (diego cervo), Calgary, Alberta; **28** iStockphoto (nolimitpictures), Calgary, Alberta; **28** Thinkstock (Wavebreak Media), München; **28** PantherMedia GmbH (Benis Arapovic), München; **30** iStockphoto (PeskyMonkey), Calgary, Alberta; **32** iStockphoto (gradisca), Calgary, Alberta; **32** shutterstock (Dmitry Kalinovsky), New York, NY; **32** shutterstock (Rainer Plendl), New York, NY; **32** shutterstock (Alistair Cotton), New York, NY; **35** shutterstock (Nataliya Hora), New York, NY; **36** iStockphoto (David Jones), Calgary, Alberta; **36** iStockphoto (Warwick Lister-Kaye), Calgary, Alberta; **36** shutterstock (Stephen Coburn), New York, NY; **36** shutterstock (rangizzz), New York, NY; **40** iStockphoto (BanksPhotos), Calgary, Alberta; **40** Thinkstock (Hemera), München; **40** Thinkstock (iStockphoto), München; **40** shutterstock (Jeff Thrower), New York, NY; **43** FESTO AG & Co., Esslingen; **44** shutterstock (Minerva Studio), New York, NY; **44** iStockphoto (Brian Jackson), Calgary, Alberta; **44** shutterstock (StockLite), New York, NY; **44** iStockphoto (Willie B. Thomas), Calgary, Alberta; **46** shutterstock (Goodluz), New York, NY; **48** shutterstock (Mihai Simonia), New York, NY; **48** shutterstock (Moreno Soppelsa), New York, NY; **48** shutterstock (Bertold Werkmann), New York, NY; **48** iStockphoto (jian wan), Calgary, Alberta; **50** www.sika.net SIKA Dr. Siebert & Kühn GmbH & Co. KG, Kaufungen; **51** iStockphoto (Dragan Trifunovic), Calgary, Alberta; **52** iStockphoto (fatihhoca), Calgary, Alberta; **52** iStockphoto (Clerkenwell_Images), Calgary, Alberta; **52** Thinkstock (Purestock), München; **52** iStockphoto (Chris Schmidt), Calgary, Alberta; **53** Thinkstock (BananaStock), München; **54** Thinkstock (Stockbyte), München; **55** iStockphoto (kristian sekulic), Calgary, Alberta; **56** dreamstime.com (Kellydt), Brentwood, TN; **56** iStockphoto (Stephan Hoerold), Calgary, Alberta; **56** Thinkstock (iStockphoto), München; **56** iStockphoto (Joerg Reimann), Calgary, Alberta; **57** shutterstock (am70), New York, NY; **60** iStockphoto (Clerkenwell_Images), Calgary, Alberta; **60** shutterstock (wavebreakmedia ltd), New York, NY; **60** Thinkstock (Purestock), München; **60** iStockphoto (Oleg Prikhodko), Calgary, Alberta; **61** iStockphoto (bluecinema), Calgary, Alberta; **63** iStockphoto (Joshua Hodge Photography), Calgary, Alberta; **64** PantherMedia GmbH (Dusan Kostic), München; **64** iStockphoto (Srdjan Stefanovic), Calgary, Alberta; **64** BigStockPhoto.com (pixpax), Davis, CA; **64** iStockphoto (zilli), Calgary, Alberta; **65** Thinkstock (Hemera), München; **65** PantherMedia GmbH (Boris Sosnovyy), München; **65** Thinkstock (iStockphoto), München; **66** PantherMedia GmbH (Bernd Jürgens), München; **66** Rothenberger Werkzeuge GmbH, Kelkheim; **67** BMW AG, München; **68** iStockphoto (YanLev), Calgary, Alberta; **68** iStockphoto (Steve Debenport), Calgary, Alberta; **68** iStockphoto (Sean Locke), Calgary, Alberta; **68** iStockphoto (Louis-Paul St-Onge), Calgary, Alberta; **69** iStockphoto (Sean Locke), Calgary, Alberta; **72** shutterstock (ag-photos), New York, NY; **72** Fotolia.com (Hein), New York; **72** iStockphoto (Steve Froebe), Calgary, Alberta; **72** dreamstime.com (Dmitry Kalinovsky), Brentwood, TN; **75** Thinkstock (iStockphoto), München; **76** Thinkstock (iStockphoto), München; **76** shutterstock (jordache), New York, NY; **76** PantherMedia GmbH (auremar), München; **77** shutterstock (2399), New York, NY; **77** shutterstock (Vladimir Mucibabic), New York, NY; **77** shutterstock (PHOTOCREO Michal Bednarek), New York, NY; **78** shutterstock (emel82), New York, NY; **79** shutterstock (Richard Welter), New York, NY; **80** shutterstock (Nomad_Soul), New York, NY; **80** shutterstock (Thor Jorgen Udvang), New York, NY; **80** shutterstock (Dmitry Kalinovsky), New York, NY; **80** shutterstock (MikLav), New York, NY; **82** shutterstock (zcw), New York, NY; **84** LinguaTV GmbH, Berlin; **85** LinguaTV GmbH, Berlin; **86** ZDF Enterprises GmbH, Mainz; **87** ZDF Enterprises GmbH, Mainz; **88** ZDF, Mainz; **88** ZDF Enterprises GmbH, Mainz; **89** Video(s) supplied by BBC Motion Gallery, London; **COVER** Getty Images (ScienceFoto/U. Bellhaeuser), München; **COVER** Getty Images RF (PhotoAlto Agency RF), München

Textquellenverzeichnis

93/94 Source: Powered Hand Tools – Pneumatic Tools – Basic Safety, http://www.ccohs.ca/oshanswers/safety_haz/power_tools/pneumat.html, Canadian Centre of Occupational Health and Safety (CCOHS), year of publication. Reproduced with the permission of CCOHS, 2012.